HOME
GAME

HOME
GAME

HOCKEY AND LIFE IN CANADA

KEN DRYDEN
AND
ROY MacGREGOR

M&S

Every reasonable effort has been made to trace copyright of photographs. The publisher would welcome information about errors or omissions.

Canadian Cataloguing in Publication Data

Dryden, Ken, 1947–
   Home game : hockey and life in Canada

ISBN 0-7710-2871-7

1. Hockey – Canada. 2. Hockey – Social aspects –
Canada. 3. Hockey – Economic aspects – Canada.
I. MacGregor, Roy, 1948–   . II. Title.

GV848.4.C3D79 1989   796.96′2′0971   C89-095273-6

Printed and bound in Canada

McClelland & Stewart Inc.
The Canadian Publishers
481 University Avenue
Toronto, Ontario
M5G 2E9

CONTENTS

Dedication

To our "home" teams,
and to "players," everywhere.

Some of the interview material in this book is derived from the television series, "Ken Dryden's Home Game," produced by Starplay Films Inc., for the Canadian Broadcasting Corporation, with the support of Telefilm Canada and the sponsorship of Imperial Oil Limited, Peter Pearson, Producer/Director, Michael Maclear, Executive Producer.

CHILDHOOD

Family album:
Ken Dryden, age 10,
front row,
fourth from right,
father
Murray Dryden
and brother
Dave, coaches.

REG CORLETT

Things eternal, St.-Jérôme.

MICHAEL BOLAND

"HOCKEY HASSLES," TAKEN FROM *A PRAIRIE BOY'S WINTER,* © 1973. WILLIAM KURELEK PUBLISHED BY TUNDRA BOOKS.

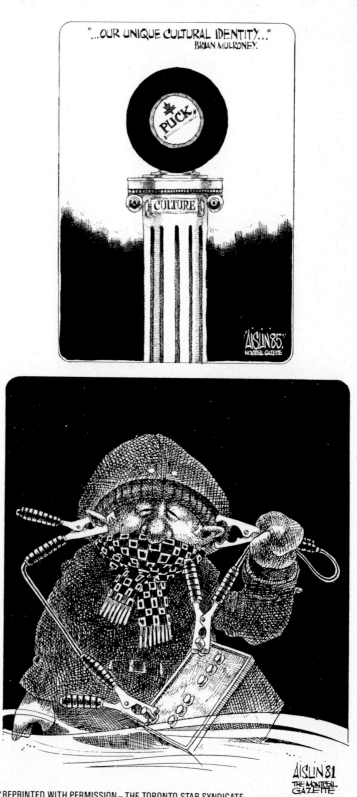

"...OUR UNIQUE CULTURAL IDENTITY..."
BRIAN MULRONEY.

PUCK

CULTURE

AISLIN 85
MONTREAL GAZETTE

AISLIN 81
THE MONTREAL GAZETTE

*REPRINTED WITH PERMISSION – THE TORONTO STAR SYNDICATE

The Forum,
Montreal.

DENIS BRODEUR

The Slough,
St. Denis, Saskatchewan.

Homecoming:
Team Canada,
Toronto, 1972.

BRIAN PICKELL

**Field of Dreams,
Islington, Ontario.**

**Getting close:
cameraman Mike Boland
and Saskatoon
and Prince Albert players.**

INTRODUCTION

HOCKEY IS PART OF LIFE IN CANADA. THOUSANDS PLAY IT, MILLIONS follow it, and millions more surely try their best to ignore it altogether. But if they do, their disregard must be purposeful, done in conscious escape, for hockey's evidences are everywhere – on television and radio, in newspapers, in playgrounds and offices, on the streets, in sights and sounds, in the feeling of the season. In Canada, hockey is one of winter's expectations.

Hockey is part sport and recreation, part entertainment, part business, part community-builder, social connector, and fantasy-maker. It is played in every province and territory and in every part of every province and territory in this country. Once a game for little boys, now little girls play hockey as well, and so do older men and women; so do the blind and the mentally and physically handicapped. And though its symmetry is far from perfect, hockey does far better than most in cutting across social division – young and old, rich and poor, urban and rural, French and English, East and West, able and disabled. It is this breadth, its reach into the past, that makes hockey such a vivid instrument through which to view Canadian life.

Its first game was played just eight years after Confederation by reluctant northerners who chose to escape winter and play it indoors. In little more than a century, hockey has moved from pickup games on rivers and sloughs to Friday nights in quonset-hut rinks, town against town, to cathedral-like arenas and *Hockey*

Night in Canada, to the spectacle of electronic scoreboards, synthesizers, and million-dollar contracts. Hockey has changed as life around it, as people in it, have changed; as Canada has changed.

This book is part of a project. About five years ago, some people at CBC asked if I was interested in adapting a previous book, *The Game*, into a television series. I thought about the suggestion, then decided not to pursue it. Such a series offered the challenge of working in a different medium but otherwise it seemed too much like going back to old familiar ground. As time passed, however, I began to think that hockey might offer some very new ground. Hockey, after all, is people and places. Look at those people hard enough and long enough, listen to them, and they will tell you stories – about themselves, about Canada. What they hope and want and fear; what matters to them and what doesn't. They will tell you about being parents and being kids, about having dreams and fantasies, about growing up and what it takes to make it to the top, to every big league, late in the twentieth century. They will tell you about sport and business and selling pure and simple – tickets, beer, T-shirts, cities, countries, values, ways of life. They will tell you about living and competing in a global world and being changed in the process; and of the need sometimes to escape that world and be someone else, creating your own rules and regulations – about the magic of play. And in so many ways, they will tell you about the joy of getting together, about the need for community. In lives filled with division, by age, income, status, neighbourhood, technology, distance, language, culture, they will tell you about the links they feel, about the feelings that bind us together.

I began to think that a careful look at hockey would tell us a lot about life in Canada – how it was, how it is, how it might be.

In this past year and more, often with the TV production crew, sometimes with Roy, sometimes alone, I have travelled this country and heard these stories. It has been a privilege. To be in St. Denis, Saskatchewan, on a slough, in the middle of a tiny French-speaking community that is unimaginably there, and that somehow survives – watching boys play hockey. To be on "coffee row," in the Red Bull Café in Radisson as people talked about their community and hockey and the rink that links them. Even to experience forty-below cold (not dry cold, not damp cold – *cold*) in Churchbridge and Saskatoon and Quebec City, wherever we went, it seemed.

It was a privilege to be in Los Angeles for the beginning of the Gretzky era, to be in Montreal as the Gretzky-less Oilers struggled against the Canadiens, to listen to Oilers' captain Mark Messier, in the eloquence of passion and conviction, talk about a team and what it means to be the best. It was a privilege to watch girls and women and older men, the blind, the physically and mentally handicapped, so long kept on the outside, playing hockey, too. And it was a privilege to be in Moscow just as two great adversaries, Vyacheslav Fetisov and his coach, Viktor Tikhonov, came to their final showdown. Hockey was my passion as a child, my opportunity. It was, and it remains, my education.

It has also been a privilege to spend time with hockey people, to rub up against their feelings and have them trust us with their stories. Igor Kuperman in Moscow, the Bentleys of Delisle, Saskatchewan, Bob Borgen, a pre-Gretzky oasis of hockey passion in Los Angeles, Joe Zeman in Saskatoon, Denis Gibbons in Burlington, Ontario, Ralph Barber in Toronto – and there are others – in communities small and large, people who *love* the game, just love it, beyond anything they get from it themselves. These people, along with the players of Huntsville's Christmas Classic and Roy's Dufferin Street regulars, along with my brother, Dave, who from the perspective of many years I know now was my teacher – he taught me how to play goal; more importantly, he taught me about play – serve as the emotional benchmarks of this book. I hope their feeling for the game comes through.

There are many people to thank: the CBC and Darce Fardy for their encouragement of this project and their patience; Doug Gibson, who understood the complications and benefits of doing a book and a TV series simultaneously, and never tried to have it both ways; Michael Maclear and the staff at Starplay Films; Peter Pearson, a self-proclaimed baseball fan, for his spirit and enthusiasms, his friendship and good sense; Mike Boland, for getting his video and still cameras right inside the action, and the rest of the dedicated Starplay staff: Mike Feheley, Guy Simoneau, Terry McKeown, Stephen Bourne, Julie Smith, Alexsandra Davies, Victoria Woods, Norah Wakula, and Adrienne Mitchell; Richard Tallman, our editor, Lucinda Vardey, Art Kaminsky, and Janet Pawson for their criticisms and support; Lynda, Sarah, and Michael Dryden, Ellen, Kerry, Christine, Jocelyn, and Gordie MacGregor for their inspiration and understanding.

And mostly, Roy MacGregor. We have known each other for nearly two decades. We share a love of hockey and writing; without his endless generosity, good nature, and professionalism, this book could not have been written.

Ken Dryden
Toronto
September, 1989

CHAPTER ONE

THE COMMON PASSION

Somewhere in our souls is a spiritual Canada. Most probably, its bedrock is of snow and ice, winter and the land. And if we were to penetrate it a little deeper, chances are we would find a game.

ON THE COLDEST DAY OF THE YEAR – MORE THAN FORTY DEGREES below by any measure – and in the teeth of what will be described in the morning paper as the worst blizzard to sweep down from Alaska in 100 years, the Yellowhead Highway is all but devoid of life. Cars and trucks travelling between Saskatoon and the Battlefords have been abandoned where they spun blind. Outside Radisson, within sight of the large red and white and black sign that in determined letters reads "Town With A Future!" there is only a rented car crawling uncertainly on black ice and, high above the slick road, a solitary black raven.

Ugly and naked on the cold wind, the bird drifts oblivious to the sheets of snow that flick off the near fields. But this is the raven, renowned for its ability to survive impossible conditions, an opportunist of enormous cunning. This is *Tuluguk*, the wise bird who, the Inuit say, created light by flinging mica chips against the sky, the one who dared to try what no one else had even imagined – and who succeeded against all odds.

Opposite the big sign sits the Red Bull Café, a combination gas station, video rental, and restaurant that serves as the Radisson "coffee row," a highway coffee and doughnut stand that is charged, along with the elevator and arena, with the care and nurturing of the town's soul. "Coffee row," Saskatchewan poet Stephen Scriver has written, "this is where it's at . . . if you want to find out about your past, present, or future, here it'll be. . . ."

And here, on a "dangerously cold" winter's day between harvest and seeding, local men – no women – have come to the Red Bull Café to talk, as always, about hockey. Usually, the talk is about last night's NHL schedule of games, especially about the Gretzky-less Edmonton Oilers if they happened to play, sometimes about the local junior team, Saskatoon's Blades of the Western Hockey League, just sixty kilometres down the highway. But more often now, they talk about their own hockey future. Radisson's old rink has been condemned as structurally unsafe. And in their voices, there is a mixture of fear for their community if they cannot raise the money necessary to build a new one, and hope that as they and their ancestors have done so often before, they will somehow find a way.

Radisson has "434 people on an early Sunday morning," according to the local school principal, Walter Kyliuk, who stirs his coffee while his neighbours burst, stomping and wheezing, through a glass door that has been painted solid with frost. Gathering here is the team that runs a typical Saskatchewan town with a Pool elevator, a Massey-Ferguson dealership, a post office, a fire hall, Co-op, Red & White, hotel, one boarded-up store, a ball diamond with local advertisers – "Bronsch Auctions"; "John Gerich MLA, Working for You for a Better Tomorrow" – providing the home-run fence and a pool hall that prefers to say "Billiards" over its entrance.

If one thing sets Radisson off from the hundreds of other small towns in the province, it is the nearly billboard-size sign at the turn by the farm equipment dealership, a painting of a Buffalo Sabres hockey player with the proud words "Welcome to Radisson, Home of Bill Hajt" – the home town honouring the local boy who went off down the Yellowhead Highway to play for the Saskatoon Blades, and from there to the National Hockey League. If there is one thing that ties Radisson to those other freckles across the face of Saskatchewan, it is that its arena – where Bill Hajt first learned to play his game – has been declared uninsurable.

"If you lose the rink," says Scotty Mundt, the retired power company employee who now as a volunteer takes care of the town arena, "people'll lose interest in the town and start looking other places. It's just as important as the elevator."

"It's the backbone of the community," says Don Harris, who runs the elevator. "That's what draws people to the town."

Around the tables, the coffee spoons stir and the men nod. "We know of other towns that have lost their rinks," says Kyliuk. "They die overnight. It's the grand central gathering place for the young and the old. The young come to skate and the older citizens come in to watch. The arena is the gathering place for the winter months."

"It's a baby-sitting place, too," adds Alfons Hajt, who, as Bill's father, has a particular place of honour at the Red Bull Café, a status that remains even though his son retired from professional hockey in 1987 after fourteen seasons with the Sabres. "Families like to leave the kids there and they'll do something else. And the children? They know they're looked after. They have a place to go."

"If I'd known that when they asked me to take on the rink," says Mundt with a wink, "I wouldn't be looking after it now." His friends laugh.

Dave Roberts listens and nods knowingly beneath his wide cowboy hat as these men from Radisson talk about the rink's value to their community. Roberts comes from Fielding, the next village up the Yellowhead Highway. "The first thing to go was our hockey rink," he says finally. "Then our curling rink went. Then our grocery stores started to go and gradually the school went and then our post office. All we have left now is a community hall which gets used once or twice a year for a stag party or a meeting. . . . Three families live in Fielding now and the rest is all deserted empty buildings."

Coffee row goes silent but for the ring of spoons being lazily turned. Roberts offers a vision more horrible to contemplate than the blizzard that bullies at the café door, daring them to come back out into a storm where even the raven must go with the prevailing winds.

Sixty kilometres east of Radisson, cars and half-tons are crawling along the Yellowhead where Highway 16 connects with 12. They move so slowly it is possible to hear the knock-knock that comes from tires that have been squared frozen on one edge as they sat through a day in which the radio warns that "exposed flesh will freeze in less than one minute." Thirteen deaths across the Prairies have already been attributed to the storm's cold and snow. A young farmer's truck has quit within sight of a farmhouse and yet he has frozen to death before he could walk the short distance. The radio stations have turned over their regular programming to endless lists of cancellations. *No bingo this evening at the Elks club . . . no Brownies at All Saints . . . Parent-teachers meeting put off 'til next Monday . . . curling cancelled until the weekend.* And the radio stations have filled in the spaces with incoming calls from listeners who are trapped in farmhouses and homes from Meadow Lake to Maymont, prairie people who talk about the food and fuel they have on hand as proof that the elements will never beat them, no matter what. *No 4-H tonight . . . no dart tournament . . . cribbage cancelled . . . choir practice off . . .*

But out here on the Yellowhead Highway on the northern outskirts of Saskatoon, the road is plugged with idling, blinking cars spewing exhaust smoke as thick as toothpaste. In this unlikely place on this forbidding night, the vehicles' occupants are almost in reach of their evening's destination, Saskatchewan Place. They park in the paved field that surrounds the arena, then hurry through wind and blowing snow and air so cold nostrils lock solid on a single breath. They are going to a hockey game.

Inside, they will cheer when the scoreboard flashes "COMPLIMENTARY BOOSTS AFTER THE GAME – BRIDGE CITY TOWING" and they will cheer again – proudly – during the third period

WELCOME TO
RADISSON
HOME OF
Bill Hajt

Coffee Row,
Radisson, Saskatchewan:
Walter Kyliuk, Dave Roberts,
Scotty Mundt,
Alfons Hajt, Wayne Rookes,
Don Harris.

Don Harris.

MICHAEL BOLAND

**Father and son:
Julian and Kevin Kaminski,
Churchbridge, Saskatchewan.**

The Gathering Place, Saskatoon.

The Mine,
Esterhazy, Saskatchewan.

MICHAEL BOLAND

The boys on the bus.

Long winter:
Kevin Kaminski (23).

Ties that bind:
near Floral, Saskatchewan.

Something in common:
Saskatoon, Saskatchewa

Visions: Kevin Kaminski.

LAURA SHUYA

when the game's attendance is announced: 5,594. They have come to the brand-new SaskPlace arena on a night when "extreme caution is advised," come to watch a junior hockey game featuring the third-place Saskatoon Blades and the seventh-place Regina Pats. They have come to cheer the progress of their home-town team as they go through a season-long training camp toward May's Memorial Cup, the Canadian championship for Junior A hockey. Saskatoon has never before been host city, the Blades, awarded an automatic berth as host team of the championships, never before a finalist.

And they have come to cheer for prairie kids with distinctly Canadian names, like Katelnikoff and Kocur, Snesar, Kuntz, Holoien, Lelacheur, Bauer, Yellowaga, Smart, and Sutton. And to wait for a nineteen-year-old named Kevin Kaminski – a young man with blue eyes and black, curling hair now skating about the warm-up with his sweater tucked big-league style into the left side of his pants – once again to strut his stuff.

They have come to a $30-million state-of-the-art hockey rink where the first sod was turned by a ninety-three-year-old World War One veteran named Johnny Walker, who as a young boy skated miles along the Qu'Appelle River with a rifle in his hand rather than a hockey stick, in search of mink not pucks. And they have come to drink Labatt's Blue beer in public in a city founded more than a century ago by the Temperance Colonization Society with the stated goal of creating a community where alcoholic beverages would never, ever be served. But they have not come to remind themselves of whom they are or how far they have come or how much they have changed along the way. They have come for the same reason people in Saskatchewan have always come to arenas: to be together.

Saskatoon's Wild Bill Hunter, who would turn this building into a home for a National Hockey League team if only the gods would listen to reason, says that on any winter Friday, Saturday, or Sunday night in the province of Saskatchewan – population slightly in excess of one million – more than 300,000 of these citizens are watching a live hockey game in some community, be it Saskatoon or Kevin Kaminski's home town of Churchbridge.

And even if Hunter occasionally deals more in exuberant truths than in more earthbound literal facts, the point is the same. Here, people love this game, and once more this damnable evening they prove it.

It is a mythic Canadian night. The land, the winter are everywhere. People are out where they shouldn't be, doing what to others seems to make no sense. But for the original prairie settlers, for Bill Hunter and Kevin Kaminski, for the people of tiny Radisson, for Canadians, what did sense ever have to do with anything?

Canada is such an improbable country. Just how improbable can be seen from an airplane drifting into Saskatoon's airport, just a few river-hockey games away from SaskPlace. The immensity of the land overwhelms. Only a few scruffs of trees and buildings distract the eye from its utter space. The land separates and disconnects, place from place, person from person. What links it all together seems so hopelessly overmatched. The broad winding rivers that brought in fur traders, the ruler-straight railway lines that brought settlers in and their grain out, the highways, the power lines, the TV antennae and TV dishes – such fragile threads to bind this far-flung land and its people. All serve to connect in some way, but these cannot create the bond. What ties us together must be a feeling that travels the waters and pavement and airwaves and steel: things we have in common, things we care about, things that help us make sense out of what we are.

It is a hard-won feeling. So much about Canada sets us apart – distance, topography, climate, language, European rivalries and cultures. The country can seem so contrary to destiny and good sense that at times we ask ourselves, "Why bother?" Canada has never worked seriously at developing the traditional instruments of community: the icons of nationhood – flag, constitution, monument – the myths, legendary figures, events and commemorative dates. Without such evidences of nation worship, without focal points for community expression, it can seem we lack a sense of nation. It can seem that what sets us apart is stronger than what holds us together. It can make our bonds seem frail. It can make us weak when we are not.

It matters little what the icon is, what the myth is about. For American nationhood, a bronze statue, the Statue of Liberty, is important, a story about a future President and a cherry tree gets passed on from generation to generation. An icon is nothing more than a symbol. It embodies and evokes what a nation feels about itself and offers its people the too-rare opportunity to express what they really feel. Canadians may seem undemonstrative and reserved, but not at a hockey game. We may seem isolated and distinct one from another, we may seem non-patriotic, but not at a hockey game. Hockey helps us express what we feel about Canada, and ourselves. It is a giant point of contact, in a place, in a time, where we need every one we have – East and West, French and English, young and old, past and present. The winter, the land, the sound of children's voices, a frozen river, a game – all are part of our collective imaginations. Hockey makes Canada feel more Canadian.

And it is here in Saskatchewan, this most Canadian of provinces, that we look for a game in its place.

To understand the phrase "Next Year Country" it helps to have been born in a sod hut. Better if it happened during a late May blizzard with no treebreak available, the gumbo laughing at your parents' feeble plough, last year's crop having failed, prices plummeting on the world grain market, white salt rings showing in the fields, the big sky of Saskatchewan clouding over with your top soil. "Man is a grasshopper here," Charles Mair wrote about the Prairies in a letter to the Toronto *Globe* in 1869, "a mere insect, making way between the enormous discs of heaven and earth." Forced to be continually in awe of the elements, prairie people, indeed, anyone in this northern land, found that their best resource was hope.

And tied to that pressing hope that things will eventually work out fine, there grew an optimism that was relentless, and to the mind of many others, often quite senseless. When Edmund Collins, a nineteenth-century Bill Hunter, went to New York City in 1887 to address the Canadian Club on "The Future of the Dominion of Canada," he informed his astonished audience that,

"Alone, the valley of the Saskatchewan, according to scientific computation, is capable of sustaining 800,000,000 souls." Next Year's Country was – and remains – a state of mind.

It was the way it had to be. If you looked prairie reality in the eye, you were too easily beaten. Pioneer farmers believed they could build a good life for themselves on the land and a prosperous community for themselves and their neighbours wherever a railroad siding or river bend or crossroads might bring them together as something other than farmers who shared an overblown sky and a bully for winter.

Having come to a seasonal, isolated life, those who set down roots sought out activities that could involve them as a community. The church was the first community centre – a place to meet each other as well as one's Creator – but it neither provided enough gathering time nor did it cut across the ethnic and religious divisions that give the Prairies a significant aspect of its character. Playing "ball" was popular at the fairs and Saturday afternoons that interrupted the hard summer labour. Curling and, later, hockey became religions of convenience during the long idle winters. They offered sources of much needed conversation, distraction, ways even of working together that otherwise happened only at harvest. They helped to create a community's bonds.

"Loneliness and the need for society brought people in from very large areas, and stirred them to extreme expressions of social solidarity," American author Gary Wills has written in an attempt to explain settler mentality in the U.S. That loneliness and separation and the need for community go a long way toward explaining the popularity of fundamentalist religion and passionate politics. To get people to slog ten miles through midwinter cold, one needed to offer entertainment as well as spiritual and secular basics. The same search for solidarity and entertainment also explains a lot about prairie people's fascination with hockey.

Hockey, in particular, became a winter passion for both players and watchers. It kept coffee row humming. It was, for many, a means of off-season fitness for the rigours of farming, the driving force behind the building of community centres, the way in which widely separate communities connected with each other. And it was a way of extending the web of community outward to regions, to the province, to the country itself, even if that web often burned with rivalry. Through Gordie Howe, the Bentley brothers, and countless more, perhaps more than any other, through Foster Hewitt, hockey was a connection to the rest of Canada more vivid and far more acceptable than banks and federal bureaucrats. And for young boys growing up on the Prairies – boys no different than Gordie Howe in Floral back in the 1940s or Kevin Kaminski in Churchbridge in the 1980s – hockey, like the RCMP and the priesthood, was that dreamed-of ticket to a bigger world.

Before there were malls, kids would hang around in hockey arenas. Before Zambonis could be found in every hockey rink in the land, it was the kids – rink rats – who would fight for the right to grab a wobbly, bent-blade snow shovel and join in the plough lines that circled the rink, for free, to clear off the snow so a barrel of hot water could be wheeled out for the flooding.

And before there were Zambonis and arenas, there was the outdoor game, played on farm ponds called "sloughs" and in schoolyards, as much in winter boots as on skates. Not so many years ago, it was very nearly the only game played in this mythical hockey heartland. Weather had created the game in the first place, but weather limited when and how often it could be played. Games awaited an early winter freeze-up, then ended for good, not when schedules were played out and playoffs won, but when the ice melted. In between, snowstorms and extreme cold temperatures – both hardly rare – cancelled many games. Jackie McLeod, a former New York Ranger from tiny Hazlet, a few miles west of Swift Current, remembers that as a boy in the late 1930s and early 1940s, he played "only three or four games a year." Gordie Howe, from Saskatoon's breakfast community of Floral, as the legend goes played on three different teams in one year. In doing so, he played fewer than half the games a Toronto Marlboro peewee, on one team, will play this year.

It was not until post-World War Two affluence, time, and technology moved the game indoors that hockey really boomed. Until then, prairie people of Howe's and McLeod's generation grew up, as most Canadians did, with a game that went on in their heads, with Foster Hewitt calling the play-by-play. Even today, those of middle age and older remember vividly the darkened kitchen on a Saturday night, a pale light washing through the doorway from the dining room, the entire family sitting around the kitchen table with the big, wooden radio sitting in its place of honour. They share a memory of the arched grill above the dial, and the burnt orange aura that came from a light behind the grill, and how as children they would sit staring at that light as if watching the very images that Hewitt's icy voice described. Men ten feet tall. Shots like Lee Enfield .303s. Passes as intricate as crewel-work. Common stories, common dreams, a mythology to share whether you lived in western small towns or eastern big cities. It was the tableau of its time. Canadian Gothic.

Hockey had become part of the Canadian imagination, an instinct, a need, an expectation passed from generation to generation, an obligation of one to the next. In 1970, a potash mine worker named Julian Kaminski tied a pair of too-large skates on the feet of a child not yet two years of age, and Sheldon Kaminski, then five, took his baby brother Kevin out onto the slough to try and teach him how to stand up on feet more used to being in his mouth than in stiff leather boots with rusted blades on the bottom. It was the same rite of passage Gordie Howe went through in Floral with his father, Ab, during the Great Depression, the same lesson that Wendel Clark would go through – with his mother, Alma, shouting stops and starts – in Kelvington. In Val Marie, Bryan Trottier would teach his border collie, Rowdy, how to play goal on the river that flowed past the family farm, and when Rowdy would die at age eleven in Trottier's last year of junior hockey, the poor dog would not have a tooth left in his head.

And out of that dream, that imagination, came the drive to build indoor arenas. Travel around the Saskatchewan landscape today and you will see countless tin-and-wood quonset-shaped rinks, "Memorial" arenas built after World War Two by communities to honour their past in the best way they knew how: by committing themselves to their own communities' future and to that of their children. A generation later, that commitment would be reaffirmed with "Centennial" arenas. The arenas went up like old-fashioned barn-raisings, the townspeople supplying as much of the material as they could, doing all of the labour themselves. For those towns which did not get their arenas, it was not that their dream was any less strong. They were smaller, or poorer. It would just take them longer.

Incredibly, in Saskatchewan today there are 459 indoor rinks, 151 of which have artificial ice. In all of the Soviet Union – a country some 300 times larger – there are only 116. With about 850 cities, towns, villages, and lesser communities in the province, nearly half can claim a rink. A closer look at the numbers offers even more startling details.

A city in Saskatchewan is defined as having 5,000 people or more. There are only twelve "cities" in the province. Together they share sixty-two indoor arenas (seventeen in Saskatoon, ten in Regina, eight in Prince Albert, three in Moose Jaw, and two in most of the rest). There are nearly 400 rinks, therefore, in communities with *fewer* than 5,000 people. Maymont, population 197, has a rink. So do Marquis, population 97, and Brownlee, population 89. None of this makes the slightest sense, it seems, but of course it does.

Each community needs a place to gather, to act and feel like a community, to remind itself of why it is a community, to strengthen its resolve to fight those forces that threaten its existence. A local arena is spirit-building, and in a time of enormous change, every bit of spirit that can be mustered is needed. Out of every three of those 850 cities, towns, and villages, one is growing, two are dying. "Memorial" rinks and "Centennial" rinks are getting old and beyond repair. It is the story of Radisson and of a hundred other communities in the province. The arena that was a symbol of community development is becoming a symbol of community transformation and dissolution.

But Kevin Kaminski has other things on his mind. The next step along his hockey dream, the Memorial Cup, is just a few months away. Last year, he got close enough to it to be hugely disappointed when the Blades fell short in the WHL playoffs. He remembers the fans that jammed into SaskPlace – it seemed as if all of Saskatoon was there. It reminded him of those Friday night games in Churchbridge, town against town, "our boys" against "their boys," and when his own peewee and bantam teams played for provincial championships. This will surely be his last chance at a Memorial Cup, and he knows it. He also knows it is his next chance to show the Minnesota North Stars of the National Hockey League, which drafted him in the third round in 1987, that he belongs. For the NHL is the final step to Kevin Kaminski's hockey dream.

That dream began in Churchbridge, a town of 1,035 people in southeast Saskatchewan, also along the Yellowhead Highway, about halfway between Saskatoon and Winnipeg. The town had its origins more than a century ago when the Manitoba and North-West Railway came through and brought with it a party of wide-eyed settlers from the Anglican Church Colonization Land Society. A century later, the Anglican Church is only one of seven thriving churches and farming is less important to the town's economic base than are the potash mines in nearby Esterhazy. The original British stock of colonists survives but shares the town with the Icelanders and Germans and others who followed. And the new business brochure, in which the town describes itself as "More than a good place to live," gives bare mention to the fact that the CPR roars through on its way to Edmonton but prominently features the curling club and hockey rink.

Julian Kaminski came to Churchbridge in 1964. A son of poor immigrant farmers from the Ukraine, he had left his family's farm a few kilometres north of town and gone to work in Winnipeg for a year but learned to despise city life. "You never knew anybody," he says. "It just wasn't my type of life." He went north to Thompson, Manitoba, working briefly in the nickel mines there, then ended up in Churchbridge when he heard that International Mineral was opening a potash mine and taking on men.

He was twenty-two years old. Within weeks he met Vicki Ellingboe, who was working in the town's beauty shop, and soon after they were married. In 1966 a son, Sheldon, was born. Three years later, Kevin was born, and in 1973, a daughter,

Lana. Now forty-seven, with a quarter-century of mine work behind him, Julian figures he will work at the mine until he retires and live in Churchbridge until he dies.

The children, however, are gradually moving away. Sheldon is a third-year history major at the University of Saskatchewan in Saskatoon. Kevin imagines a future in Minnesota with the North Stars. Lana, now sixteen, also plans to go to university, and, like her brothers, doesn't plan to go back. The local mines are doing well, its workers stay on and rarely leave, openings are rare. But their desire to move on is an instinct. Young people do not dream of small towns and potash mines down a short, familiar road. "When I get older and do settle down," says Kevin over dinner one night, "I think it'll be in the city."

"Yeah," says his father, jumping in from the far end of the table, "until you start having kids of your own – and then you'll wish you were in a smaller town."

The son says nothing to his father. There is no animosity, just echoes of a conversation repeated in every small town over so many other evening meals.

Kevin Kaminski lived the mythical Canadian boyhood – on skates at twenty-one months; on the streets in road hockey games through much of every winter, half a block from his house where Sunset Street meets Vincent, with his older brother, Sheldon, the Sakundiaks, Troy and Todd, the five Sopkow brothers, Ray, Ronnie, Glen, Barry, and Randy; the local rink, just a few hundred metres away; the town teams, his father the coach, Kevin the star and often the captain, on his back the jersey number (19) of his hero (Bryan Trottier of the New York Islanders); the trophies, team pictures hanging in the arena, the championship seasons. And at fifteen he was a kid with a future, moving away to Saskatoon as had so many before him.

Kevin developed into a tough, scrappy player with a frightening temper. He was known around the Churchbridge area as "Killer" Kaminski, a nickname that sticks today. His passion for the game and slickness with the puck, coupled with a genuine meanness, made him a star with but one main liability: his size. Listed at 5′ 9″ and 190 pounds in the Blades' guide, he seems smaller. Size is his father's one regret, almost as if he blames himself. "I wish he was bigger," Julian Kaminski says. "Six foot would help."

It was size that convinced Kevin Kaminski that he would not be selected in the NHL draft, if at all, until near the end of his junior career, even though, at eighteen, he would become available in the 1987 draft. That June 20th, when the other stars of the Western Hockey League were sitting with their agents and parents in Detroit's Joe Louis Arena waiting for the NHL teams to announce their selections, Kevin Kaminski was in Regina playing a ball game.

The ball game over, Kevin hitched a ride with a fellow player, Brian Glynn, who had been drafted a year earlier by the Calgary Flames. Kaminski was sitting in the back seat trying not to think about the draft. Glynn turned on the radio and danced the dial straight into the announcement: *Minnesota North Stars select Saskatoon's Kevin Kaminski in the third round.* "My heart started beating," remembers Kaminski. "I wanted to shout but I was speechless." Instead, Glynn turned from the front seat and punched him. *"Awwwrigghhht Killer!"* No NHL sweater from a smiling general manager, no photographers, no applause – but that didn't matter.

He attended the Minnesota training camp that fall, returned to the Blades for the season, then was back again in September, 1988. This time he felt he would make it. Minnesota had had a dismal season the year before and was in desperate need of the kind of fiesty spirit that Kevin offered. He played in several exhibition games and was in the North Stars' lineup as they opened the season against the Canadiens in the Montreal Forum.

Kevin remembers the night: "Guys like Larry Robinson and Bob Gainey," he says, shaking his head, his voice pitching higher. "It's just amazing. While they're playing you'd just like to stop and shake their hands, you know, because you watched them on TV when you were just a little kid and now you're all of a sudden skating and playing against them." Even if he never plays another NHL game, he will never forget the first time he stepped out onto the Forum ice for the warm-up skate. "Big leagues," he says. "No helmet on and you get your hair blowing and it's just – you just pump, the adrenaline's flowing, you're so hyper, you have all the energy in the world. It feels like you're skating about sixty miles an hour. It just seemed like all eyes were on you, especially around ice level because all the men have suits on and their wives are all dressed in fur coats and diamonds and everything and everybody was just watching you. And you didn't want to make a mistake because everybody would start laughing or something."

The North Stars lost the game by a goal. Kevin Kaminski was used only sparingly, and a few days later he was sent back to the Blades for another season. So he could work on his skating, they said. Intellectually, he understood. Emotionally, he remained in Minnesota. Back in Saskatoon, the points didn't come. He didn't seem as tough as last year. He didn't seem as important to the team.

In January of 1989, *Star-Phoenix* sports columnist Dave Komosky put down in print what Kaminski had been hearing from the stands, even in the whispers of his teammates. Kaminski's play, Komosky wrote, "has some people . . . asking whether Kaminski is a liability the Blades can do without. . . . Something is terribly wrong. . . . Fans look at him and wonder why he doesn't drive down the ice any more. They look at his stats and wonder why they're only half of what they were at this stage last season."

Putting on his media face, Kaminski professed little concern – "I've just got to work harder, that's all" – but he was deeply puzzled. Other guys were tough; he was always tougher. They would go *this* far; he would go farther. It was a point of pride. He did what it took, whatever it took, to win. And everyone knew it. Some guys came back from NHL camps with a big-shot swagger about them, too big for junior hockey. He would be different. But this year, he wasn't. *What's wrong with me?* he agonized.

Searching for an answer, Kevin has even begun showing up each game day at 3:30 in the afternoon in the office of Flo Lavallie, a Saskatoon reflexologist. There he lies back with his shoes and socks off while Flo massages his feet, using the 4,500-year-old Chinese secrets of foot kneading to relax his back muscles, improve his circulation, ease his mind, clear his thoughts. While Flo works his toes and twists his heel, Kaminski closes his eyes and plots his revenge, imagining himself standing at the podium during the team's end-of-season banquet, the star centre who came back so dramatically in the last half of the season, Kevin Kaminski, on his way to certain glory with the Minnesota North Stars.

But now he must produce. On the verge of realizing his dream, one he has shared with his father and mother and brother, with the Sakundiaks and Sopkows and most of the neighbourhood kids in most of the towns and cities of this country, one he got close enough to taste that night in Montreal, he can suddenly feel it slipping away. He must fight to get it back.

Saskatoon is barely 100 years old, a settlement founded in 1883 high on the banks of the shallow, muddy South Saskatchewan River. The river, before the railroad, is what connected the fur traders to the rest of the country. The railroad came later, in 1890, and was what made this bend in the river more than a convenient place to camp. In 1901, Saskatoon's population was 113. Nearby Rosthern's was 413. The locating of the main switches for the Canadian Pacific Railroad line meant that Saskatoon, now 177,000, would thrive while Rosthern, population 1,594 today, would be fortunate to survive. Then as now, especially on the Prairies, things came to those who went and got.

"At Rosthern," a correspondent for the *Montreal Herald* reported in 1905, "the population seems to sit around thinking what it may become when destiny comes to pass; at Saskatoon it is so busy bringing it to pass a few decades earlier than scheduled, that it has no time to think about what will be at all." By 1912, Saskatoon's population was 28,000, an "instant" city, the self-proclaimed fasting growing city in the world.

The city's blessing, of course, was to be situated where it was during the "Wheat Rush," but that in itself was not enough. Other cities were just as well positioned. When Sir John A. Macdonald's National Policy moved into the settlement of the West, enterprising Saskatoon merchants built warehouses and the railway stop became a distribution centre. In the fifteen years between 1901 and 1916, the area that became the province of Saskatchewan in 1905 grew from 90,000 to 650,000, a vast number of them immigrants from Britain. A wave of eastern European immigrants followed a decade later. Those who tried prairie farming but decided to leave it fell naturally to the nearest urban centre, which in the north of the province was Saskatoon. In time the city gained hospitals, schools, a university, government centres, each new development serving to attract others.

It sounds easy. It wasn't. A hundred years ago, one flat piece of prairie looked pretty much like another. Why then settle *here*, not *there*? Why build the capital in Regina, the university in Saskatoon? There was no good, natural, indisputable reason. Each community had to create a reason. Sometimes it was real, sometimes fanciful. It was a time for promoters, dreamers, crackpots, and the communities that got in behind them. "Prairie spirit" or "Saskatoon spirit," it was called, depending on where you lived. Anyone who doubted or questioned or criticized was avoided. He was a "knocker." You had one chance to make your case, to promote yourself better than the next place in line. There would be one hospital, one school. If the other guy got it, you never would. The province's history of co-operation and solidarity had its roots in pragmatism, not ideology. It emerged out of need. Competition and rivalry were directed outward, not at neighbours but down the line at the next town. Nothing much has changed.

One person who understands prairie spirit and boosterism is Bill Hunter. Known across the Prairies as "Wild" Bill Hunter, he much despises the nickname. He is the small-town guy who has big city ideas, a community builder with hockey his chosen instrument. Like Professor Harold Hill in *The Music Man*, Hunter's way is to persuade people that they can do anything – start up a new hockey league, bring an NHL franchise to Saskatoon – but first they must *believe*.

Hunter was the driving force behind the formation of the junior Western Hockey League that the Saskatoon Blades play in today. Nearly twenty years ago he was a main player in the birth of the World Hockey Association, upstart rival league to the

National Hockey League. In 1979, a merger brought four of those WHA franchises into the NHL, and one of them, the team Hunter founded – the Edmonton Oilers – turned out to be the dominant NHL team of the 1980s. And it was Hunter who, in 1983, decided that little Saskatoon should go after the floundering St. Louis Blues franchise and bring the NHL to what would be the league's smallest city.

It made no sense, but he almost pulled it off. The huge American manufacturer, Ralston Purina, was anxious to divest itself of the money-losing Blues, and a local buyer could not be found. Hunter wanted to give them a home where the game truly mattered. In doing so he was attempting to fight more than a hundred years of history. Things come *from* the Prairies. Every Canadian school kid knows that. Wheat, minerals, people – raw materials get nurtured and cultivated here, then sent east or west, but always someplace else. It is the same with hockey players. Eddie Shore, Bryan Trottier, Gordie Howe – "You saw the best of him down east," Johnny Walker, the ninety-three-year-old Qu'Appelle River skater, once said of Howe. He spoke with no bitterness or resentment, with just the truth. It was the way it was, it was the way it always would be.

But the Saskatchewan Blues would be different. Something *finally* would be grown and developed and *finished* at home.

Hunter built his pitch on a tantalizingly plausible premise: if the people of the province can support the Saskatchewan Roughriders of the Canadian Football League and average more than 20,000 fans a game, they will surely support an NHL team. The analogy, however, is far from exact. An NHL team would ask the Saskatchewan sports fan to get to, and pay for, forty home hockey games a season, as opposed to ten (including pre-season) in football, and to travel to those games over winter roads. Hunter was unimpressed. *Fans will come from Gull Lake and Foam Lake and Punnichy and Raymore as well as from Saskatoon and Regina*, he sang. *We'll get special buses, arrange special packages . . .*

And the Saskatoon people listened. Many were a bit surprised that they listened. They had heard such things from Hunter before. Still, the more they listened, the more sense the whole thing seemed to make. Why not? The professional enthusiasts –

politicians and business people – slowly, then in a rush, jumped on board Hunter's bandwagon. The professional sceptics – academics, media – went curiously silent. Prairie convention took over. Its code spread about the landscape as it has for a hundred years. *We've got to stick together. This is a long shot. We may make it, we may not. But if we have any chance, we need everybody. We've got to show the NHL that their population/market size mumbo jumbo just doesn't apply here. There's no place for any clear-eyed columnist or politician with perspective to doubt. Naysayers, nonsayers never built this land. With the first bad winter, with the first drought, they were gone. They're just "knockers," and who needs them? Let them move to Toronto, where everyone can afford to be so reasonable, where there's always a second chance, where nothing needs to matter much. This may seem like so much nonsense to anyone there, but let it. We make our own sense out here. We have to.*

Hunter's failure was not in Saskatchewan. The people took off their John Deere caps and put on Saskatchewan Blues caps instead. More than 18,000 pledged to buy season tickets. People carried "Go For It Bill!" placards, wore buttons, and wrote to the NHL. Hunter struck an agreement-in-principle with Ralston Purina to buy the team for $14.5 million, pending approval of the National Hockey League Board of Governors. He did not get it.

The *market* wasn't there, the league decided. Putting thousands of bodies into arena seats was one thing, making TV couch potatoes out of millions more was something else again. Only one million people lived in the whole province. Modern sports franchises need large TV revenues, they need to sell T-shirts and key chains and every sort of knickknack, and for that they need large markets. Besides, travel would be difficult – not winter roads but scheduled airline runs for incoming opponents. It would mean another Canadian team when the league was already concerned with hockey's too-Canadian image. And if that wasn't enough, imagine aspiring in the U.S. to the big-league status of baseball and football, and a marquee at Madison Square Garden reading: "Tonight! Rangers vs. Saskatchewan Blues." That one image alone was enough.

The people of Saskatchewan felt they had been done in by the NHL owners and NHL president John Ziegler the way their ancestors had been done in by eastern banks in the depression – never given a fair chance. Worse, they felt put down. They had caught Hunter's dream. They were proud of their community. Saskatonians had never thought of Winnipeg, Calgary, or Edmonton as being much different than they were. An NHL team would be just recognition of Saskatoon's past, its growth and increased importance, and would be a catalyst for the future growth they could feel was coming.

Instead, they felt mocked. In trying to be bigger than they were, they were made to feel smaller than they are. Stephen Scriver, in "Nobody Cares Who Got The Blues," had this to say:

> *The way I got it figgered*
> *well you see money talks*
> *an Yankee money is a hell of a lout louder*
> *than ours so we gotta go after the buggers*
> *some other way*
>
> *like number one*
> *no more going across the border*
> *an loadin up the spare tire*
> *with American beer me*
> *I'm strickly a Moldon's man*
> *from here on in*
>
> *then Satudday night*
> *we all gotta switch off the CBC*
> *an boycott "Hockey Night in Canada"*
> *this boy'll be watchin "Hymn Sing"*
> *before he supports that crap again*
>
> *. . . but mostly we gotta stop growin our boys*
> *to go an play on their teams*
> *I say we just save em up*
> *for a couple years*
> *make our own team an then show em*
> *just think – no more Gordie Howe*
> *or Tiger Williams fillin the stands*
> *for those blood-suckers*

. . . so what it all comes down to
is that Yankee Board of Governors
don't know if their butts
is punched, bored, or shot out
by the Lone Ranger an none of em
better show their faces in Saskatchewan
or they'll have a halfton
ridin their tails all the way
from Moosomin to Maple Creek

"We were disappointed and shocked," Hunter told a huge Saskatoon rally when he returned. "But believe me, we will never quit." Ralston Purina eventually sold the Blues – for less money than Hunter was offering – to Canadian-born Beverly Hills businessman Harry Ornest, who promised to keep the franchise operating in St. Louis. So Hunter turned his vision away from St. Louis and toward the oft-rumoured NHL expansion into places like Dallas, Milwaukee, San Francisco, Seattle, and Hamilton – and, with Bill Hunter always fuelling the rumour, Saskatoon.

It is said about Bill Hunter, "He can make you blind." He is the modern-day version of yesterday's temperance society land flogger, the man who is bringing the railroad. He is the distant rain cloud during drought. He is Next Year Country incarnate.

"If you look at the map of North America today," Bill Hunter says from a Saskatoon office littered with the memorabilia from his bid to bring in the Blues, "there's no community and no area better fitted for an NHL franchise than are we in the province of Saskatchewan. We're the only province west of the Maritimes without a major-league franchise. You take a look at our two neighbouring provinces – Manitoba with the Winnipeg Jets and Alberta with the club that I founded, the Edmonton Oilers, and the Calgary Flames – two NHL franchises and two of *the most successful* NHL franchises. I'll never forget when [former NHL president] Clarence Campbell and I met many years ago when I was going to buy the Pittsburgh Penguins, who were at that time in deep financial trouble, and move them to Edmonton. Campbell said, 'There's no way Edmonton could support an NHL franchise.' Well, from day one they became the leader in the NHL – in attendance *and* excitement." Hunter chuckles at the memory he has shared once again.

Hunter is not fazed by the fact that Alberta has a population almost three times that of Saskatchewan. Hunter does not faze. "We in Saskatchewan are unique," he argues. "The Saskatchewan Roughriders draw from across this province. In hockey we would draw from all areas. We have 18,694 season ticket requests recorded on the Price Waterhouse computer. We would sell out our 16,000-seat building. We can stand another 1,200. We would build sky boxes and we would be one of *the* most successful franchises. We'd be a strong financial asset and we'd be an exciting draw, too – because people *love* an underdog."

It goes on and on. The listener begins with the urge to interrupt him at most every point: *Why would you say that? You don't really believe . . . Oh come off it, Bill . . .* but the urge slowly fades.

Saskatchewanians, Hunter believes, are special. "We love our sport," he says. "We are located at the heart of North America, a cold, cold province with extreme winters. I think that pulls Saskatchewan people together. They have to huddle together to get warm. But it created a community atmosphere. The 'Riders have thrived when others in the CFL have been stumbling and falling. With a team that missed the playoffs for eleven straight years, our crowds were always in the top three, outdrawing cities like Ottawa, outdrawing Hamilton, outdrawing Winnipeg, outdrawing Calgary. Why? Because of the *spirit* and the *enthusiasm* of the Saskatchewan sports fan. It's unique. There's no question about it. And there's no question that we *will* draw. Our drawing area is not twenty-five miles. It is not fifty miles. Our drawing area is a *300*-mile radius of Saskatoon."

It may well be. Prairie people measure their miles differently from people in the rest of the country. When Prince Albert Raiders' team president Ken Webster was asked if the Raiders ever considered chartering buses to accommodate the 300 or so fans that follow the team down to Saskatoon for games against the Blades, he laughed. "Buses? It's only ninety miles!"

But in a smaller place, there is only so much of everything to go around; and the pie doesn't expand so easily. If one gets too big, it is usually at the expense of someone else. For all to survive, each must share and forgo great ambition, or leave. What then if Hunter is right? If somehow the province could support an NHL team?

"It would be like putting a patient on life support," says Guy Vanderhaeghe, the Saskatoon-based novelist. "All that support would have to go to the franchise. . . . My guess is that it would be bad for the city and, in some ways, bad for the province. There are only so many resources and you can only distribute them in certain ways. An NHL franchise would have to monopolize resources that could go into other areas."

"Bringing in a National League team?" says Ken Webster of the Prince Albert Raiders. "Not only would it destroy junior hockey, it would decimate to some degree the fibre of Saskatchewan rural life." Prince Albert, he believes, is like Saskatchewan in microcosm. For the junior team to survive its people must work longer and smarter than those in bigger areas. Prince Albert must also draw from surrounding communities, many of them nearly as close to Saskatoon as they are to Prince Albert. Already since SaskPlace opened, attendance at Raiders games has slipped by around 400 a game, and the suspicion is that most of these lost fans are now attending Blades' games, which they can combine with shopping in Saskatoon's bigger and better stores, eating in its more numerous restaurants, using all of its bigger city's amenities.

An NHL team in Saskatoon would monopolize far more than the hockey money and time of the province, Webster believes. For all to survive, each must share and forgo great ambition – or leave. It is the vulnerable nature of life on the margins, what prairie people have had to understand and cope with all their lives.

It is the universal city-town dilemma, and a classic Canadian dilemma. Is it better that the next aerospace plant be built in Toronto or in Simcoe, Ontario; in Ontario or in Saskatchewan or Newfoundland? To the extent these things can be influenced, do we want to encourage people to live in Toronto or Saskatoon, or is it important somehow that *someone* live in Simcoe or Prince

Albert? Should resources go to the few to trickle down, it is hoped, to the many? Should they get spread around to the many, but more thinly? Do we fight prevailing winds or go with them? Does it really matter anyway?

Bill Hunter believes there is more than enough for everybody. He has *faith* that Saskatoon's good fortune would be for all the province to share. He believes that Saskatoon was turned down earlier because the timing was not quite right. The league was in the process of negotiating a national television contract and the loss of St. Louis would mean the loss of much of the Midwest market. All that has changed now. Saskatoon has proved itself by building its NHL arena, and when the time comes for expansion, Hunter is convinced, the NHL will opt for two American cities and one Canadian. And that Canadian city will not be Hamilton but Saskatoon. How soon will this come about? "*Amazingly* soon."

But just as before, Hunter's biggest obstacle, more insur-mountable than small markets and population, than winter and prairie distances, is *the outsider*. The outsider, in Ottawa or Toronto, New York, Washington, London, or Tokyo, determines much of life here. What the outsider does and thinks matters absolutely. And Hunter knows the outsider thinks of Saskatoon and Saskatchewan the way the slightly more distant outsider thinks of Canada: the archetype, the myth, the land of ice and snow and great open spaces, of great resources and not many people and small unimportant markets. And so even if the people of Saskatchewan can deliver the improbable, they will not likely be given the chance.

Bill Hunter would not likely take consolation from this, but, succeed or not, his attempt to bring an NHL team to Saskatoon galvanized the community, in the city and province. It made it think and act and feel like a community the way few things ever have. In the meantime, Bill Hunter, an insatiable devourer of biographies of other visionaries, will comfort himself with his favourite anecdotes, mostly concerning Thomas Edison, the inventor of the electric light that stands as a symbol for all great inspiration.

"History records," Hunter notes, his own smile rising and flickering like a Jacob's ladder, "and don't hold me to this, that Edison discovered light sometime after 3,978 attempts, somewhere along that. Well, that perseverance has been behind all great, great things in this world. History has shown that all great achievements or accomplishments have been built of dreams. I have a dream to bring the NHL to Saskatchewan. I was born and raised here. I come of a hockey family. My father was a great sportsman in this province for many years before me. And we were all taught by our grandparents and forefathers that in Saskatchewan *you persevere*. We have come through droughts. We have come through heavy rains and blowing snow and everything else, and this province has continued to rise and produce great happenings and great people. I believe we'll be in the NHL because we have the guts to persevere.

"The critics don't understand that. But what have the critics ever built? I'm saying I can see it now that on opening night there will be thousands standing outside the building who can't get in because they didn't believe. . . . That's the heritage of western Canada – when others say it can't be done, we know *it can be done*."

> *When the railroad comes – it cannot come to all of us;*
> *Some will mourn in far-off valleys, some will curse on*
> *distant slopes.*
> *For the tinkling of the hammers filling many hearts with*
> *rapture*
> *May be spiking fast the coffin lid on other people's hopes.*
> W.A. MacLeod, "When the Railroad Comes"

It can be done . . . That is what they say in Radisson as well. But the men who sit over coffee in the Red Bull Café say it not only *can* be done, *it must be done*. The story, told by Dave Roberts, of how Fielding disappeared as a community is for the outsider. The real thing is just down the road, and it haunts them. They can almost imagine the same future for themselves: the neat houses of Radisson boarded up, the post office closed, the paint peeling off the outfield fence, never again chatter in the field, cheers from the stands, the hollow sound of a puck rapping against boards in an early morning practice.

There is something different here. In Saskatoon, in Toronto and Antigonish, hockey helps to make a community feel like a community. Here in Radisson, the hockey-community connection is literal and absolute. If a new arena doesn't get built, the community may die. "That's why our recreational facility is so crucial to our town's survival," says Walter Kyliuk, the school principal. "Because there are teachers and policemen who will apply for jobs in small towns if there are adequate recreational facilities. Then we get quality applicants. But if you don't have a focal point in the community – a recreation centre – then we don't get quality applicants and everything starts to deteriorate after that."

These men seek a new arena for themselves, for their jobs and homes and futures, and because they believe in continuity, in the importance of shared memories. You can sense the feeling of community at the Red Bull Café, see it even in the fire hydrants around Radisson painted to resemble townsfolk – there is a Bill Hajt hydrant, a Walter Kyliuk and a Don Harris one, even one of a priest in front of the church.

"The kids will never forget the years they played against the neighbouring communities," says Don Harris. "They're going to have friends wherever they go, somebody they played hockey against. These are the best years of their lives. Somebody has to provide that for these kids. . . . These are things that communities have to do in order to survive. Maybe they'll some time farm here and have kids of their own and they'll remember that somebody built a rink for them back in 1989."

"Somebody got one for us in 1960," says Wayne Rookes, "so somebody's gotta replace that one."

It was the rink that put Bill Hajt into the NHL. Without an indoor arena, it could never have happened. And they know it. They also know what else is at stake. They prefer not to think about the fact that others will surely lose if they are to win, because that only muddles the mind that can't afford the muddle.

"Right now we're struggling for survival and trying to stay

ahead of the pack," says Walter Kyliuk. "We'd rather cohabitate with our neighbours and support each other so that everybody could have some facilities and everybody would be able to survive . . . but we unconsciously have become involved in the survival game because of the trends we face. If we had any way to influence the trends we'd work on that part of it. But . . ."

The survival game . . . The fact is that the province's 850 communities reflect Saskatchewan of another time. The size of a farm historically bears some relationship to the capacity of a family and its equipment to cope with it. The existence of a local town bears some relationship to the ability of local people to get access to its services. Technological advances have allowed farmers to handle larger farms with many fewer people and to travel greater distances to gain access to a town's services. As a result, farm families have gotten smaller, and many children who grow up extraneous to the needs of the farm move to the cities. This leaves many fewer people living in the same geographical area. Services that have sprung up to support these people – car dealerships, banks, barber and beauty shops – must, to survive, increase the size of the area in which they do business. This, of course, means an overlap with the services offered by other towns that also must extend their reach and, consequently, direct competition. There is not room for everybody. The simple fact of today is that, economically, Saskatchewan does not need all of its 850 communities.

It is a story told again and again – school consolidations, post office closures, grain elevators shut down. The Wheat Pool, a farmer-owned co-operative, has been closing elevators at a rate of about fifteen a year. In 1972, there were 1,200 Pool elevators across the province; today the number is about 800; and by the turn of the century it is predicted there will be only about 300 elevators in operation. The larger implications are predictable. "When you take out the elevator," the Pool's Jim Affleck admitted to the *Globe and Mail*, sounding like Dave Roberts of Fielding, "it's sort of like putting the stake in the cemetery. That sort of marks the end of the town."

The arena is part of the same story. It is another of those

essential services a town has needed to provide in order to survive. But farm populations have shrunk, people are able and willing to drive farther for what they want, and, simply stated, the province no longer needs all 459 of its indoor arenas. The arenas have been built so they will continue to operate. The fork in the road comes, however, when, because of age or instability, they must be rebuilt. Even the barest of facilities now costs upwards of $500,000 to build. What to do, especially if you are Radisson or a few hundred towns like it and have only 434 people or so to share your burden? It may well be that the province does not need all its arenas, but each town surely needs its own.

More than a community centre, the arena has become an important community symbol. The arena went up to reflect and encourage a community's bonds. Now it goes up again in communities anxious to sustain those bonds. A new arena is a ringing message, ambitious and defiant, to banks, car dealers, farm equipment dealers, stores, people in town and people out of town, that "We will make it."

One will make it, two will not. These are the unblinking odds for every small town in Saskatchewan surviving long into the next century. These are the prevailing winds that not even the cunning raven can brave. Who will make it and who will not? As always in Saskatchewan, things will come to those who go and get.

In the fall of 1986 the Radisson rink campaign began. It started slowly. The first year was a learning process. "Penny ante stuff," Walter Kyliuk now describes it. Such fund-raisers as bottle drives and box socials attracted little money, but gradually the campaign began in a new direction, and in earnest. The arrival of Bill Hajt into the NHL had put Radisson on the hockey map. His retirement could ensure its future. The committee decided to stage a "Bill Hajt Retirement Dinner" as an official kick-off to the rink campaign. The dinner featured Hajt as guest of honour, and Bill Hunter, *Hockey Night in Canada*'s Don Cherry, and Hartford Whalers GM Emile Francis as special guests. In 434-person Radisson, 420 sat down to dinner and 800 came to the dance that followed. More than $8,000 was raised.

As an unexpected bonus, Hajt had been in contact with his old team and the Buffalo Sabres had pledged a further $5,000. When the cheque hadn't arrived in a few weeks, Walter Kyliuk, Don Harris, and Wayne Rookes flew to Buffalo to meet with the Knox brothers, owners of the Sabres, and pick up the cheque personally. On their way home, they stopped off in Toronto and got themselves interviewed by the *Toronto Star*.

"We see on television every night that Ontario is on the upswing," Harris told the *Star*. Added Rookes mischievously, "We figured if everyone in Toronto gave $1 off their paycheque, we'd have it made." Kyliuk painted an evocative picture of the town rink as Radisson's "community living room." The article went on to say that the people of Radisson were still $500,000 short in their rink campaign.

Through former Saskatoon Blades player Wendel Clark, they also tried to arrange a meeting with Harold Ballard, principal owner of the Toronto Maple Leafs, but Ballard was ill and in the hospital. Leaving Maple Leaf Gardens disappointed, they walked across Carlton Street for lunch at the Golden Griddle restaurant. The manager recognized them from their picture in the *Star*, picked up their meal tab, and arranged for every other Golden Griddle in the Toronto area to do the same, should they drop by. He also called Toronto's Radisson Hotel and persuaded them to provide rooms for fellow travellers from Saskatchewan's Radisson.

"It was unbelievable," Wayne Rookes remembers. "These people knew nothing of us. They never had to worry about losing their rink. Yet somehow they *understood*." He shook his head and took a deep breath at the wonder of it. "You know, it's hard for us to know what people in the East are really like. It's hard for them to know us, too, I guess. Sometimes we get these ideas in our heads . . . " And he paused. "You know, we really don't understand each other very well, do we?" And then he brightened. "Yet *this* they really understood." He shook his head again and, a little embarrassed, he said, "You know, I never felt so Canadian as I did that day."

The initial response from Toronto was a mere $300, which served to interest the national media all the more. The Canadian Imperial Bank of Commerce offered to accept contributions to the fund at any of its metropolitan Toronto branches, and more money began flowing in. Wayne Rookes was interviewed on CBC's *Midday*. Watching him in Milton, Ontario, was Joe Tutt, a twenty-five-year-old driveway contractor. He decided for his part to embark on a fund-raising journey by bicycle from Milton to Radisson, more than 3,000 kilometres. A mobile-home dealer in North Battleford offered a vehicle to accompany him. Several weeks later, when Tutt arrived, he was met by his wife, whom the Radisson organizers had quietly flown out to greet him. They had also purchased for both of them non-refundable return air tickets to Toronto. Tutt had raised about $25,000 on his trip to Radisson, short of his goal, so he refused the ticket and decided instead to pedal back to Milton – and $10,000 more was raised.

"What Joe Tutt did for us was much more than raise money," Walter Kyliuk said a year after the bicycle marathon. "He injected a pride and spirit into this thing that captured everyone. We started to believe we really could do it." And as perhaps their ultimate tribute, the town of Radisson painted a fire hydrant to resemble Joe Tutt, who cared enough to bicycle out from Ontario.

Every day following the trip east, the post office at Radisson would find another few letters arriving on the morning truck, with postmarks from little towns in Ontario or cities further west. "I just finished reading the *Star* this morning," Hilda Sibthorpe wrote from R.R. 1, Wyebridge, "and wanted you and your community to know that we from Ontario are not heartless. . . . I live on a pension, so even though the enclosed cheque is not large, it goes with good wishes for success in raising the necessary funds." Five dollars from another pensioner in Ontario, $25 from a small office in Calgary, $100 from "a fellow Canadian" – and invariably with comments that made the people of Radisson feel a little less alone. "Growing up in a family of eight on a mortgaged farm and our mother a widow," an anonymous pensioner who sent $100 wrote, "we darn well knew the importance of a rink in a small community."

New fund-raising ideas kept coming, often from sources least expected. Area grain farmers who were cash poor but equipment rich came up with a scheme that will eventually see them rent twelve sections of farmland they can seed and harvest and sell, letting all profit go into the fund. Senior citizens decided they would take over ten acres near the town and go into a small market garden operation, likewise funnelling any profits back into the rink campaign. The committee started making plans to hold a huge dance and to stage what they would call "The World Mud Volleyball Championships." What began as "penny ante stuff" had taken on promising life.

By January, 1989, after the Bill Hajt dinner and the Joe Tutt ride, after the box luncheons and bottle drives, after a large gift from Bill Hajt himself and other donations, the Radisson arena fund stood at $300,000. There was still a long way to go. But Radisson, it seemed, was going to make it.

Twenty-five kilometres further along the Yellowhead, Maymont was digging out from under the first blast of the great blizzard. Its arena, appropriately situated on the corner of 1st Avenue N. and 1st Street E., had not yet been ploughed free, not at all accorded the priority of Main Street. "Welcome to Maymont," the green, white, and yellow sign at the turnoff said, "The Village with a Big Heart." On the bulletin board stationed by the Lucky Dollar, puppies were being offered for $10, a house was up for sale for $14,000. There was also a hand-made poster: "Kaiser Tournament and Box Social in Maymont Hall, Feb. 18 at 7:30 p.m., $5.00 per person. Women who bring box lunches will be admitted *FREE*! Auction of Box Lunches will take place after the tournament. Refreshments available. 64 team limit. PROCEEDS TO THE RINK." But with the wind blowing and the rink road unploughed, it seemed it would take far more than box lunches and a big heart for Maymont to beat Radisson at "the survival game."

"Everybody's threatened with the same demise," Walter Kyliuk says back on Radisson's coffee row. "The town that gets the jump on things will likely wind up with the facility."

"It's survival of the fittest," says Wayne Rookes.

It is a bittersweet story. We cheer on Radisson, its dreams and schemes and triumphs. Maymont, a little further down the sur-

vival chain, without a Bill Hajt, and with 237 fewer souls, struggles along silently. It's all part of the survival game, just as it has
always been in Saskatchewan, now with rinks the chosen
weapons.

"It's amazing, isn't it?" Bill Hunter says, sitting back in Saskatoon. "Here's Radisson, forty miles away. You know, they're
going to do it – and *we are going to do it, too.*"

It is late at night when Kevin Kaminski plays his own survival
game. He lies in his bedroom at the home of his Saskatoon hosts,
Jim and Joanne Johnston, and he thinks about how he has played
this season and how he has always played in the past, and he
cannot reconcile the two. What has gone wrong? Where does
the answer lie? Can he find it himself through the cliché answer
to every mysterious slump: dedication and hard work? Will it
come tomorrow as surely as good weather is on its way, as
certainly as Bill Hunter thinks his NHL franchise is coming, as
absolutely as Radisson feels its own luck is finally about to pay
off? Or will Flo Lavallie find it somewhere between the third
and fourth toe of his right foot?

Kevin Kaminski lies there and lets the thoughts tumble
awhile, but when they show no sign of falling into any order that
leads anywhere useful, he leans over, pulls his earphones on, slips
Alabama's *Roll On* into the tape slot of his ghetto blaster, turns
up the volume, and tunes out reality.

He is not the only one worried. His parents cannot understand
it and phone constantly with encouragement. Joanne Johnston,
his "mother" while Kevin lives in Saskatoon, frets so much he
has grown more worried himself over her concern. The morning
mail often turns up a quick handwritten note from Hughie
Scobie, the Churchbridge area scout for the Blades who first
tapped Kevin Kaminski as a comer, good old Hughie sending
along a little inspirational pep talk for Kevin's consideration.
Dean Lombardi calls from Minnesota, where he is the assistant
general manager of the North Stars, and Lombardi has yet
another proposition he figures might get his young draft choice
back on track. Forget that bet we had of $50 if you score fifty

goals this year, he tells Kevin, who will end the game at Sask-
Place with sixteen for the year. Forget all that – you get fifty
points in the remaining games and the cash is yours. Score ten
points in the next five games, Lombardi says, and I'll send you a
dozen new sticks – maybe there'll be a few goals in them. . . .

Meanwhile, the Blades are not doing well. "We just kind of
hit a rut," says coach Marcel Comeau, "a tailspin." The Swift
Current Broncos are the talk of the Western Hockey League.
After fifty games they had won forty and were averaging more
than six goals a game. The Saskatoon Blades did not have a
scorer in the top twenty. Still, for the Blades and Kaminski, their
place in the Memorial Cup was assured. It was their season-long
second chance.

Saskatoon is now one of the largest cities in the country with a
junior hockey team. Teams have gone from Edmonton, Calgary,
Montreal, Vancouver, and Winnipeg, and at the end of the 1988-
89 season even the storied Toronto Marlboros packed it in and
moved to Hamilton, making Hamilton junior hockey's largest
surviving centre. Junior hockey had been a way for town to
compete against town, small city against small city, but when
towns and small cities grew up and found higher levels on which
to compete, junior hockey lost its sense of importance. That,
combined with a city's carnival of alternatives, doomed junior
hockey in larger centres.

But it has made a comeback here, thanks to SaskPlace. This
new arena is to the typical Saskatchewan hockey rink what a
combine is to the hoe. Located in a quarter section of solid
parking near the airport – so far from downtown that critics
have dubbed it "Radisson Square Garden" – it is the contemporary arena, a complete entertainment centre designed to compete with personal and private interests and modern activities
for the spirit of the community. Where the traditional small-
town rink had only to go up against euchre parties and the beer
parlor in the local hotel, SaskPlace faces such competition as
vcrs, theatre, movies, fine dining, Nintendo, and water slides. It
can't take a single seat for granted.

SaskPlace is big-city Saskatoon and perhaps best symbolizes

how the city and hockey, as part of it, have changed. SaskPlace replaces the Saskatoon Arena, built in 1937 as a depression-era project, now lying locked and idle, an "Asbestos Dust Hazard" sign taped to its door, awaiting its unlikely future. It was the typical town arena of its time. Except for a few more rows of seats or a few less, rinks in Huntsville, Ontario, Red Deer, Saskatoon, or much larger Hamilton all looked the same: quonset-shaped, steel rafters slung low over a band-box ice surface, its tall boards sloping up the ice from its end zones like Gordie Howe shoulders. Fans in the cheap seats, all of ten rows or so from the ice, like boxers on the run, had to bob and weave from behind metal posts to see snatches of the action below.

To the outsider, the old Arena was wonderful nostalgia. The coffee spills, the stink of tobacco smoke, the crust and gum on its walkways, the dusk-dark lighting – these all gave it a texture, a rare intimacy. Fans seemed to hang over the very ice. But the 2,500 or so steeply pitched seats were only part of the reason. Here was no game played by strangers before strangers. These were friends and neighbours and many were family.

The Arena was small-town Saskatoon. Today, ask about its future, hint to Saskatonians that it would be kind of sad to see the old barn go, and they will screw up their incredulous faces. *What are you talking about?* their expressions ask. *Nostalgia may be nice, but it doesn't get the crop in. If you have an arena, it had better work, because there's not money enough for two. The old arena was fine for its time, but that time ended years ago, and still we were stuck with it. Let it be torn down, redeveloped into malls or condos. Out here, we can't afford nostalgia. We have to worry about now.*

SaskPlace is an ingenious engineering feat. Currently, it seats about 8,000, but for special events like the Memorial Cup or the Brier, Canada's men's curling championship, which it hosted in March, 1989, it can be expanded to 9,100. Perhaps more importantly, it can also be "contracted." People want closeness, to have their sounds and emotions connect and blend together. And so curtains can be drawn like enormous black capes and the upper mezzanine will disappear, leaving a lower bowl of about 4,000 tight-to-the-action seats.

Few of its seats are, in fact, permanent. Should a SaskPlace event demand fewer seats, no seats at all (such as for a car or home show), or a configuration other than a bowl, each section of seats can be unhooked, tipped upright by a forklift truck, and rolled out of the way under the concrete floor of the mezzanine above. If a city is too small to have more than one arena, what it has must work and work for many years, through different times and circumstances. There will be no other.

SaskPlace has one more essential feature. Above the lower bowl is an open walkway and lobby area that skirts the building, and above that, the upper mezzanine of seats. These seats, in parallel straight lines, run the length of the ice surface on either side, with each end of the arena remaining open. Ask a Saskatonian the capacity of SaskPlace. "About 8,000," he or she will say, then point to the open expanse at either end, "but it can be expanded to 16,000 *if we get an NHL team.*"

If we get an NHL team. . . . It's a phrase one hears all the time, everywhere, in this city, in this province. And those vast open ends of the new arena, like two black holes, serve as the inescapable reminder of what isn't – and what might be. Adaptable and hopeful like its patrons must be, SaskPlace is the right building in the right place. *When the railway comes . . .*

In the beginning, there was considerable doubt that Saskatoon needed an arena even close to this size. The city had had a long history of short-lived professional teams – the Crescents, the Sheiks, the Quakers. It seemed that 2,000–3,000 people a game was all any hockey franchise could count on.

When the Blades opened SaskPlace against Brandon Wheat Kings on February 9, 1988, 9,100 fans were in the arena. This year, season ticket sales – at $225 a seat for thirty-six home games – have reached 4,650, and the team is averaging about 1,000 additional non-season ticket fans per game. Some fans drive two hours solid, on good, clear nights, from Lanigan or Elrose, then back again. Even on the night of this extraordinary blizzard the people of Saskatoon lined up at ticket windows to see how close they could get for a game against the lowly Regina Pats.

Why? The real story is not the hockey crazies from Elrose or Lanigan. They have been doing the inexplicable for years and will continue to do so. It is the 3,000 or so others that each game, since SaskPlace opened, have decided to watch the Blades. Who are they? And why do they come? Many are university students in a university city, able for the first time to drink beer while watching a game, able to turn the event into an inexpensive social evening. But mostly they are women. It was women that were missing in the old Arena.

Back when it was built in the late 1930s, men expected to venture into town; women were expected to stay home. Even later, when expectations began to change, certain places retained their "off-limits" feeling. The Arena was one of them. Like a boozey old honky-tonk, its message to women was clear – hockey is a man's game, played by men, watched and talked over by men, played to male tribal expectations and self-image. Women aren't wanted. Travel to England even today and attend a soccer game. You see old men, younger men, some boys, almost no women.

When times changed and women began going out more often, they were attracted to more welcoming surroundings – movie theatres, restaurants, Centennial Auditorium – and families came to take their business there. When SaskPlace opened, it offered bright lights and comfortable seating; it was clean, fresh, and wholesome. It met contemporary standards for an entertainment setting. "Welcome to All!" it said. So women, in numbers, began coming to hockey games for the first time.

But will they continue to come, will the university students and other new fans as well? Ed Chynoweth, president of the Western Hockey League, voices a common concern. He contrasts Saskatoon with small-town Swift Current. There, "you can't get in the building. I mean, it doesn't matter whether it's thirty-nine below zero or nine above," says Chynoweth. "Everybody in Swift Current loves the Broncos. You go into a smaller centre and they're really rabid home-town fans. They're all wearing a club jacket or a club hat. They eat, sleep, and drink that team. I'm not sure that you ever get that in a larger centre other than the fact that they do like to have a winner. But I don't know if you ever get that closeness. Now Saskatoon – it's no knock against it – they're averaging maybe about 5,500 a game, but I really wonder if we could honestly say that there might be 2,000 dyed-in-the-wool Blades fans that eat, drink, and sleep it?"

He fears that these new fans are not hockey fanatics. They are *soft* fans, drawn by the novelty of a new building, by the promise of a chance at the Memorial Cup. To them, hockey is just entertainment, a night out like bowling or bridge or the theatre. You will never see any of them in a convoy of cars along the road to Prince Albert or Regina, supporting their boys when they need it the most. Next year, there will be some new entertainment, and they will be gone, and SaskPlace will be filled with empty seats. Maybe.

Yet in today's urban world, this may no longer be the point. Who says you have to "eat, drink, and sleep" movies or television or anything? What's wrong with just watching and enjoying – and not even all the time? In a city the size of Saskatoon, there are plenty of things to do. Three thousand more people come to see the Blades now because the Blades are as entertaining as a good movie, because SaskPlace is as comfortable as a living room, as Centennial Auditorium, and the old Arena was not. Because women are now welcome. How many people in Toronto "eat, drink, and sleep" the Leafs or the Blue Jays?

In SaskPlace, the people of Saskatoon got Rod Stewart and the Harlem Globetrotters as well as the Blades, they got an entertainment centre for the *whole* community, the Saskatoon of today. It just so happens that along the way, SaskPlace has led more people to rediscover hockey.

They are doing so in the modern way – as fans. For like everywhere else in the country, in Saskatoon fewer kids are playing hockey than before. There are more old-timers playing, and women, but minor hockey is no longer where all new fans are cultivated. In 1968 there were 163 minor hockey teams in Saskatoon. By 1974, that number had more than doubled, to 330 teams involving some 6,000 children. At the time, Saskatoon could claim more kids per capita playing hockey than anywhere else in the world. But no more. Today in Saskatoon there are around 200 teams.

There are reasons for this, but the movement of people out of the province is not one of them. Saskatoon itself has grown dramatically. Nor does an aging population or a smaller number of kids explain the change. More kids now live in Saskatoon than fifteen years ago. But the demands of minor hockey – increased time, above all – have been too much for many Saskatoon families as they have for families in other provinces. Many people have chosen to do other things. There are now dozens of other activities to capture the interest of the Saskatoon child and his or her parents, from Suzuki violin lessons to French lessons to gymnastics. Hockey once ruled by default and winter circumstance as well as by pleasure. Now it has competitors.

This game, like this country, was built on its natural resources: water and ice, the land's wide open spaces, time and the winter. Those natural resources seem not to matter so much any more. More prosperous economies are built on other things. Winter has been moved indoors and tamed, and people are able to get out and about and do mostly what they please even when the weather is horrendous. The game flourishes now because of our own creations – indoor rinks and artificial ice, the spectacle and dream-making images of hockey on television, and the penetrating myths of the game that are passed from generation to generation. But what has not changed is the dream, or the faith that it will all work out. Somehow.

Out on the ice, Kevin Kaminski plays as if the gods are playing a table-top game with him and are testing to see how long he can accept being one turn of the wrist short of scoring. He comes in on the left side, his little tuck move working to let him slip past the defenceman, but just as he dances past the puck falls harmlessly into the boards. On a Saskatoon power play he carries the puck in from the blueline until there are two defenders sprawled on the ice and the goalie is flopping across his crease in the wrong direction. Kaminski feathers the puck through his legs into a crease where no Saskatoon blade is waiting to rap it home.

But then, on another power play with the Pats ahead 2–0, Kaminski works a corner until the puck moves free and out to the point where a Blades' defenceman fires a low, hard shot that is deftly tipped in, blind, by Kaminski. Skating to the bench as his name thunders over the public address system, he wonders if perhaps now he will begin to play the game as everyone has always said he would.

To the outsider, the important outsider who determines so much of the boundaries of life in this province, the phrase "Next Year Country" sounds ironic. It strikes as the cry of the forever loser – "wait 'til next year" – and to the outsider's superior perspective it seems a joke. To the outsider, it is the insider's way of hiding from the reality that "not now" means really "not ever."

And so, since the depression, Saskatchewan and the Prairies have been *wink-wink, nudge-nudge* "Next Year Country." Its relentless winter, its distances, its bountiful but punishing land, its competition from everywhere else, all the forces, all the prevailing winds, have been too much for any other destiny.

And maybe so. Certainly "Prairie Spirit" or "Saskatoon Spirit" is not always enough. It wasn't enough early in the century and every year since to give Saskatoon the industrial base to its economy that it sought. It likely won't be enough to give Bill Hunter an NHL team for Saskatchewan. Despite his *need* to make it, Kevin Kaminski may not be big enough or fast enough to make the NHL. Some way or another, it does seem that Radisson will get its new rink. One *will* make it, maybe more. No winks or nudges, no irony, "Next Year Country" is real.

Hockey will never hold the monopoly of time and attention it once held in Saskatchewan and Canada. Yet people still have a need to come together – in Radisson and Churchbridge, in Saskatoon, Toronto, and Montreal – to feel close, to share something in common. Look around at the crowd this snowbound night in Saskatoon. Amidst a variety of men of different ages and generations, there are a father and his daughter; a young girl, probably a university student, and her boy friend; a grandmother and granddaughter and the grandmother's friend – young and old, male and female, city people, and country people, businessmen, mine workers, and farmers. In no other place in Saskatoon do so many people of so many different backgrounds gather together so often. And if Saskatoon can never be Swift Current or Prince Albert, SaskPlace and the Blades can make it feel that way sometimes. In a few months from now at the

Memorial Cup, these people will be back – louder, more passionate, and in even greater numbers.

To this community, hockey is part of a shared imagination. Even among those who don't watch it or play it or care about it in any way, it is *there*. Water and pavement and airwaves and steel are instruments of that community, and so is the hockey arena. But move inside the arena on a Friday night or Saturday morning, or practically any time between November and March almost any place in the country. Come to SaskPlace for the Memorial Cup in May, for a hockey game, and there you find a community of the spirit, a feeling that binds.

The game between Saskatoon and Regina, tied 6–6, goes into overtime and, with only a few seconds left, the Blades' captain, Tracey Katelnikoff, bats a puck out of the air and in behind the Regina goaltender for the Saskatoon victory. The crowd cheers quickly and immediately begins hurrying out the exits, worrying that the extra overtime may have killed whatever life was left in their batteries.

The game over and other Blades laughing and joking in the showers, Kevin Kaminski wanders a back corridor, talking about his slump and how good he felt out there tonight. "I only got one point," he says, "but I was on for six of the seven goals, you know."

He stands in the corridor, his helmet, gloves, and sweater off, the suspenders of his pants hanging down over his hips like clipped wings. His chin oozes blood from a scuffle. The knuckles of his bare hands are as raw and swollen as those of the first pioneers who came to work this land. He wipes his chin, smiles a big smile, and begins chewing on a fingernail.

"Well," he says, and smiles a big smile, "I guess it wasn't bad. So long as I'm there one of these days."

Meanwhile, out in the SaskPlace parking lot, two tow trucks from Bridge City Towing move slowly down the lines offering a boost. The people of Saskatchewan drive off in the winter's night. A few wait, knowing that soon it will be their turn.

CHAPTER TWO

PLAYING FIELDS OF SCARBOROUGH

When he was a kid, he'd be up at five
Take shots till eight, make the thing drive
Out after school, back on ice
That was his life,
He was gonna play in the Big League
The Big League . . .
     Tom Cochrane, "Big League"

THE CAPTAIN OF THE TORONTO MARLBOROS PEEWEE HOCKEY CLUB IS IN his room working on his "imagery." At least that is what Greg Koehler is supposed to be doing. But he is having some difficulty concentrating. The captain of the Marlies lies in his unmade bed listening to the baby cry upstairs; she needs a diaper change. He did the last one; someone else can get this one. He can hear the tinny pounding of the Walkman his older brother wears in the next bedroom. He can hear Chip 'n' Dale nattering on the television in the next room over. He can hear his two youngest brothers strangling each other on the basement floor. He can hear the car doors slamming out in the driveway, meaning his parents and two more brothers are about to shatter the shell of

53

concentration he is supposed to be building on a cold winter afternoon when imagery has more to say in the clouds than in the mind of a thirteen-year-old boy.

He opens his eyes – eyes as blue as the familiar maple leaf crest he wears, white as the sweater it graces – and his vision fills with the sultry pubescent looks of Alyssa Milano of *Who's The Boss* as she steams down from five separate posters on his walls. In the bedroom of an adolescent whose entire life has so far been hockey, the poster score has changed dramatically over the past few months: Alyssa 5, Wayne Gretzky 1. But Gretzky still has the place of honour: the first image Greg Koehler sees in the morning as he sits up in bed and stares out into the jumble that is a small bungalow shared by two adults, six hockey-mad boys, and a baby girl. Gretzky, still in an Edmonton Oilers' uniform, is gliding into eternity on the far wall, his wary blue-heron profile as comforting as the words over which he skates: "May Your Years Be Filled With Happiness and Luck." Happiness, yes. Luck, yes. But *imagery*?

Paul Lewicki, the head coach of the Marlboros' three-man coaching staff, issues "imagery" sheets before each important game. And tonight's game against the North York Canadiens is vital, the normally doormat Canadiens having beaten and tied the Marlies in the two previous meetings between these two teams in the Metropolitan Toronto Hockey League's top AAA division. Imagery – or "visualization" – exercises are what each Marlie is expected to do in the quiet hours before a game. He is to play the game in his head. He is expected to lie very still and connect possible problems to practised solutions. A defenceman gets caught pinching. What should the captain of the Marlies, a centre, do? As the Marlies' finest playmaker, he must look for the open man on the move and not forget a trailer on a two-on-one break. He must watch the Canadiens' slot man in his own zone. He must make sure he goes to the net after rebounds, leads his wingers.

Greg's left winger and good friend, Chris Taylor, says this imagery exercise is "like you're playing your hockey with little knobs and someone's controlling you and you don't think, you just do it." But Greg Koehler can't concentrate on his imagery.

He can't lie back and close his eyes and pretend to be totally under someone else's control and play a game that isn't taking place. Besides, the idea of this being his quiet time before the game is nothing short of lunacy in this throbbing home on the western edge of the vast suburb of Scarborough. If the head of the captain of the Toronto Marlboros is filled with anything this Sunday afternoon it is of the noise from other rooms. And if he manages to cut through the noise, there is always school to think about – there ought to be a law against science – or Mac's Milk, the convenience store where the owner treats the neighbourhood kids more like marauders than customers. Just last night the police were around knocking on doors wanting to know if anyone knew anything about an assault that was supposed to have taken place there.

Who can possibly concentrate? Thank God for the bob of Billy Thompson's black fedora as he passes by the basement window, Billy coming to call like Billy comes to call a dozen times a day. Billy Thompson skips across the frozen lawn and up and through the door for a short, sugar-coated visit with Mr. and Mrs. Koehler and the baby and then three hops and his boney frame's downstairs melting into the chesterfield in front of the television. No wonder Greg's dad calls Billy "Eddie Haskell" after the trouble-making, ingratiating (depending on whether his audience at the moment is kids or their parents) character on the old television series, *Leave It To Beaver*. But at least he makes everybody laugh with his dopey fedora and his endless "Sirs" and "thank yous" and, if the truth be known, Billy Thompson has as good a glove hand as any goaltender the captain of the Toronto Marlboros has yet faced on ice or raw pavement.

"Ya wanna go out and shoot?" Billy asks as he tumbles down through the basement and into Greg's room.

"I guess."

Out through the house they head. Out past three-year-old Brandon and five-year-old Christopher, now so tangled on the floor it is impossible to say which scream comes from which mouth, out past fifteen-year-old Ben, about to head off with his Walkman to meet his pals at the mall, out past eight-year-old Darrin and ten-year-old Richard who are coming in with their hockey bags, out past the baby, Danielle, who now burbles contentedly, having been changed by Billy Thompson as he bobbed through the house, out past Greg's parents, Ed and Cathy Koehler, who are just settling down over steaming cups of coffee, cigarettes, and the photocopied sheets, calendar scribbles, crayon and pencil notes, and remembered phone calls from coaches and managers and teammates' mothers that mount up to the coming week's impossible schedule.

Billy Thompson and the captain of the Toronto Marlies go out to the driveway, into a dumping ground of broken sticks, foam pads, old baseball gloves, goalie sticks, extra pads, and punctured tennis balls that once were electric green and fuzzy and bounced with upper-class smugness but now are black as ash and shaven clean by the pavement and bounce, if at all, with the hollow, weak sound of a rimless, tubeless tire. Put another way, road hockey perfection.

"Look what some son of a bitch done to my stick!" Greg Koehler shouts to Billy Thompson.

Billy comes over, his head shaking from an overload of sympathy. Another kid on the street has taken Greg's stick without permission, and the moment Greg picks it up he senses the abuse that has taken place. The stick is a handle really, a handle attached by two loose wood screws to a wonderfully, wickedly bent plastic blade. The captain of the Toronto Marlies – who in a few hours will be wearing $200 skates and carry a new $20 stick – is nearly in tears as he stares at his precious road hockey stick. He set the screws himself, sawed the handle, taped the knob. He himself doctored the blade with hot water and pressure, sticking it into a crack and bending it until the curve was illegal by NHL rules but, for rule-less road hockey, "amazing." And a few hundred thousand goals on the corner of Pachino Street and Amberley Drive had slivered the blade and polished the handle down until it was as much a part of Greg Koehler as his high-back sneakers or the dark breaking wave he nurses each morning over his forehead.

"Bastard," says Billy Thompson, as he dips down into the pile for a goaltender's stick and a baseball glove.

The captain of the Marlies steps on his blade and resets it. He slams the screws tight against the concrete walk, cuffs the stick twice on the driveway, and is satisfied. Pulling the best of the hockey nets over his shoulder, he heads out to prepare himself for the coming game. Not *imagery*, but *imagination*. Not memory, but creativity. Not work, but play.

Billy Thompson crouches deep into the net, his eyes set, his glove cocked. The captain of the Marlies dribbles the ball, scoops it, sweeps it, dances with it as he runs stickhandling headlong into the contest. One on one: Billy and a glove, Greg and the ball. The lone spectator is a black mutt that grins sheepishly as she wiggles, still crouching, away from the steaming proof that she has once again gotten out and onto the neighbour's lawn. The captain of the Marlies dekes, drops the ball back from the blade of his stick to the heel of his foot, slides the ball soccer-style past his stepping other foot and back magically into range where he snaps a shot high and true that glances off Billy Thompson's glove and heads down the street in the endless roll that has cursed road hockey since its first goalposts were ground into powder by winter snow tires.

The captain of the Marlies runs down Amberley and across Pachino, where he retrieves the ball by slamming it against the far curb and catching the rebound in his hand. Still running, he turns and begins flicking the ball ahead and catching up to it as he returns to the space where Billy Thompson is still complimenting himself on a brilliant save. Greg Koehler sees his brother Richard coming down from the driveway to join in, and he fires a quick, surprising pass to his brother that momentarily catches Richard off guard. Richard cuffs at the tennis ball and it rises high and again over the net, only this time the captain of the Marlies is coming back the other way in full flight and he picks the flying ball clean out of the air with the blade of the stick, sending it tumbling back over the net and falling in an arc to the front of Billy Thompson, still gloating. But the ball does not even reach the pavement. The captain of the Marlies has come back faster than the ball he struck can fly. He turns midair as he leaps past the net, twisting blind but still able to pluck the ball a second time, clean and neat, and before Billy Thompson's mouth can even fall open in surprise the frayed net behind him bulges with a tennis ball that was supposed to be dribbling harmlessly off into the distance.

"*Awwwriggggghhhhttt!*" screams the ever-courteous Billy Thompson.

The captain of the Marlies says nothing. But a small smile has something to say. *This* is "imagery" – pictures painted in the mind – and it is not an anticipated error remedied by a studied solution. It is Greg Koehler, spinning at centre ice. Maple Leaf Gardens. Billy Thompson, now Grant Fuhr of the Edmonton Oilers. The sheepish dog now 16,182 fans rising like a jack-in-the-box as the Great Koehler does the impossible yet again and scores the overtime goal to win the greatest Stanley Cup ever played.

> *My boy's gonna play in the Big League*
> *My boy's gonna turn some heads*
> *My boy's gonna play in the Big League*
> *My boy's gonna knock 'em dead.*
>   Tom Cochrane, "Big League"

"The Tradition Lives On," the sign in the lobby of St. Michael's College School Arena brags. Inside the glass are a half dozen old National Hockey League programs and a dozen glossy photographs of Leonard "Red" Kelly, a good ol' St. Mike's Boy who will be guest of honour at the upcoming Alumni Celebrity Dinner, tickets $100 each. Around the corner and past the snack bar is a plaque commemorating the St. Mike's players who have been drafted by NHL teams over the past decade, names like Vancouver's Tony Tanti and Philadelphia's Rick Tocchet, Hartford's Kevin Dineen and New Jersey goaltender Sean Burke. Beyond that, there is the St. Mike's Hall of Fame: Joe Primeau of the famous Maple Leaf "Kid" line is there, and Ted Lindsay, Kelly again, Tim Horton, Frank Mahovlich, Gerry Cheevers, Dave Keon.

Into this Toronto arena come the Toronto Marlboros peewee AAA hockey team, each boy in a matching blue jacket over matching blue Marlboros sweaters, a tie, white shirt, pressed pants. The Toronto Marlboros date back to 1903, when a group of Toronto sportsmen formed the Toronto Marlborough Athletic Club, which they named after the line of English noblemen who inherited the title, Duke of Marlborough. The team's nickname became "The Dukes" and the crest on the jersey was the family crown set against a blue maple leaf background. Since Winston Churchill had family connections to the House of Marlborough, the Dukes of Toronto liked to think their name and logo were synonymous with leadership and the ability to rise to the challenge in times of adversity. More than 200 players have gone through the Marlboro system and on into the NHL, including coach Paul Lewicki's own father, Danny Lewicki, who played in the early 1950s for the New York Rangers, Chicago Black Hawks, and Toronto Maple Leafs. For more than sixty years the club has had a junior team, and for more than forty years it has iced peewee, minor bantam, bantam, minor midget, and midget squads. Seven times the Marlboro junior team won the Memorial Cup, more than any other junior club in the country.

"It's kind of like being the Edmonton Oilers," Chris Taylor says. "Some people liked the Marlies at the start, but then they won everything and now they hate them."

They are a diverse group, the best players the organization could recruit from all over Metropolitan Toronto and slightly beyond. They come from Mississauga, Etobicoke, Weston, North Toronto, the city of Toronto, and, of course, Scarborough. They represent a wide assortment of ancestries: British, Italian, Yugoslavian, Irish, German, Polish, Greek . . . They are the sons of policemen, realtors, homemakers, teachers, entrepreneurs, contractors, store clerks, bureaucrats, actors, restaurateurs. They come from rich families, from middle- and lower middle-class families. None comes from a poor family, none from a family being held together by a single mother on a tight budget. They are a team in personality, a single entity identifiable by their jackets, sweaters, ties, and cockiness. In the team, these boys find something beyond friends, beyond family, an identity that rides above who they might be at home or at school. The persona they prefer is that of a Marlie, second a Taylor or a Koehler, third a student of a particular school or a kid of a certain age. They may not be recognized on the streets: few of the kids in their classes may even play the game at thirteen years of age. But the fact that they are Marlies is known in their circles and what it means is understood. As Ed Koehler says, "Hockey is still the hero sport."

The captain of the Marlies, Greg Koehler, walks in the new desert boots that have yet to pick up a crease, his shoulder carrying a team bag that repeats the message his jacket and sweater and swagger have already given out: these are the stars of tomorrow. *The tradition lives on.*

Behind the captain of the Marlies comes his family, a team in itself, and the younger boys scatter through the arena like wild ponies who have just broken corral. There are six Koehler boys in total, like the six Sutters of Viking, Alberta, who made it to the NHL.

While his son goes off to change, Ed Koehler buys a coffee and stands behind the goal area while another game is played out. The children on the ice are seven years old, ten skaters who move over the huge St. Michael's ice surface like wasps over spilled pop: frantic, concentrated, without the slightest order. The puck slides in behind the net and several players bear down on it, one player accidentally falling over his own stick and into an opposing player. A young mother who stands nearby with a toddler in an Edmonton Oilers' tuque slams her fists against the glass nearest the referee, screaming for a penalty on the play. Ed Koehler shakes his head. "First competitive experience," he says with a grin, nodding toward the young woman who still pounds and screams. "They get a little caught up in it."

The Koehlers pride themselves in not getting so caught up in it, at least not so it is visible to the casual observer. Cathy sits alone, apart from the other parents who instinctively herd into two opposing bunches behind their sons' team benches. She says she cannot stand to hear the criticisms that are launched against players, coaches, and parents who don't happen to be within the protective circle at any given moment. But she also sits alone because a hockey game is as close to an hour of peace as she will get that day. Ed stands with other fathers along the back railing. Since the status of the child accrues to the parent in minor hockey, Ed Koehler is treated with special deference in the stands just as Greg, the captain, is deferred to on the ice by his teammates, for Ed – who once played junior B hockey himself and who has sired six promising young players so far – is, by association, a starting parent.

Out on the St. Mike's ice come the Marlboros, the Canadiens entering from another gate, each boy imitating that quick, soft shuffle the pros use as they step onto the ice, a signal that they are now creatures moving in their natural element. Chris Taylor, however, is not with his Marlies teammates. Instead, he is spending his fourteenth birthday leaning against the same back railing his father and Ed Koehler watch from, his left ankle in a cast. During a game earlier in the season, his skate caught in a crack in the ice and his ankle snapped in two places as it twisted under him.

"When they were helping him off the ice," his father, Bob, remembers, "he looked up at his mother and his mother looked down at him. And he had that look on his face like, 'Mom, please don't let it be serious.'" When the doctor at the Sunnybrook Hospital emergency ward said it would require an operation and the insertion of a screw, Chris thought for one awful moment that his hockey career was over at thirteen. But the doctor had been quick to assure him the cast would be off in six weeks and Chris might even be playing before the season was out.

But would it be in time for "Quebec"? For thirty years, the Quebec International peewee hockey tournament has been a gathering place for the best twelve- and thirteen-year-old players in the world. Once that meant just Canadian kids. This year, there will be teams from many parts of Canada, the United States, France, Switzerland, Finland, Czechoslovakia, England, and the Soviet Union. The Marlies will be one of them. Centrepiece of Quebec City's Winter Carnival, the tournament attracts crowds of 14,000 for games played by children who, until this moment, have stared into stands that contain few people who are not directly related to one of them. Some have argued that such tournaments force unhealthy pressures on too-young children. Not many who have actually taken part, however, as players or parents, would agree. For them, it is a fantasy – an NHL arena, NHL-size crowds, TV cameras, autographs, girls – a taste of the dream.

For some, the memory of Quebec becomes their inspiration. Asked about the first time he knew he wanted to be an NHL player, former Montreal Canadien and Toronto Marlboro Steve Shutt had no hesitation: "At Quebec. When I walked down the corridor to the ice and looked up and saw all those people – that's me!"

Guy Lafleur played at Quebec; so did Wayne Gretzky and Mario Lemieux. Alex Legaré, president of the tournament, estimates that 300 of the tournament's players have gone on to play in the NHL. For kids and parents, Quebec is the first checkpoint along the fantasy road that began with that first NHL team sweater under the Christmas tree. What does Quebec mean to this year's Marlboro team? "It would be like playing in the NHL for a week," dreams Chris Taylor.

Then he broke his ankle. But his dad has a plan. Bob Taylor has worked it out on his fingers. If Chris's ankle heals, his cast could come off the week before Quebec. If Chris spends these few weeks leading to the tournament using weights to build up his knees and thighs, once in Quebec City, he and Chris could ask Paul Lewicki if Chris could put on his skates and go out for the warm-up. He would not actually play, but staying on the bench during the game, cheering on his teammates, he could get close enough perhaps to feel the dream. "If he could just go out," Bob Taylor says, the fear of loss already in his voice, "he'd be able to say he was there, eh? Like Chris says, 'If I never make the NHL, well, okay – but at least I'd be able to say I skated in the Colisée.' "

From where Chris and Bob and Ed stand, and with only a little imagination, these thirteen-year-old peewees might be the Montreal Canadiens and the Toronto Maple Leafs skating out onto the ice of Maple Leaf Gardens. At this competitive level coaches look for big kids, and by age thirteen, with skates and pads on, the players are almost adult size. They bodycheck and skate and play with adult-like skill. Only their faces would betray them, but hidden as they are behind helmets and face masks, they offer no hint.

It is a mini-adult world, with adult coaches, adult fans and referees, adult sensibilities, expectations, and ambitions. And yet, today in Canada there are fewer parents and their kids who want to share that world. Minor hockey registration is falling, by 30 per cent across the country, by nearly 50 per cent in Quebec in the last decade. The declining national birthrate is only a small part of the explanation.

Research by François Bilodeau of l'Université de Laval has found that while Quebec minor hockey registration was falling by 24 per cent from the 1983-84 season to the 1987-88 season, the male population for these age groups fell by only 6 per cent. More interesting was where the dropouts occurred: atoms (aged up to 11) down 10.4 per cent; peewees (to 13) down 18.5 per cent; bantams (to 15) down 27.5 per cent; midgets (age 16) down 40.9 per cent; and juniors down a remarkable 63.4 per cent. "When we compare the number of atoms or peewees in 1983-84 to the number of bantams or midgets in 1987-88," Bilodeau said, "we notice 56 per cent left along the way."

Canadian Amateur Hockey Association data argue almost precisely the same point nationally. Over the decade that spanned the mid-1970s to the mid-1980s a quarter of the country's peewees vanished, more than a third of the country's bantam players disappeared, half of the midgets were gone. Yet in recent years, the total number of Canadians playing organized hockey has actually increased, to over one million, because of hockey's growth among women, male old-timers, and very young boys. Why do so many fewer young men during their peak physical years, 14-25, play hockey?

Besides demographics, cost is a factor: hockey is a more expensive game to play. The Canadian population is more urban. There is no local rink around every next corner. A city's traffic makes distances, and time, seem greater. All have had their impact. But mostly, the way we live in this country has changed, and hockey has changed with it. Life is busier and more competitive; kids are asked to grow up sooner. Making it to the big leagues, to every big league, takes more time, demands more commitment. If one dream is not to be, parents and kids believe, it is better to cut your losses and change dreams.

Some things are universal and timeless and do not change. The other night, when Bob Taylor was helping his son into the bath, Chris Taylor looked down at his broken ankle and broke down himself. Bob Taylor stood there holding his son in his arms while the boy sobbed, and Bob did not know what to say except that everything would be all right. It is a parent's hope. Parents want the best for their children; that never changes. In the midst of what can often seem like bizarre behaviour by parents and their children, it is this point that should not be forgotten. What provokes the bizarre in this more competitive and complicated world is the ongoing quest for what is best and how to achieve it.

We live in a time of what might be called Power Parenting. No longer can the relationship between parent and child be simply benign and supportive; it must be involved, committed, directed. It is what "making it" demands. As a result: Prenatal University opened in Hayward, California, claiming parents could be taught to shout through the mother's abdominal wall so that baby will enter the world, Dr. Rene Van de Carr asserts, with "a ready-made set of verbal sounds that can be attached to things later." Playful Parenting franchises have been established in such cities as Montreal to show new moms and dads how to pack as much quality "play" into an hour as experts could devise. Gymboree fitness clubs have opened up in Coquitlam, British Columbia, and elsewhere, offering a full fitness regime for children aged three months to four years. Newspapers run fitness columns advising new parents to take a toothbrush to their new baby's legs and rub along the insides and outsides of the tiny limbs "to tone foot muscles and stimulate body awareness." According to Janine Levy, the French author of *Exercise for Your Baby*, only a fit baby would be able "to face the initial difficulties of life in the best conditions." Beginning in the 1980s, the human offspring would be grown more like a Japanese bonsai tree. In a competitive, uncertain world, it would seem, human development cannot be left to chance – *at least not with my child*.

As baby becomes child, the pressure intensifies. In Ottawa, a

The Kid:
Greg Koehler,
Scarborough, Ontario.

MICHAEL BOLAND

Home Team:
Christopher, Ed, Brandon,
Danielle, Cathy, Darrin,
Greg, Richard –
and Billy Thompson (in back).

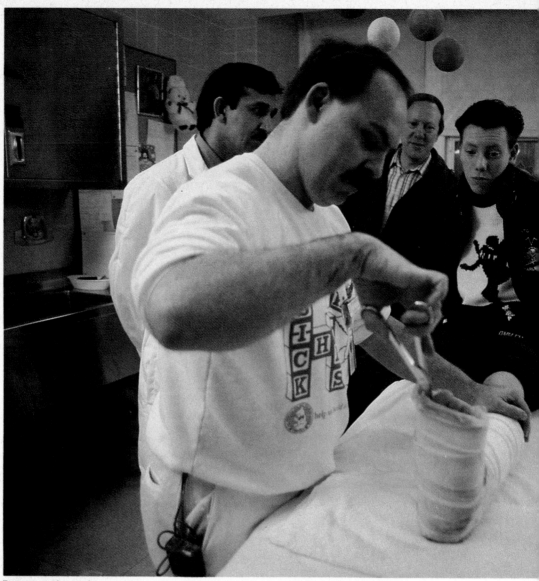

Bumps on the road:
Chris Taylor and father, Bob.

Echoes:
The class of 1973 –
Scott Parker, Kerry Pim,
Lloyd Dyson, (Ken Dryden),
Curly Davies,
and Jamie Gilmour.

Hockey father:
Walter Gretzky.

The trophy room:
Brantford, Ontario.

In the wings.   MICHAEL BOLAND

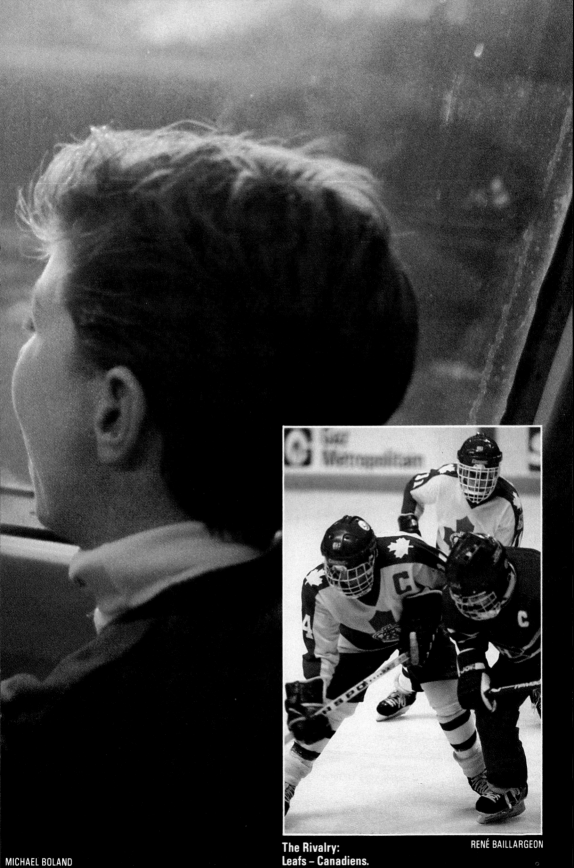

MICHAEL BOLAND

**The Rivalry:
Leafs – Canadiens.**

RENÉ BAILLARGEON

THE BIG LEAGUES

RENÉ BAILLARGEON

mother admitted that she and her husband – with three university degrees between them – had been staying up into the early hours of the morning sweating over a school project on Egyptology that their grade-four son would be handing in on Friday morning. In Edmonton, a computer-on-wheels company called Kiddie-Komps started up, offering computer classes – including word-processing – to day-care centres throughout the city. *Tim Learns About Mutual Funds* could be found in the children's section of any neighbourhood library. A mother in California was reported by the *New York Times* to be booking her five-year-old's play time through her secretary. Efficiency matters; direction is demanded; time is too precious to waste.

These curiosities are not the point – why people do what they do is. Families have more breadwinners, more money, and less time. Services spring up to save time and attract the available money. Heightened international, national, and backyard competition brings a sniff of fear, greater rewards, the taste of ambition. Add to those the risks of an *un*busy life – television, video machines, and drugs – and the result is parents who feel a desperate need to control every outcome.

In this context, is the minor hockey system and the behaviour of minor hockey parents surprising? The endless season of games, pylon-ed practices, and summer off-ice training and the coaches who are allowed to talk to the kids the way no teacher can – all seek to instill in a "soft," less guided life some discipline and direction. Just as with Prenatal University and the Kiddie-Komps kids, is this not all about "being the best you can be"? And what's wrong with that? If your child skates well and wants to skate better, shouldn't you as a parent search out power-skating clinics and hockey schools to help him skate better? To be the best he can be? Isn't it wrong, as well as too painful, to do nothing and see others pass him by? To see his unhappiness and frustration? To see a child's always fragile self-esteem erode before your very eyes, affecting the rest of his life as well?

You are a parent. You want the best for your kid. The best in hockey is the NHL. And so you push for that – not too hard, you hope. You do your best to hedge your emotional bets about him making it to the top, and make sure he does, too, but if he can make it, and if you can help him in anyway, why not?

And so the rest follows.

"For parents at this AAA level, hockey takes over their entire life," says Marlboro coach Paul Lewicki. Parents are expected to gather in a rink an average of about four nights a week. A weekend tournament – hardly an irregularity – increases the commitment. Each game is most of an hour long. Add to that the half-hour it takes to get to the rink, while the players change the half-hour wait for the game to begin, the twenty minutes or so it takes for the coaches to rehash the game and for the kids to change, and the half-hour home, and there is not much time for finishing the basement, bowling, or browsing through the evening paper. "In our particular case," says Lewicki, "the coaches take a look at the calendar each month and try to make sure we have 'mental health days.' A boy" (and though he doesn't say it, his parents) "has to want to come to the rink."

It becomes habit. For the Koehlers, a rink is almost as familiar and comfortable as home, a place where shouts and screams fade into the rafters, where nothing can be broken, where the lure of a single stop at the snack bar is enough to guarantee co-operation getting ready, relative peace in the station wagon, and, for Cathy, being left preciously to herself when the troops arrive. So accustomed has Ed Koehler become to this ritual that, if spring comes and none of his sons remain in the playoffs, he has found himself driving around checking Toronto arenas for a game in progress.

It is their social life as well. "If I didn't have a hockey game to go to at night, I would go bonkers," Cathy Koehler says. "Cooped up all day and all night, I'd go crazy." The other kids who trail along to their brothers' games come to know the other kids who also must trail along, and instead of watching the game that brought them together they run around and play their own games. As Cathy explains, "It's a night out for them, too."

"There's probably not a rink in Toronto that we don't know somebody," Ed says.

Cathy brightens: "On the door, at the snack bar, you always

know someone. They give the kids stuff. They know who it's for." When Danielle was born, her presents came from maintenance workers and timekeepers as much as from family. But then, if the rinks have become a second home, it follows that a second family would be found within. The Koehlers, like many others, feel little sense of community where they live, even where they work. They have found their community in a hockey rink.

They do what they do because their sons love to play hockey and because they grew up believing that sports were important in a child's life. In a neighbourhood such as the one where the Koehlers live, or in any other, hockey is a way to get kids off the streets, out of the malls, up from the basement. It is a chance to place a child under the control of another adult, a coach, who is able to be tougher, more demanding, more prepared to deal out discipline, and have it accepted by the same child who will permit no "coaching" from parents. They know that kids learn in different ways – about people, hard work, winning and losing, themselves. Some learn best in school, some at home or work or on the streets, and some in sports. They know that what kids learn they come to apply to everything else they do.

They like the way hockey helps kids learn about teams and teamwork and common goals, giving them the chance to share bad moments and good and to work toward something. They like that it is active and healthy, it is "doing something," superior by any account to watching television or playing video games until dawn. "If they didn't like hockey," Ed Koehler says of his six sons as he watches Greg play, "I'd find something else for them to do."

There is *the dream*, of course. *Making it*. The dream has been passed on from generation to generation as if it is in the very genes of the species – *homo sapiens canadiensis*. Ed Koehler remembers his own childhood days in London, Ontario, particularly the year he was invited to the training camp of the London Knights of the Ontario Hockey League Junior "A" division. Darryl Sittler was there, and so were Dan Maloney, Rick Kehoe, Jim Schoenfeld, Pat Boutette, and Dan Bouchard. They all made it. And as he looks at each of his sons, he wonders/hopes, *Maybe he can make it, too*. Imagine, earning money and fame for *playing a game*. Imagine, having a job that is *fun*! What else could any parent want for a child? In the cultural currency of Canada – or anywhere else – a sports career has come to seem infinitely superior even to those of doctors or lawyers. Who, after all, is the most revered Canadian in history? Easy – a Bell worker's son who lives and plays in California.

The Koehlers and Taylors, plus Chris, look out onto a listless game. The smaller Canadiens are hungrier than the Marlboros. The Canadiens forecheck more, work harder, and while the goals that result are far from pretty, they still add up to a 2–0 lead by the time the teams switch ends. The captain of the Marlies, Greg Koehler, is having a poor game, but that is nothing new lately. He lost his left winger, Chris Taylor, when Chris's ankle snapped on him. He lost his right winger, Jeremiah McCann, when Jeremiah was suspended last week for rough play. Greg plays now with an assortment of wingers, all of whom fit like new church shoes. He prides himself on his play-making and his patience, but his soft, carefully threaded passes slip under sticks or clatter against his new wingers' skates. His perfect sliding set-up of a winger to the side on an empty net goes unrewarded when the shot is missed. His drop passes are unexpected. His patience runs thin.

Along the back railing Ed Koehler watches, his left hand flexing on an empty styrofoam cup. This is the most difficult moment for the hockey parent. He can sign the kids up, keep the schedules, navigate the route in perfect time, cheer the kids on, savour their victories and comfort their losses, but his direct cause-and-effect dies the moment a puck is dropped and his son skates toward it. He is left with only his eyes watching, and they cannot warn, protect, pass, shoot, comfort, or argue for the child. They can only witness the child, entirely on his own.

A parent must split the brain to watch his or her own child. The social side, the mature side, the acceptable side, must keep track of the game and watch it as a whole, alert and supportive of the *team*. The self side, the parental side, is aware of the baby out there. It is like sitting through a one-man play, all eyes on the only player on stage, all ears aware of what is being said. The parent soars and dies with each awkward step of the plot. When the child is on the ice, it is as if he is there alone. When the child is on the bench, mother and father strain to sit with him, each as aware of the body and actual language of the coach as they are during a difficult teacher-parent interview. The way the child plays matters absolutely; the game is secondary.

For a parent who has played hockey at a high level, as Ed Koehler has, watching a son play hockey must come close to the sensation felt by those who have suffered strokes that make them incapable of movement or speech. The mind is clear, the eyes fine, but all they can do is watch, unable to engage. One experience, one emotion, stockpiles on another, with no chance of release. By seeing too much, the parent overreacts to both the good and bad moments. Good games appear better than they are, bad games worse. With young kids, everything moves slowly. Everything takes longer to develop. The parent sees the bad play about to happen, anticipates it, fears it, feels helplessly caught in it, and then must watch it in every excruciating detail. There is also more time to savour the good moment, to see the sudden opening and *will* it to be taken, watching it happen, feeling a part of it, treasuring the moment. It can be one of the most intensely shared experiences a parent ever has with the child, and yet the child can remain completely oblivious to it ever taking place.

For parents watching their child play for the very first time, it is a shock. The child, it seems, is suddenly on his own as he has never been before. Elevated and distant, the parents look down with rare and dangerous perspective. The child, in the midst of the uncontrolled, uncontrollable play of life, lies exposed. Is he a puck hog? Is he useless? Does he keep trying even when the game is lost? Does he quit? In the comfortable, controllable environment of the home, none of this is clear. Here, it is on display for all to see. The cliché has a corollary: sports may *build* character, but more often it *reveals* it. To everyone.

And, of course, what is revealed on the ice reflects back into the stands. A son's skills may seem somehow up to him, but his character seems up to his parents. How indeed, then, is the parent doing in the parent game? Do the others in the stands stare out and see a poor skater, or do they see a lazy kid? Do they see a star to cheer or one to resent? The parents of ten and more years ago, who were never there, never saw any of this, never had the irresistible urge to act out their feelings. Today's parent sees it all.

From the distant perspective of the player's bench, the child, as well, can watch a parent watching him. He can see a father who at home is always calm and reasonable, a mother warm and loving, now out of their parental habitat. His shock is no less. Today's hockey parents are endlessly held up as the model of pushy behaviour, but they are no different from their baseball or football counterparts, or from any parents given the privilege and challenge of watching their kids grow up. If classrooms were revamped to add bleacher seats and parents were permitted to watch their kids in school, the results would be no different. Is he paying attention? Does he know the answer? Why do other kids' hands go up faster? Is the teacher fair? Should I shout, maybe, or gesture the answer to him? Am I proud when he is right? Embarrassed when he is wrong?

These are parents who have advised and directed their children forever. They have protected them from pain and harm and even slight. They have coaxed them, encouraged them, rationalized for them, wept with them. And now, suddenly, unexpectedly, these children are beyond their control. It is a shock because it is witnessed. The same things happen at school – intellectually, parents have always known this – but at school parents cannot stand to the side of the class and watch. What they don't know, can't hurt. Here, in a hockey rink, everything can.

What does a parent do? Some yell, sometimes in encouragement, occasionally in fury, just as they would over a messy bedroom floor or a broken basement window. Some stand silently, shifting, hoping beyond hope that the child will stare up into the stands and seek them out so that with a series of body gestures they can, like third-base coaches, get the appropriate message across. It is the parental instinct that if they could, they would not only sit on either side of their child when he is on the bench but be his protective wingers when he is on the ice.

The *involved parent* has changed the environment for minor hockey. A few years ago, only a few fathers and fewer mothers would attend their kid's games. Now most of the time both are here. Coaches coach differently when parents are around. They feel a need to account for everything they do. They know when a game ends they will need to explain – why Johnny wasn't on the power play, why the team forechecked with one man, not two, why the team lost – to parents who have come to apply the attitude and ambitions of the workplace to everything in their lives. They have committed more to their child's activities and so expect more from them. Kids and parents relate differently, too. The passion, pride, and disappointments stored up from the game don't recede very quickly when it ends, so their journey home has little of the easy, breezy feel that other rides do. Sometimes the closeness of such an intensely shared experience will cement parent-child bonds like few other things can. Sometimes it will destroy them.

Does the involved parent make for a better or worse environment? It can be much better, or much worse. It depends on the parents and kids and coaches involved. It does make for a different environment. Parents will always be parents; and when they are, kids usually won't be kids. It is the difference between kids playing in a backyard and in an indoor arena. Backyards are for fantasy and play; rinks are for aspiration and making it. Backyards, in today's mind, seem idle and unproductive; rinks are organized, maximized, busied, and directed. Backyards are a kid's world; rinks belong to adults. More and more, the playing fields of Scarborough have been moved indoors.

It is hard to be thirteen years old. It is also hard to be the parent of a thirteen-year-old, for so many things are happening in their lives on the ice and off. Somewhere along the road to Quebec, puberty struck the Marlies. Hockey-mad and obsessed with Gretzky at the end of last season, suddenly half the team seems under the spell of Rob Boyko's older sister, Melanie, who comes to the games and sits patiently behind the players' box, her long blonde hair and blue eyes more intimidating than any opposing player in the league.

On the ice, the emotional, psychological, and playing crunch has come. The rules changed the year before: bodychecking is now allowed. Size has come to matter more and, with puberty, growth strikes each child dramatically and unevenly. Moreover, after perhaps six years in the game, a child's past begins to foretell his future. He scored ten goals this year and last; next year he will not score fifty, and for the first time both parent and child are beginning to know it. Lifelong hopes and expectations get challenged; self-images go on the rocks. It is not an easy time for anyone.

This year's Toronto Marlboro peewees, in fact, have had a turnover of fifteen players from the previous season's team. One who remained, moving up from assistant captain to captain, was Greg Koehler. The changes were mostly the result of both parents and children proving incapable of coping with the realities of higher competition. A star at eight owns the puck. Faster and stronger, he will likely score several goals a game, often on end-to-end rushes with his teammates little more than cheerleaders to the action. He will dominate his game more than Gretzky does his, something he and his parents will not fail to notice. In time, the cheerleaders get streamed away and the stars come together on one of the MTHL's eight AAA teams. But there is still only one puck and now five young prodigies who, with their parents, feel they still should own it. Gradually, the prodigy stops looking like Gretzky, and he and his parents wonder why.

"People get so wound up about their kids when they are younger," Ed Koehler explains. "And when they're older and they begin to tail off, who are they going to blame first? The coach, of course. There were a lot of big heads on last year's team. The parents were used to seeing their kids scoring and all of a sudden they're not scoring like they used to. They hadn't learned how to play a team game or to pass the puck. Parents aren't going to blame their own son, but they might blame someone else's kid because he didn't do this or that."

This year, Greg Koehler is struggling, too. He was always the one kid on the ice that understood the game. He could see its patterns, anticipate them, and direct them like a quarterback. Now he is bigger, but others are bigger still. He can see evidences of it every day along the basement walls of his family's home. Greg had always been dead centre in every team picture, the grinning captain of the best team. Now only Greg seems to be shrinking. He worries that he might have inherited his mother's size and not his father's.

He is finding it harder to gain open ice, to give himself the time he needs to direct the game. With less open ice, he is getting hit more often and hurt, and he doesn't know why. He had always been able to separate himself from his teammates and his opponents. Now he must play in the pack, and that isn't much fun.

"He's frustrated," Ed Koehler admits. "He's so used to being able to do things with the puck that the other kids couldn't do. I mean, five years ago he was head and shoulders above them as far as thinking the game was concerned. Now they are catching up."

The pressure is palpable during a game such as this, both on and off the ice. You can sense it in the small Taylor family as they stand cheering on the Marlies their son is unable to play for, yet they are here at every game showing the flag. If they did not come, Chris might be forgotten. If they did not come, the other parents might notice. You can feel it in the way Ed and Cathy Koehler look at each other when they both realize three shifts have passed and the captain of the Marlies has not come back onto the ice. "I guess he's in the doghouse," Ed says. He is. Coach Paul Lewicki is hoping that sitting his captain on the bench for a while will cure Greg of whatever ails him. Sitting forlornly on the bench, Greg rubs his right thigh. An opposing player's hip caught him early in the game, and the longer he sits on the bench the larger the injury grows. The more he rubs, the more he is trying to persuade himself and, he hopes, his teammates that he is not being used for reasons beyond his control. But it is doubtful that anyone, Greg included, is fooled.

Ed Koehler sometimes stands on the rear railing and wonders, as do so many other parents, how this game he loves has become such an awesome commitment. How did it get away on us? He had played with some ability as a child, but it had never consumed his family back then as this is consuming his family now.

"I can remember carting a bag over my shoulder and walking about a mile to the rink," he remembers of his own youth in London, Ontario. "My dad took me occasionally and my mother didn't drive, so I was pretty much on my own. Often the coaches would pick up three or four of us, so parent participation was next to nil. I could probably count on two hands the number of times my parents went the whole time I was playing hockey."

He is so involved now partly because the distances require it, much more so because he and Cathy made up their minds that they would be *involved parents*. "Whatever," he says, "we're going to do it."

It is the style of a generation. But why has the price been pitched so high? What was the trigger that set hockey loose from its past, leaving it open to the irresistible instinct for *more* – time, sophistication, commitment – that was building in our society? It was a hockey series, more precisely one game, September 2, 1972, when the Soviet Union's hockey team beat Canada, 7–3. It was the first game ever played between our best and their best. It did not matter so much that twenty-seven days later Canada could claim victory in the series on Paul Henderson's goal with only thirty-four seconds left in the eighth and final game. For on September 2, Canada entered the world and felt its competition for the first time, and changed forever in desperate need to meet it.

Just as electricity had brought day to night, the indoor ice surface can turn summer into winter. Yet, until 1972, Canadians had failed to take much notice. Tradition and culture had made hockey for us a winter game. The Soviets, faced with our seventy-year head start in hockey, extended their season on the ice and off to eleven months a year in an effort to catch up. Secure in what had seemed like a mandated superiority, Canadians felt no need to change until the Soviet series. Then, in a panic to meet the unexpected challenge, unconventional thoughts emerged. We have all these indoor arenas, where pipes and compressors can simulate winter even on the hottest summer day, so why not use them? Why not extend the season and play more games? To compete against the Soviets, who have now caught up to us, we will need to work as hard and as long as they do. All that was stopping us was tradition, and the Soviets had already demonstrated the prison that outdated tradition can be.

So the cultural barriers came tumbling down. Teams that had been practising once a week and playing once or twice more gradually took to playing two or three times a week with more than the occasional weekend tournament. The season, which had run from October to early March, began to expand. September tryouts were moved back to May, and once a child had made his *next year's* team he was expected to work out on his own during the summer, on ice and off, to be *ready* when the team's workouts began in late August or early September. The result is that child and parental commitment has nearly doubled in recent years. In 1960, a child playing in the THL (predecessor to the MTHL) played about fifty games a season and practised once a week, in total committing seventy to seventy-five nights to hockey a year. Yet because no one played more, he still had every chance to realize the dream of playing in the NHL. The price for reaching the top, as for everything else, has gone up. This year, Greg Koehler will play seventy-four games and practise and work out with the team on seventy other occasions. He will also attend power-skating school in the summer.

Competition can make us all blind. Because the other guy is doing something, or might do something, whether across the ocean or across the street, we are driven to do the same, almost irresistibly, whether it seems to make sense or not, whether we like it or not. To compete, and win, becomes reason itself, the only reason that we need. And each year it takes more to win.

Once the competitive genie is let loose, what is to stop it? Who is there to say "no"? No more? Too much? The Koehlers and Taylors grew up believing that sports were somehow part of that elusive mix of what was best for children. They have told their children that if they are willing to commit to something, they, as parents, will do all they can to help, and they have. Sometimes, sure, they help too much. Sometimes the commitment made can seem more like theirs than that of their children, but that will always happen. AAA minor hockey is what the kids and their parents aspire to. It carries with it, someone has decided, a lengthy, at times exhausting, schedule. If the Marlies were to cut back their schedule to fifty or sixty games, the team might no longer be a contender. If all the MTHL teams did the same, the other Ontario leagues and leagues in other provinces might not do the same. Who then would have the edge in realizing *the dream*? Whose players would make it to the NHL? A matter of inches can separate the best from the rest. The risk is great. What parent is willing to take it, especially when the child loves playing so much? Especially when *the dream* still burns? And what about "being the best you can be"? Isn't doing less just a deliberate acceptance of mediocrity?

Furthermore, what would the Soviets do?

And so everything makes sense, and nothing does. And the irresistible force powers on. Parents love hockey; their kids love hockey; they are mostly happy in the game. If they didn't, if they weren't, it would be simple. They would just pack up their station wagons and head them down a different highway. And many more are doing just that. Still, for those like the Koehlers and Taylors who stay hockey's course, they sometimes wonder, isn't it an awful lot to ask?

Greg Koehler is a prodigy. Together with his parents and family, they live a prodigy's life. Chris Taylor and the other Marlboros and all the kids who play in the AAA level of Toronto's MTHL are prodigies, too. They would not likely agree. To them and to most, prodigies play the piano or violin or dance ballet. Sports is different. It is play. It is what *they* want to do. Music and dance seem like things that *parents* want their kids to do when their kids really want to be out playing hockey.

But both Greg and his parents put in a prodigy's time and make a prodigy's commitment. And they have made a prodigy's choice – hockey, and not much of everything else. If they did not make that commitment, Greg couldn't play major-level hockey. He wouldn't be on the road to Quebec – and perhaps beyond. And as it is with all prodigies, he will go as far as his mind will drive him, as far as his body will allow, as far as his parents will scrimp and encourage and push him.

Such commitment leaves the family continually living on the edge. Greg has practised speed-dressing until he can put on all of his equipment, skates included, in less than five minutes, and there have been times when he has had to do it in the back of the station wagon on the way to a practice that has followed one of his brother's games. Ed Koehler figures that hockey registration alone for all the boys costs him more than $1,500. Once he adds in skates, necessary new equipment – family friends often contribute free hand-me-down pads and gloves – sticks, skate sharpenings, laces, tape, gas, he ends up with around $4,000 a year just in hockey expenses. And that does not include depreciation on vehicles, the need for a second car, hotels for out-of-town tournaments, or treats at the snack bar. He sometimes stretches the salary he takes home from the data-processing centre of the Bank of Nova Scotia almost beyond its limits. Cathy, fortunately, carries with her a special "team manager" card that means she no longer has to pay out the $1.75 admission that is charged to each minor hockey game.

This financial commitment has meant that the Koehlers will never have a new car, will never take a southern vacation, will never get around to redecorating their home as long as the children are in hockey. But they don't mind. "It's in your blood," Ed Koehler says.

There is not much that identifies Greg Koehler as a prodigy. Few would ever guess it as he walks down Pachino Street with Billy Thompson on their way to Mac's Milk. The two boys are walking along a street where the average Canadian is Greek, or Italian. There are no men dipping out of car hoods to wipe the grease from their hands, smile, and shout out to Greg that he would have potted a great goal the other night if it weren't for that darn goalpost. At Mac's Milk there are no customers to ask how the team is going, no owner to slip him a free chocolate bar because being captain of the local team is something special. The cute girls that pass by with their leather-frill jackets and black pumps are impressed by the design on the hood of a black Pontiac Firebird, not much by a Toronto Marlboros crest on the breast of a blue hockey jacket.

The small-town hero is an unknown quantity to Greg

77

Koehler. Still, watch how he walks. See how he rolls on his feet, how his shoulders seem always set and static, how the walk is so different from that of Billy Thompson, who bobs and drifts as he walks, or other kids on the street, who move as if walking were a vehicle they have out on loan. Greg Koehler's walk is that of the elite athlete, that nearly knock-kneed walk of someone who, even at thirteen, is totally at ease with his body, confident of his motion, sure of his place. Even if those who pass do not know he is captain of the Marlies, he knows. And inside of him this knowledge burns with an intense, and intensely satisfying, glow. Has all the time, all the effort put into hockey, been worth it? For Greg Koehler, part of the answer is there in his walk.

There is no middle ground in a family of six boys and a baby girl. There are only the loud and the silent, and Greg, second of seven, has always been the silent one. Words do not come as easily to him as pucks; he expresses himself better on the ice than in person. And yet, what is there that he needs to say? He is thirteen years old. He is a grade eight student at Terraview-Willowfield Public School, a C student who could, and should, do better. He likes his homeroom teacher, Greg Gourley. He belongs to the chess club. He likes to hang around malls with Billy Thompson and look at girls. He likes rap music and the Beach Boys, the same group his parents used to dance to when they began dating in London, Ontario. He doesn't see enough television to join in on the schoolyard talk and doesn't much care that he isn't as wrapped up in *Who's The Boss?* or *The Cosby Show* as is the rest of the class. When they talk about parties on the weekend he tunes out, knowing there is no use even thinking about them.

What drives Greg Koehler is hockey. When he talks fast and easy, it is about hockey, whether recounting the night at Maple Leaf Gardens when Leafs' forward Ed Olczyk gave Greg and his brother Richard the high-five, or speaking of the different joys of rink hockey and road hockey: "In a game I like to pass; on the street I like to deke around and see how long I can hang onto it." And when he wakes up in the morning the first thing he sees is the Wayne Gretzky poster.

Still, does he love it enough? Does he have that "monstrous

itch," as U.S. dancer and choreographer Paul Taylor once put it, to make it to the top? It has been fairly easy for Greg and Chris until now. There are not so many things to do in a thirteen-year-old's life, not so many things to miss by playing hockey. That is changing by the minute. Dating, more homework, other activities – real choices must soon be made. Then they will find out, and if the "monstrous itch" is there, are the talent and size?

It is when the dream begins to flicker, of course, that kids and parents drop out. They come to ask themselves "why?" Why all these games and practices and nights on the road, why do all this if it doesn't lead anywhere? It is here, as the statistics point out, that kids leave in numbers, between the ages of fourteen and seventeen, when the search for other directions gets hottest and heaviest.

Once upon a time for Greg and his teammates, hockey was an NHL jersey under the Christmas tree. It was proud, anxious fathers, backyard games and games in their heads, hockey cards, posters of heroes on bedroom walls, scoring titles, gleaming trophies to display – a world as remote and magical as King Arthur's and Luke Skywalker's, a world cultivated and fuelled by adults with books and toys and TV screens. Now for Greg and his teammates, in the NHL-like jerseys, with adult referees, coaches, and fans, these fantasies become real and start to disappear. Create the dream, buy the dream, now Greg must live with the dream and do what it demands.

> *Never can tell what might come down*
> *Never can tell how much you got*
> *Just don't know, no you never can tell.*
>   Tom Cochrane, "Big League"

Who makes it? Who combines that talent, size, and unquench-able desire and becomes an NHLer? As the words in the song go, we "just don't know," though we do have some hints. We know that out of all the 120 peewees playing major AAA MTHL hockey this year, perhaps four or five will make it to the NHL. The MTHL – with 303 minor hockey teams in 1988-89 – has produced propor-tionately more NHL players than the rest of the country but bewilderingly few superstars. Long-ago, the Leafs' "Kid" line of Joe Primeau, Charlie Conacher, and Busher Jackson moved up from its ranks; in more recent years Carl Brewer, Rick Middleton, Steve Shutt, Paul Coffey – all fine players, but none a *great* player.

The reasons have something to do with the nature of life in a big city. If you were to dredge your memory for the greatest players of your lifetime, names like Rocket Richard, Gordie Howe, Jean Beliveau, Bobby Hull, Frank Mahovlich, Bobby Orr, Guy Lafleur, Wayne Gretzky, and Mario Lemieux might come to mind. All but the first and the last, Montreal's Richard and Lemieux, are from small towns. All, without exception, are from working-class families. It has to do with time, mostly. There is more time in a small town because of fewer things to do, and in a working-class family because there are fewer choices. And with fewer other dreams, working-class kids will stay in the game longer. And whether in the field of music, literature, business, law, or, for that matter, sports, time is the incubator of creativity and greatness. Lessons with coaches or teachers do not make the crucial difference, though they help to set forth the right direction. It is the time spent between the lessons, time alone, when you can go beyond the "how" of something and just do it, when the stick-like scold of practice – "practise your piano!" – becomes the carrot of play. The philosopher and educator Northrop Frye was once asked the main purpose of the school system. It is "to instill a love of learning," he said, for the love of something keeps you at it in a way no coach or teacher or parent can. And keeping at it means spending time, where the key to specialness resides.

"He practically caved in the old foundation, before we had it rebuilt," Walter Gretzky recalls, talking about his son Wayne and his favourite spot at the side of the family home in Brantford, Ontario. "He would always have a puck out there, just firing it against the wall. And you'd go out and say, 'Wayne, no more. Okay?' A few minutes later you'd hear, 'Bang, bang.'"

We have come to distrust time, especially in the cities. It is open to such easy, unforgiving abuse. Parents have come to associate time on one's hands with drugs in one's pockets. They feel a certain security in "busy-ness," in treating play like work or school – highly organized, structured, filled with penalties and rewards. It seems more productive, more purposeful, more useful in the long run. For those who fear time, an arena or a swimming pool or a gymnasium takes on the aura of a sanctuary. For them, a kid hanging around the backyard in 1989 is much the same as a kid hanging around a pool hall in 1959. Trouble brewing.

So we play more hockey now in arenas, on teams, with coaches and referees, and less on the streets, backyards, or driveways. Another cultural change is involved here, which has nothing to do with time, and despite our frequent outbursts of nostalgia it will not be reversed. We prefer to escape winter and spend it indoors, and now we can. It changes the way we play.

"Every time we teach a child something," Swiss psychologist Jean Piaget once wrote, "we keep him from inventing it himself." A hockey school or a highly organized practice and game structure can teach skills – the fundamentals – but the creative side of play, the imaginative, cognitive side that provides the special breakthrough moments in a game, comes mostly from somewhere else. Hockey schools and closely organized practices teach the language but not the idiom, the notes but not the music.

Paul Lewicki is part of the post-1972 hockey revolution in Canada. His practices are crisp and sharp and engage the attention of his players. No player, it seems, stands around longer at any moment than it takes for him to catch his breath from one drill before going on to the next. The carefully planned drills, repeated through the season, are intended to work on the game's fundamentals – skating (turning and acceleration), passing (the passer *and* receiver), and shooting – the very fundamentals, flaws in which the Soviets exposed so clearly in 1972.

It was then that hockey's "back to basics" movement began. If in education its symbol was the dunce cap, in hockey it was the similarly shaped pylon. Put pucks on the ice and kids will play a game. Add pylons, and maybe their attention can be distracted from games long enough to learn what they need to know first – to skate, pass, and shoot. The pylon can expose flaws that a game never can. The philosophy of every game is to hide your weaknesses and expose your strengths. If you happen to be a poor skater, you learn the patterns and rhythms of a game, anticipate well, and few will notice. But put out a pylon and smarts can't help you. You look hopeless.

So you work on your skating and other skills and get better. Games become the place to practise your skills, except games are not very good for that. Few players, other than goalies, will be on the ice for more than fifteen minutes in any game. And these are highly pressured minutes, where there can be little on a player's mind other than to try to score and keep the other team from scoring.

At the next practice the player will work on his skills again, but where is the time between lessons to go beyond the "how" of something with the pylons gone, where individual skills can be put together in some uniquely personal way and applied to a game? The "back to basics" movement makes most sense when it is applied in the context of a more informal, complementary side of life. In hockey, it presupposes the mythical winter life of a child that does not exist much now, particularly in a city. It presupposes street hockey.

Pylon hockey and street hockey represent a mix of the organized and unorganized, the formal and informal, the goal-directed and fantastic, the disciplined and undisciplined, the time-pressed and timeless. They combine the skill and cognitive functions of the brain, the "how" (skill) with all the creative ways (cognitive) in which the "hows" get put together. This happy mix characterizes the childhood of most great players. To the extent that Wayne Gretzky was made, not born, it happened far more in his backyard and sideyard than in all the arenas of Brantford.

Today there are more skilled players than ever, but despite technical improvements in coaching and equipment there are no more great players. The difference between the "skilled" and "great" is the difference between the "smart" and "wise." A "back to basics" movement, whether in education or sports, produces the skilled person and is of itself only part of the answer. It means that in large Canadian cities, where in hockey the rest of the answer is more elusive, many young boys will be developed whose skills will make them into competent NHL players. But the great players will come from someplace else.

The captain of the Marlies is out of position. At least, he is out of position as far as the "imagery" play might have it. The Canadiens are deep in their own end, behind their net, and Greg Koehler should be in forechecking, but instead he is looping lazily around the ice by the blueline. The Canadiens' defenceman shoots the puck out to his winger by the hash marks, just as the set play demands, and the winger fires a high pass to the centre who is breaking up ice, just as the set play demands.

But suddenly there is the blade of a stick snaking out. It is Greg Koehler's stick, catching the pass in mid-air just as he caught his brother's high shot on the road, snicking it out of the air as he ran back from down the street. Here, in St. Michael's College School Arena, Greg tucks the falling puck in tight to his own skates and heads over the blueline, slipping around the sprawling winger who sent the pass out. He steps in toward the defence, tucks again, and in a moment is clear of both defenders, heading in alone on a goalie who assumes the fighting-scorpion position. Another shift and the goalie is himself out of position. As delicately as he snapped shots earlier that day on the road, the captain of the Marlies cuffs the puck at the space that grows along the goalie's left side.

The puck clangs against the post and skips back out toward the blueline. Greg hustles to get back in the play.

If culture affects who makes it and who does not, the hockey system does as well. At present, for example, the system rewards those parents who are able to time a pregnancy to begin in the spring and come to its happy fruition in the early months of the new year. Hockey registration, you see, goes by the calendar year, and each child born in a given year is considered the same age for purposes of setting age limits. Yet a child born, say, on Wayne Gretzky's birthdate of January 26 is likely to be a better player on the first day of hockey tryouts than a player born on December 25th of the same year. The January child is almost a year older, a year stronger and more mature. At age six or seven this represents an enormous advantage, the January child being nearly one-sixth or one-seventh older. Greg Koehler's birthday falls on February 27. Chris Taylor turned fourteen on January 22, 1989. The older child has the best chance to be the first star of the game, to develop a star's skills and attitude and expectations of success. The younger child – smaller, weaker – must first learn to cope, and later, when the age difference matters less (for example, at fourteen the same January child is only one-fourteenth older), he is often unable to undo his and others expectations, reprogram himself, put to one side his coping skills for a star's skills, and become a star. The same situation and problem exists, of course, in the schools.

If streaming came at a later age, the effect of birthdates would be largely outgrown. But streaming comes early in hockey. As a result, the system rewards the older child and penalizes the younger. From age nine onward, better players get streamed into competitive teams, and the competitive teams get the better coaches and more ice time. The lesser players get streamed away from higher expectations and more ambitious goals, and the gap between the mediocre nine-year-old and the gifted nine-year-old begins to widen, and widen fast. In Canadian minor hockey in the late 1980s, if you don't make it by age nine, you likely won't make it at all.

The effect can be seen by comparing the birth charts of NHL players over different periods of time. Professors T.E. Daniel and C.T.L. Janssen of the University of Alberta found that for the 1961-62 NHL season, when the registration date was August 1, slightly more than half of the players in the NHL were born in the second half of the year. By 1972-73, after the registration date had been changed in 1969 to January 1, the results were inconclusive. But for the 1985-86 NHL season, with the registration date still January 1 and the effect of transition gone, Daniel and Janssen found that of the 775 Canadians who belonged to NHL teams, 495 were born in the first six months of the year and only 280 in the later months. January, with ninety-two players, had the most players born. December, with only thirty-four players, had the least.

"Players born in the early months," Daniel and Janssen concluded, "are naturally more developed – bigger, stronger, heavier and better coordinated – than those born late in the year. As a consequence, the older kids do better at any early age and are placed on the higher level or 'rep' teams; the younger boys in the same age groups are shuffled off to 'house league' teams. For 6-year-old children, twelve months of development makes a big difference in motor skills. This in turn tends to give positive reinforcement, more ice time and better coaching to the relatively older players, and negative reinforcement to the younger ones. As a result, the former group progresses more rapidly, lending to an ever-widening skill gap and to a greater number of players from the older group continuing in hockey, and to the younger group dropping out, causing disproportionate representation in the junior and major leagues."

The Alberta professors also looked at the Canadian Football League and found no evidence of a relative age effect on its players. In football, organized play comes at a much later age than in hockey (often not until high school), so an up-to-364-day age difference created by a registration date will mean far less. Streaming in school as in hockey makes early differences – age, physical and emotional maturity, economic circumstances, parental interest (or non-interest) – harder to reverse and leaves a child few second chances. Only in hockey are children streamed at so young an age and with such unfair effect.

The high number of dropouts and a nagging sense of unease over the present system brought the government of Quebec in 1988 to establish a fifteen-member task force on minor hockey. Under MLA and chairman Robert Thérien, and including Montreal Canadiens' captain Bob Gainey and Quebec Nordiques' Michel Goulet, the task force spent seven months travelling the province listening to wide-ranging, often passionate opinion. The task force offered its recommendations in the fall of 1988, generating fierce interest and controversy. The report suggested that the current system of highly organized, competitive hockey was too stressful for Quebec children under the age of twelve and should be eliminated. Further, to break the lock of the elite system and make the game more recreational, it advised that minor hockey be taken out of the hands of private volunteers and placed instead in the schools as part of their physical education programs.

Criticism of the report was harsh. Some parents argued that such a unilateral de-emphasis of hockey only ensured that Quebecers would no longer be able to compete in the NHL race. Some said they would keep their kids out of hockey if there was no real goal to aim for. Hockey survives on volunteers, others charged. With hockey part of the school system, the interest of volunteers would fade and the game would collapse. Moreover, commented others, the report challenged basic human nature and as such its recommendations were bound to fail. Kids love to compete; even in road hockey they play to win. Hockey for kids is play and fantasy, and part of fantasy is pretending to be your heroes. That means sweaters and games and scoring goals and winning. Not pylons.

It is not yet clear what the province of Quebec will do. The Thérien report offers many doubtful answers. It does, however, ask the right questions. Who is minor hockey for, and for the time, money, and dreams we invest in it, what are its purposes?

Minor hockey's falling registration has something to do with lower birthrates and rural-to-urban population shifts, with split families and the cost of equipment. More significantly, though, registrations are down because the minor hockey stakes have gone up. "Being the best you can be" is the prodigy creator's creed. It means always *more*, and it means a *dream* that is harder to come by. Minor hockey parents and kids are asked to live a prodigy's life, and how many want that life? How many piano or ballet prodigies are there? How many kids, and parents, are willing to put in four nights a week and occasional weekends, all weekend, for a dream that almost certainly will not be? Not many. Count them, in music or dance – a few thousand perhaps, maximum. There are hundreds of thousands in hockey. This more than anything demonstrates the power of ambition, the strength of the dream.

Minor hockey parents and kids accept the contortions of this life right up until the dream dies. Only then does the cost of equipment and commitment of time seem too much. So kids drop out and search out other dreams. They become fans until, as old-timers, they can come back to hockey on *their* terms, able to slot hockey into their busy lives and not the reverse.

Minor hockey has become largely an exercise in prodigy creation, its demands driven by the needs of the elite player, by the competition, driven by the dream. In this country it is a mass activity, and so masses of kids and their parents are affected. A mass system making elitist demands brings many kids to drop out entirely, when with demands better scaled to their childhood circumstances they might continue on. More troublesome is what happens to those who are good enough to pursue the dream. Hundreds will make it and receive incredible rewards, which in the future will only get larger. The tens of thousands of others who won't make it are the problem. They have committed as much time, and there were just as many other things they chose not to do, as many things they never learned, as the stars who made it. Now they must go on to something else.

Think of minor hockey as a lottery. Compared with other lotteries, the odds are good: maybe one in a thousand will win and make it. But the cost of each minor hockey ticket in time, in choices not made, is not the usual $1 or $10, money that otherwise gets spent on things that don't matter, money that will never be missed. Buying it means not buying many other things that do matter; it means borrowing against the rest of your life for some hoped-for payoff in the future. Imagine its dollar-value cost at $10,000 or $50,000 and rising each year. For the few winners, it is a good investment. But for the thousands of losers in this lottery, life is not the same. And like other lotteries, this bargain appeals most to those with fewer chances of winning any other way. The middle- and upper middle-class parent will stay in the game until the writing on the wall becomes clear, then back away. Working-class parents and their kids hang in longer.

Or think of minor hockey as a poker game; the parents are the players, their kids the cards they play. With poor cards, most minor hockey parents will fold right away. With good cards, they stay in the game, seeing, raising, and as the stakes go higher each dollar already gambled becomes another reason to stay in and gamble more. And at the end the winner takes all, and the biggest loser is the one who thought and hoped and stayed in, but whose cards were not good enough. And until the end no one can know who has "second-best" cards.

The dream will not change much, nor will the numbers who realize it. If anything can change, it is in the demands made of those who play. There are some who are always willing and wanting to do more. And in the future, with greater and greater rewards for those who make it, they will be asked to do more. Elite hockey will survive, but the minor hockey system needs to gear itself more toward those who will not make it, not toward those who will. If its registration numbers are not to continue to drop precipitously in the future, the system will need to separate into two nearly distinct categories, with a few elite players streamed, at a later age, toward the NHL for their benefit and our entertainment. The great mass of others, still competitive and wanting to win, still fantasizing about being Wayne Gretzky and Mario Lemieux, will play less often but learn the lessons of the game and have the time to apply them to the rest of their lives.

It is the difference between treating minor hockey as a means or as an end. Once "being the best you can be" had to do with being the best *person* you could be. School, church, Cubs or Brownies, sports were all considered as important ingredients in a recipe of means that could help achieve that end. If sport came to offer the wrong experiences or teach the wrong values, then it lost its purpose. Now "being the best you can be" means being the best you can be *at something*. It can be as a student, business-person, accountant, video games player, or bottlecap collector. Being the best is its own goal and reward. There is no bigger picture. Everything becomes an end.

And so minor hockey does, too. It matters less, then, that a child spends more hours a week, more weeks in a year, at something and not at everything else. A graduate of minor hockey may offer the maturity and life perspective a good doctor or teacher needs, but he has had less time and is less likely to qualify and get his chance. He develops the means for no attainable end.

Being the best you can be is a notion easily abused. Built into it are the incentive and rationale for exaggerations of all sorts – workaholism, prodigyism, etc. An attitude of the times, this drive to be the best strikes at minor hockey as well. Children reaching their young teenage years will continue to drop out of hockey in large numbers. This has little to do with hockey's excesses and a lot to do with a stage of their lives. The number of dropouts will be higher than before, in part because each year there are more other things to do, so each option gets sliced thinner.

The more time hockey demands of its mainstream player (and family), the fewer will get involved and stay involved. Minor hockey faces this haunting irony. Once, parents found hockey appealing for their kids as an outlet for fun and learning, and as a way to avoid all the destructive things a child might otherwise get involved in – alcohol, drugs, hanging around. Hockey was a way to keep them busy and off the streets. Now, one sees parents of young boys actively encouraging their kids into cross-country or downhill skiing as a way to distract them from the demands of hockey. They see minor hockey as another of those destructive things to avoid.

Kids love to play hockey. Parents love to watch them play. But they also worry about where their future leads and what effect a hockey life has. Minor hockey, so long as rinks are more than walking distance away, is about kids *and* parents.

Sometimes one can love something too much. It can hold us in its thrall and make us do what we really shouldn't do (and likely will continue to, whether it changes or not). That is the power of this game. It makes the responsibility of those who administer it all the greater.

Years from now, how will Greg Koehler and Chris Taylor look back on this time? In 1973, another Marlboro peewee team also went to the Quebec tournament. Called "Shopsy's" for their long-time commercial sponsor, they were the subject of an hour-long CBC documentary, *It's Winning That Counts*, that chronicled their season.

Their coach was Curly Davies, a crusty, old-school type, about fifty at the time, who would prove to scandalize his CBC audience not used to marine-sergeant ways of dealing with twelve-year-old boys (the peewee age was later raised to thirteen). This was the intent, for the series was commissioned shortly after the 1972 Team Canada-Soviet series, and Shopsy's and Davies were intended to symbolize all that was wrong with Canadian hockey. If anyone cared to look at Davies closely enough, however, every mean-sounding word he delivered came with a serious twinkle in his eye, which his players, if few others, could always see.

Eventually, Shopsy's made it to the tournament final where they met their Toronto rivals, Dorset Park, in front of a Colisée packed with screaming fans. Shopsy's scored first, Dorset Park tied the game, and the teams went into a sudden-death overtime. Finally, on a shot that deflected off a Shopsy player's skate, Dorset Park won. Later that year Shopsy's won the MTHL title, beating Dorset Park in the finals, and then the all-Ontario championship. But they had lost Quebec.

Sixteen years later, four of the players from that team and Curly Davies got together to remember. Most of them had not seen each other for several years. Jamie Gilmour, one of the team's goalies, had changed the most. Always the smallest, he was now easily the tallest. Lloyd Dyson, also a goalie, was there. He had played most of the games in Quebec, including the overtime loss to Dorset Park. There, too, were Kerry Pim, a pint-sized defenceman, and the team's captain, Scott Parker.

Today, they remember Quebec with wonder and delight, and some sadness. "The most exciting moment I ever had in hockey," said Scott Parker, "was in Quebec when I walked along the long corridor from the dressing room to the ice. When you look up and all you see is a wall of people." The others murmured at the memory. "It was mind-boggling," said Pim, "here we were twelve years old and kids are coming up asking for *our* autograph. They couldn't even speak English." "Everything after that year was anti-climactic," mused Parker. Then he smiled, and remembering the Andy Warhol line, said with pride, "That was *our* fifteen minutes." They thought they would have many more, that Quebec would be only their *first* fifteen minutes, but it didn't turn out that way. Only two team members went as far as junior A hockey. None made it to the NHL. Asked whether this surprised him, Pim shook his head. "Yes, very much," he said. "I figured at least four or five guys on the team would make it."

Gary Dillon, playing for Dorset Park, was considered the best player in Toronto, perhaps in all of Canada. He played thirteen games in 1980-81 with the NHL's Colorado Rockies. Dillon's teammate, less highly regarded at the time, was Charlie Huddy, who became a fine defenceman on the Edmonton Oilers' Stanley Cup winning teams. He was the only one who truly made it. "It's great to see Charlie doing so well," Parker said, "but you figure out of two complete hockey teams, the best in Canada at the time, to have only one go as far as he has, I would have expected better odds, frankly." Why did Huddy make it? "Desire," said Parker. "Pure desire," echoed Lloyd Dyson. "I think it's like anything else in life," Parker went on, "if you want it, you go out and get it. There's no excuse. I just had enough. I didn't want it anymore." "I think myself," Gilmour said, "I just more or less lost interest once I got into high school and there were so many other different things going on. . . . "

The regret they felt at not making the NHL remains, but it is not so close to the surface as it once was. At twenty-eight, they are now more content with what they are than disappointed at what they are not. Even the loss at Quebec hurts less, though not by much. "More than the thrill of winning the Ontario championship," said Pim, "I remember the devastation of losing Quebec. I'll never forget that. I just can't get over that. It was all the hope and everything and the week there and the big dinners, and all the hype just like the pros. And we lost." It is particularly hard on goalie Lloyd Dyson. He had been a standout in the rest of the tournament. He had played a strong game right up until that one moment in the overtime. He has learned to come to grips with it over time, preferring to recollect all the other good things of that year, the MTHL and Ontario championships. Still, it haunts him. "It was my fault," he said. "I let everybody down."

But they all hold fonder memories. "That year we all spent together will be with us always," said Scott Parker, still the captain. "We can always pick up the phone," then he interrupted himself and started again. "There was this camaraderie on that team that I've never experienced with any other team. I can't think of half the people I played minor sports with, but I can always tell you who was on that team." He paused, then, filled with great pride, he murmured: "The Shopsy's Peewee Team."

Their fifteen minutes, their cup of coffee: it wasn't much of a dream come true, but it would be hard to persuade them that it wasn't worth it. Once they were prodigies like Greg and Chris, now they lead normal adult lives. All are married, only Kerry Pim has a child, none has a university degree, all have played recreational hockey in other years, none does now. Today, they are an electrical installer, assistant controller, school maintenance man, and firefighter. Would their lives have been different without hockey? Was the dream worth it? What about Greg and Chris?

"I have a three-year-old son that's taking skating," Kerry Pim tells his old friends, "and I want to get him into hockey just for the kind of experiences we had. Never mind the NHL, never mind anything, just to meet the people in hockey. . . . They're good people. And the times he'll have . . . "

It was as if a conversation that had begun many years ago had simply been put on hold. Already "The Shopsy's Peewees, 1973" were talking about putting together an old-timers team to play in some tournaments. "Hey, we could play Dorset Park," Dyson said, and they all laughed.

"As long as you don't ask me to coach," growled Curly Davies.

"We wouldn't," chirped Pim, and they laughed even harder.

When they got up, they traded addresses and phone numbers, and left.

On a Sunday afternoon the current Marlie captain, Greg Koehler, sits in his basement, showing little interest in what is supposed to be the sports event of the year, the Super Bowl. His father, Ed, fiddles with the VCR and keeps switching back and forth between the game and a rough videotape of Greg playing hockey when he was eight years old. But Greg Koehler is concentrating on neither a live U.S. football championship nor his own immediate past. He is thinking instead to the future and what it might be like if his dream ever comes true. "I want to go as far as I can," he says. In five years the dream is to be in junior hockey. He will be eighteen then, old enough to be drafted by an NHL team if it all somehow works out. "I don't know – I just want to make it. As high as I can go."

Billy Thompson is at the door, his goofy black fedora tipped back on his head the way Leo Gorcey liked to cock his in *The Bowery Boys* more than a half-century earlier. Billy changes the baby and flops down in the couch but cannot get caught up in a game he does not play or a past he does not share. Billy begins fidgeting, playing with his hat, playing with the baby, staring back and forth between the flickering television and Greg Koehler's flickering attention.

"You want to go out and shoot?" Billy Thompson asks.

Greg Koehler turns from the television, knowing that he should, if anything, be in his room working on his "imagery," not his shot with a punctured tennis ball.

"Sure," the captain of the Marlies says. "Why not?"

CHAPTER THREE

MERE PLAYERS

IT IS 5:17 P.M., SATURDAY, NOVEMBER 26, 1988, AND CHARLIE HUDDY and Greg Adams are sitting in their underwear. They are alone in the Montreal Forum, two solitary fans among 16,072 empty seats, two professional players who know there is something special about being where they are, doing what they are about to do.

They sit in the best seats in the house, between the Forum's distinctively patterned centre ice where, fifty-one years ago, Howie Morenz lay in state while thousands wept, and the blueline over which, on the night of March 23, 1944, Rocket Richard burst to score his fifth straight goal in Montreal's 5–1 playoff victory over the Toronto Maple Leafs. Above them, twenty-three white banners – each one declaring "Montreal Canadiens, Stanley Cup Champions" – hang from the rafters. Around them, in paintings on the lobby walls, in dressing-room photographs, but mostly in the memories of those who have spent even one night in this storied building, swirl the ghosts of Joliat, Vezina, Morenz, the Richards, Beliveau, Lafleur . . . It is here, in the Montreal Forum, that so many of this country's finest performances have been staged.

Around them, too, in this semi-darkened arena, are colourful billboards – Provigo, McDonald's, Tip Top, Molson Export,

Bell Cellulaire, Pages Jaunes, Laurentide, Caisse Populaire, Loto 6/49. There are no billboards on the ice, only the Canadiens' distinctive logo. In hockey's greatest home, sport and spectacle, myth and commerce, meet comfortably. It is perhaps the Montreal Canadiens' greatest achievement that for the player and fan who perform here there is never a question but that hockey comes first.

Huddy and Adams know there will be no hockey history made three hours from now, when their Edmonton Oilers, the team of today, meet the Montreal Canadiens, the team of forever. It will be the only time the entire season that these two teams face each other in the Forum. The result will not affect the standings much, nor will it prevent either team from making the spring playoffs. Still, these two young men hardly need to be told it is a moment for them to savour.

"Is this the national game?" Adams asks, as he notices a camera high in the seats above. He is wondering if *Hockey Night in Canada* will be taking him more than 3,000 miles into his home town in British Columbia.

"Yeah," Huddy says, his head nodding.

Adams laughs. "Remember running down into the basement to play in between periods?"

"Yeah, sure."

They are remembering a shared, but hardly exclusive, past. Charlie Huddy, twenty-nine, grew up in the sprawling eastern city of Toronto and played his entire minor hockey years in Ontario. Adams, twenty-eight, grew up in the western small town of Duncan and played all his early hockey in British Columbia. Their link is the game, the country, and . . .

"The dream, eh?" Huddy says, smiling.

"The *Great* Dream!" Adams corrects.

Both men, sitting in their underwear in this hockey shrine, lean back their heads, laughing – two National Hockey League veterans who still, deep down inside, harbour more than a little surprise that, for them, the Great Canadian Dream somehow came true.

The evening before this late November game in Montreal, an

earthquake registering 4.8 on the Richter scale struck the Chicoutimi area of Quebec along the North Shore. It damaged buildings and roads all the way to Quebec City, cut electricity in sections of Montreal, and rattled windows and china all the way west to the small village of St-André Est along the Quebec bank of the Ottawa River.

There, in a bedroom where hockey is played on the wallpaper, on the sheets, on the pillows, and in the posters that have turned this small room into a tiny shrine itself, Cameron Lowe, age eight, was settling into his own dream. Come the morning he and his mother, father, cousins, uncles, aunts, and grandmother would be driving from nearby Lachute to Montreal for a visit with his father's cousin Kevin, assistant captain of the Stanley Cup champion Edmonton Oilers. It was almost too exciting for a youngster of eight to imagine. He could not make time move fast enough. He could not get to sleep.

At 10:45 p.m., Noreen Lowe checked on her son and found him still awake, lying on his hockey sheets in the dark with nothing but the dull glow of his cousin's glossy poster to occupy his staring eyes. Not only would Cameron be meeting Kevin and taken into the Oilers' dressing room before the game, but for the first time he would be meeting another relative, Mike McPhee of the Canadiens, a distant cousin of his mother's from Sydney, Nova Scotia. It would be, as much as a trip to the Forum, a family hockey reunion for a large Québécois family linked through three generations to an outdoor rink eight Lowe brothers built more than thirty years ago, burying beneath it refrigeration pipes from the nearby family dairy so they could have ice from late October until Easter.

Cameron had already selected what he would be wearing: his red cap and the blue jacket with the "Lachute Hockey Mineur" crest over his breast so his cousins would know his heart was in the same place as theirs. And he would be carrying his Count Dracula pen for autographs, praying for Mark Messier's, his hockey hero since the summer past, when the patron saint of Canadian minor hockey players, Wayne Gretzky, had departed the Oilers for distant Los Angeles.

Early Saturday morning, when the Lowe family was still

assembling the convoy that would head down Highway 148 into Montreal, the Forum was already awake, time now as much a factor for the people who work there as it was for Cameron Lowe, bouncing in his seat on the drive into the city. Oilers' trainer Barrie Stafford was perfectly on schedule. He had just inserted an inspirational tape on the art of negotiations into his Walkman and begun work on the team skates. Behind the thirty-two-year-old Stafford the visiting team's dressing room was open and had been meticulously prepared by Stafford and the team's other trainer, Peter Millar, so it would appear precisely as every other dressing room the Oilers would enter this season, anything to make the road feel a little more like home: two pots of coffee brewing inside the door, blue and black and white tape set out on a table in order and size, Spearmint gum, Minute Maid and Pure Sun cold drinks, five bars of soap opened and set out on the step leading into the showers, two cans of Right Guard set by the sinks with their tops already off, two cans of Gillette Foamy shaving cream, four razors, Fabergé Brut cologne, Gillette "The Dry Look" extra-hold hair spray, an open jar of Life styling gel, Alberto Mousse, and European Styling Foam for the hair of the team for today.

While Stafford sharpened his players' skates and his own negotiating skills – "It's good to stay on top if you can" – a lone player took to the ice in this still early morning: Bob Gainey, the captain of the Montreal Canadiens. Three weeks away from his thirty-fifth birthday, Gainey was nursing a long, distinguished career that most had thought at an end the previous summer when he had been rumoured as the next general manager of the Minnesota North Stars. Ironically, he had of late been playing almost as well as he ever had during his sixteen seasons in a Montreal uniform.

Yet that was not so clear as it once had been. In the late 1970s, on a powerful offensive team, Gainey's meagre goal totals had seemed unimportant, even irrelevant. The Canadiens needed more his ability to bump and struggle to an unnoticed standstill the league's best opponents – Esposito, Clarke, Bossy, Sittler, Dionne. And, with linemates Doug Jarvis and Jim Roberts, he had succeeded remarkably. Now, without great scorers, the

Canadiens of the 1980s have needed goals from everyone and Gainey's eleven goals the year before – not far off his seasonal average – did not help much.

Gainey now has to wrestle with the complementary plagues of the athlete, age and injury. The fate of athletes and dancers and scientists is to see their brilliance flash and fade while still in their youth. It has to do with the sheer physical demands of greatness and our fleeting capacities. Isaac Newton was in his early twenties when he discovered the law of gravity. Albert Einstein offered his theory of relativity at age twenty-six. Wayne Gretzky scored 212 points at age twenty-one. What the great ballet dancers gain in nuance and depth by their mid-thirties, they lose in sheer power and flexibility. But dancers, like hockey players, learn how to do best with what they have left.

Gainey badly twisted a knee two years ago, and though the pain had gone away soon enough, the leg didn't feel right until recently. It had been a troubling time for Gainey. When he had felt the pain, at least he could pinpoint some reason why his body did not move the way it had before. But when the pain left and still his legs could not power him up the ice, his decline seemed permanent and irreversible, his career over. Then time, surprisingly, became his ally. After weeks and months his legs began to feel stronger, and his powerful skating stride, always his trademark, returned.

But to push legs that are able to move again, Gainey, a team player in a team game, needed a purpose. He had seen many fine players struggle with time and change. Those who managed best, he noticed, had found a role for themselves. "You have to realize [a career] won't all be played at a peak," he once told *Montreal Gazette* writer Michael Farber. "But there have been a lot of players who contributed even after they were on the downside."

First, however, they had to want to contribute and put on display their downside skills. They had to be willing to slide back into the anonymous pack of the team and let new solo stars take centre stage. Age had robbed Jean Beliveau of his powerful stride and shot, but exaggerated his *presence*. He could lead and others, trusting him, would follow. He could help pass on the Canadiens' championship state of mind that had been passed on to him two decades before. That night in Uniondale, Long Island, another former Canadien, Guy Lafleur, was playing the twenty-second game in a comeback season with the New York Rangers. Once Lafleur had been unwilling to accept the downside and retired. There was to him only one way to play – headlong, helmetless – and only one contribution, *goals*, he wanted to make. When the goals stopped coming, Lafleur had seen no reason to continue. It took him more than three idle years to change his mind.

For every veteran player, age depends on how he decides to look at it. For Lafleur, it was as if staring into the morning mirror, he could see the buttons on his shirt straining at their button holes and, fixated with that sight, seeing only what he *had been*, turned and walked away. Beliveau, looking into the same mirror, just bought a bigger shirt. Gainey seemed willing to do as Beliveau had done, but to have much impact on his team, first his play had to improve.

So far in 1988-89, it had. A quarter of the way through the season, Gainey had already scored five goals, but the team, after a messy and disappointing previous season, was sputtering. To make matters worse, the Canadiens, a disparate group of twelve Anglo-Canadians, two Americans, one Swede, one Finn, one Czechoslovak, and only five French Canadians, and made more disparate by two non-winning seasons, had a new coach, Pat Burns.

Burns and his players were still going through the awkward ritual dance of introduction, feeling and testing each other out. Burns had not yet learned to trust his veterans, and his veterans had shown themselves reluctant to learn Burns's new tricks. Gainey's role could be as conduit. But while age and past Stanley Cups count for something, producing in the here and now counts for a lot more. For Gainey to lead he had to feel the team's respect, and his own. He had to prove to himself, and to them, he still had something to offer.

Tonight – less than eleven hours from now – would be a new test. The Oilers were the defending Stanley Cup champions, as they had been in four of the last five years. They were without Gretzky for the first time since they had entered the NHL in 1979, but such stars as Mark Messier, Jari Kurri, and Grant Fuhr remained. If the Canadiens and Gainey had championship aspirations, now was the time to begin to prove it.

Wearing a white jersey and full uniform, Gainey has come to the rink earlier than any other player to work, once more, on the weakest part of his game: the moment when puck meets stick. He has come early to dump a hundred or more pucks around the net, to skate and swoop and dart in quickly and from a dozen different spots to hit the top corners of the net.

Gainey grew up with the conventional wisdom that a good hard low shot was best. Like most, he hadn't noticed that goalies had begun "cheating" – bringing their bodies into a deeper crouch and closer to the puck. High, much harder slapshots had brought real danger to a goalie, whose face was then protected by only a flimsy, face-formed fibreglass mask. Goalies and their coaches, seeking better protection, bullied practice shooters to keep the pucks low, a routine the shooters found they could not shake once a game turned them into opponents. And so for a while goalies managed to do what rule-makers would never allow. They had created the three-foot-high net.

The cage mask changed all that. Now a goalie's face is at least as well protected as the rest of his body, and once-chastened shooters have gotten their revenge. As Gainey is doing in his time of private practice, they have come to shoot high, often, and with great effect.

Gainey comes out at this time regularly on the day of a game, a little after nine in the morning and about an hour before most of his teammates arrive, often with nine-year-old son Stephen. This weekend, however, Stephen is in Boston at a hockey tournament. This is Gainey's time to be alone. No one else has call on the ice. Arriving as early as he does, few teammates will ever share it with him. At thirty-four, he is still ambitious. If his well-developed skating and power skills can only diminish with time and his prodigious team skills need no further practice, he has decided to work on those he has long neglected. Now, at an age of physical decline, he actually feels himself getting better.

It is a scene of great solitude and peace: the crunch of just two blades, the thwack of just one stick and puck at a time, the sounds of one person, where normally there are many, echoing through the sweep of empty seats. Time moves slowly this many hours before a game. Young players, inexperienced and unburdened with time, cut time's corners and come to the arena only when they need to. An older player too often has felt time speed by and take control of him. So Gainey comes early to get ahead of time to control it, if only for a few moments so that time won't matter. Time is endless, yet time is running out. For the players, this is the inescapable tension of the day. The game is coming and nothing can stop it.

It is only the morning and yet Gainey's mind is already firmly fixed on a game he has already played 1,134 times, more times than all but two other active NHL players – his older teammate Larry Robinson and Marcel Dionne of the New York Rangers. More than a thousand times he has gone through the purposely vacant hours that lead up to a game. But as Gainey says during a break, "My mind is constantly ahead to eight o'clock. It's a slow burning fire that goes all day."

Hockey is Canada's game. It may also be Canada's national theatre. On its frozen stage, each night the stuff of life is played out: ambition, hope, pride and fear, love and friendship, the fight for honour for city, team, each other, themselves. The puck flips one way, bounces another, and the players set out to control and direct it. It takes them where they never planned to go. It tests them. And in struggling to get it back, with the millions who watch in the arena or by television, the players find out who they really are. Like the bearpits in Shakespeare's time, we attend hockey games as our popular theatre. It is a place where the monumental themes of Canadian life are played out – English and French, East and West, Canada and the U.S., Canada and the world, the timeless tensions of commerce and culture, our struggle to survive and civilize winter.

But a game is different from a play, in that no one can know what is ahead. There is no script. This may be theatre, but these are not actors. They cannot control time, and when they are cut

they bleed. In a game's frenzied hours, the players give a performance of their lives.

The Canadiens' players drift in through the Forum doors past
the fifteen or so kids who seem always to be there. In the cold or
snow, in the early morning or late at night, win or lose, they
come from Anjou or Outremont or from the South Shore on a
special winter pilgrimage to see in the flesh their only team.
Their faces grow to be as familiar to players as those of good
friends, but when each brief exchange ends, they go off to their
own distant worlds until the next time. Players watch them
grow up; they watch players grow old. The autograph tells them
and others that once they got right up close. It tells the player
that he is important. These fans give at least as good as they get.

At 10:36 a.m. the Canadiens' dressing room is filling. The
Oilers, who will practise when the Canadiens are done, are still
at their hotel. This is the mellow of the day. The pounding
rhythms of rock music pour out of the room's sound system;
players fix sticks, talk, laugh, and slowly get ready. It is like a
Sunday afternoon at the club. Goaltender Patrick Roy sits where
Canadiens' goaltenders have sat since the Forum was rebuilt
more than twenty years ago. Gainey has hung up his clothes on
the same hooks in the same spot since he joined the Canadiens in
1973. Everyone has his place and knows his place. There is one
new face in the room. Jyrki Lumme, from Tampere, Finland,
will play his first NHL game tonight. It will come against his
countryman and hero, the Oilers' Jari Kurri. Lumme has been
put beside Scandinavian neighbour Mats Naslund to make him
feel more at home, but he has the shy eyes-on-the-floor look of
someone who thinks he doesn't belong.

It makes little sense, it seems, to bring players in from distant
homes to risk injury in a short and shapeless practice. Nothing
will be learned, no skills will be honed beyond what they were
yesterday. But the morning skate gets players out of bed and puts
them here among friends where the energy of the day can get at
them. It gets them into the comfort of unhurried routines and
brings the mood of the game closer.

Gainey, who left the ice to share the dressing room with his later-arriving teammates, has returned to the ice and others have followed. Together, they ease their bodies into the day, feeling them grow warm and loose and wet with sweat. Half-watching them and half-swapping stories with each other are Montreal's press, as relentless on the Canadiens as London's Fleet Street is on the royal family. They sit, scattered about the arena, their legs over the backs of the seats in front of them, scribbling notes to themselves like backstretch veterans watching an early morning gallop. And as "hockey people" of nearly any stripe happen by, they attach themselves to them, looking for a quick comment to fill vacant lines at the end of tomorrow's stories.

Hockey Night in Canada broadcasters Scotty Bowman, Brian McFarlane, and Dick Irvin sit together and talk, as everyone is talking this morning, about the NHL's decision to suspend Canadiens' defenceman Craig Ludwig for five games for using his elbow to knock Chicago Blackhawk Trent Yawney unconscious the previous Saturday at the Forum. The injury was more serious, the collision more violent, than many involving sticks that had brought about the league's most recent suspensions, and so it seemed impossible to overlook. Still, Ludwig had used only his elbow, not his stick. To the gathered, it seemed that the league had entered disturbing new territory. Everyone was wondering what was next.

Oilers' president/general manager/coach Glen Sather is not sympathetic. "You elbow a guy and it's five, you hit a guy with your *fists*, it's gotta be worth at least ten," he says sarcastically. Canadiens' president Ron Corey sees the suspension as "a dangerous precedent." The Canadiens have announced they are considering an appeal, so Ludwig can play tonight, but once the Oilers game is out of the way they intend to accept the league's ruling.

Pat Burns stands back slightly from the action, letting his assistant, Jacques Laperriere, handle the practice. Burns looks uncomfortable. His face wears the look of someone who is still asking himself – why am I coaching this team? He grew up a poor kid from St. Henri, not many blocks but worlds away from where he now stands. He used to hang around in back of the Forum, like so many other kids, looking for autographs. It was as close as he would get, as close as any kid like him would ever get to the real thing. He played hockey but not well enough, and until two years ago he was just a small-town cop in Gatineau, Quebec, and a junior hockey coach.

And this is the Montreal Canadiens, not only a team of legendary players but of legendary coaches as well – Dick Irvin, Sr., Toe Blake, Scotty Bowman. Their portraits cover Burns's office wall. Every day he sees Jean Beliveau, Jacques Lemaire, and Serge Savard walk the halls of the Canadiens' offices. At games, he sees Rocket Richard, Henri Richard, Doug Harvey. How dare I coach this team, he wonders? Even its journalists are legendary – René Lecavalier and Danny Gallivan and Jacques Beauchamps from the past, now Red Fisher, Dick Irvin, Richard Garneau. Even the fans have a mythical dimension. Everyone he passes stops to shake his hand, wish him well, and always there is some little suggestion. *Pat, don't you think that . . .* Who am I not to listen, he wonders?

Yet the more he listens, the more he finds himself lurching this way and that, confusing himself and his team. He has yet to make this team his own. He simply cannot shake the big question from his mind – why me? His face looks it; his players see it. Unless he finds his own answer soon, he will fail.

The Oilers arrive. Some go directly to the dressing room; others hang around in the Forum's corridors, fixing sticks, talking; still others grab empty seats and watch the Canadiens practice. For Kevin Lowe, the pressure of the day has already begun. As a visiting team player he gets two tickets for the game, for which he must pay. Yet he has scores of family and friends in Lachute, all anxious to see the Stanley Cup champion Oilers in their only visit to Montreal this season, to see the relative and friend they followed loyally and encouraged proudly since he was a little boy, to see whether the NHL star is still "little Kevin Lowe," the kid next door, or whether *he has changed*. Lowe knows it is an opinion they are sure to share, and one that will get bound up somehow with how they feel about getting a ticket or not getting one. It has taken him many seasons, but now most of Lachute knows his ticket dilemma, even understanding its implications, if not that those implications must apply to them. He has negotiated several extra tickets from his teammates, but still Lowe hasn't quite delivered his miracle. He keeps trying, flitting from one group to another, to another.

Shortly before noon, Burns and Laperriere disappear into a room off their offices to watch videotapes of the Oilers' last game, a 2–1 win in St. Louis, in which the Oilers managed only thirteen shots on net. They look at the images on a big projection screen, slowing them down, sometimes reversing them several times to examine them more closely. Burns already knows the way the Oilers play, and the way he wants his team to play against them. These images put picture to thought and feeling and only leave him more certain. He must now come up with a plan for the game. Nothing complicated, nothing step-by-step, for a game changes too fast and he knows that hockey's fates mock anyone who tries to control them. He needs a plan that is clear yet adaptable, something his players can believe in. Burns and Laperriere talk it through as they watch.

The Oilers skate with the self-assured air of champions. Their drills are mostly the same as those of the Canadiens, but their practice chatter is louder and they laugh when something is funny. The Canadiens, as last year's also-rans, went through their drills wearing faces that seemed not to catch the joke. Yet the Oilers are just now beginning to realize how much their championship swagger was because of one man, Wayne Gretzky. This is a team that has won four Stanley Cups in five years, that should have nothing more to prove, but it has. And so has each of its players.

Mark Messier is the team's new captain. He feels the need to honour a friend and mourn his passing, but he knows that he and his team must get on with it. They must find strength in their championship past, yet not live in its wistful mire. He has leadership to provide, more goals to score, and now he must do it against tougher opposition for he has inherited Gretzky's "shadows," the best defensive players every other team has to offer. Even as he cruises the practice ice, one can sense his animal power. With features chiseled and over-sized, he appears to be an indestructible force. Once when he was asked how he understood intimidation, he said plainly, it is "playing tough, like no matter what happens I am going to go into that corner and get that puck. No matter how hard you hit me I am going to get up and come at you again. No matter how hard you slash me, I am going to play through the pain."

He is the league's most intimidating presence. Everything Gretzky did said, "I am magic. You cannot beat me." Messier says it with a bone-chilling *look*. But it was Gretzky that helped give meaning to the look. The question on everyone's mind, and more and more on his, is *now what*? Too much lately, Messier has tried to pick up Gretzky's slack by playing with Gretzky-like finesse, but it doesn't suit him. The Oilers need the real Mark Messier, now more than ever.

Glen Sather also has something to prove, and at least outwardly, nothing could please him more. He must show he can coach a Stanley Cup winner without Gretzky. Sather played his ten NHL seasons in hockey's trenches, the invisible foot soldier. Now a four-time Stanley Cup winning coach, he is finally a star. He looks and dresses like a star. He swaggers like a star. And being cocky and clever and witty enough, he has gathered to him an army of willing detractors, anxious for him to be exposed as overrated and lucky, a Gretzky-creation. Sather wants to win again for his own pleasure and to tweak the noses of his critics once more. He wants to hold onto his star's spotlight.

In private moments Sather admits that this year is very different. "We are still the Stanley Cup champions," he says, "but the perception of the team has changed. Without Gretzky, others don't see us as a *great* team at the moment." Nor even do his own players. Sather can see once confident, self-assured players now doubting themselves. They knew that Gretzky was the centrepiece to the team's success, but they didn't know just *how much* he meant. In past years, when they scored more goals, they took their success personally. They could feel themselves becoming stars, too, and others treated them that way. It was a fantastic feeling. But now, as they get fewer chances and score less often, they think back and wonder if they ever were stars and how much winning those Stanley Cups really had to do with them.

They can feel themselves and others rewriting their own history, and they don't like the way it is turning out. Last year, and every other Gretzky-year, they had fewer injuries. Is this year just bad luck, is it the law of averages finally catching up to them, or is it that without Gretzky distracting the attention of their opponents there is less space on the ice, less time, and so they are getting hit more often? Is it, as their owner Peter Pocklington has suggested, "creative avoidance"? If the ship is going down, abandon it for your own injury lifeboat. Never, in other years, would they have imagined such things. Now these thoughts never go away. Everything that was precious to them is now in doubt. This is no slump they are battling. This is a crisis of self-image that won't soon pass.

It is Sather's job to direct the team ahead, to what can be, not back to what once was. He tries to get his players as excited by the challenge as he sometimes feels. "What a psychological opportunity for these guys if they can win without Wayne. I mean, what a coup that would be. That's the flip side to all this. If we can win with all the changes and all the injuries and all that's happened . . ." He believes what he is saying and his players believe it, too. But none of them yet feel they can do it. "We don't have the rhythm," Sather says, explaining their current problems. "We don't have five moving together. We have one here and one there. We don't have that system. We have a group of players that are trying hard, but we don't have any flow."

The Oilers' practice ends. Lowe wanders out of the room to retrieve the long line of young cousins who have been watching the Oilers skate and brings them to the dressing room – fathers hurrying alongside with video cameras – and he makes sure each leaves with autograph-proof of the visit and of who his cousin is for all those doubters back home in Lachute. In exchange, the dressing room is flooded with packaged ice cream cones fresh from the Lowe family dairy.

Cameron Lowe, his red cap pulled tight to wide brown eyes and his hockey jacket collar raised in the hope of making him look larger than eight, gets his poster of Mark Messier signed, then is taken around the Forum to the Canadiens' side, where he meets his other cousin, Mike McPhee, and while McPhee signs his autograph with the Count Dracula pen the two cousins who have never met talk about the one thing they have in common more than family.

"What are you going to be when you grow up?" McPhee asks, knowing the answer.

"A hockey player," the boy whispers.

It is now 12:32, and in thirty minutes the Canadiens' tough right winger, Claude Lemieux, will be home. There he will eat, sleep for two and a half hours, and listen to music. Then, precisely at 5:30 p.m., he will get back into his car for the return to the Forum. He will have the same radio station on he listened to the last time he drove, and he will take precisely the same route – unless he hasn't been scoring or the team hasn't been winning, in which case he will alter his route to the Forum and keep altering it until things improve. He has the same routine for every home game. In an uncontrollable life, he controls what he can.

Bob Gainey goes home for a near-formal family dinner with his wife, Cathy, and three of their four children. Son Stephen calls from Boston to say that in his own game he scored six goals, more than this season's total for his father. This does not go unnoticed by the rest of the family, particularly daughter Anna, ten. "Stephen gets six in a game," she giggles, "and you're at five." The others laugh, too, except Bob. There is silence. Bob looks at Anna severely. "Can I have the salt and pepper, *dear*."

Gainey is not tired or sick, but after lunch he goes to his room for a nap anyway. "You have a certain routine," he says. "You eat certain foods, energy foods. You nap to make sure you still have some energy left at ten o'clock when it's late in the game. It's a mental exercise preparing yourself, physical, too. Everything's all pent up and when the gate opens at eight o'clock you've gotta be ready to let your energy loose. You get it all out in three hours, and then your tank is empty."

A few miles away, across the city, the Oilers sit down to their team meal. It is the same meal they eat forty times a season for each road game. It is ready when they are, whenever they are ready. In fifteen or twenty minutes, they are done and filled up and gone. Nutrition matters; taste, volume, and speed matter more, for nutrition will not make them feel better seven hours from now or in the hours in between. To a player who must face a game's uncertain fates, if he feels good he has one less thing to distract his mind and make him wonder.

As they eat, the players, who must live with its implications, talk of the Ludwig incident. "It's like Ludwig says," says Kevin Lowe, "the more they show it, the worse it gets."

"Whaddya mean?" Messier asks.

"On TV. They show it and show it and they slow it down – and it looks like you deserve *life*, not six games."

Their lives run in parallel, the Oilers in their hotel, the Canadiens in a scattering of homes and apartments about the city. And they keep moving in those parallel lines until late in the afternoon, when suddenly the lines turn and, like mountain rams, run at each other. The players eat many of the same foods, watch the same football games, even cheer for the same teams. And for the day of a game, they have the same unambitious purposes. They want to get through it – unsick, unhurt, untired, unbothered, to escape from the game, and from time, by eating, sleeping, walking, watching Miami play Arkansas, thinking of other things or, better yet, of nothing. Time is their enemy. They have nothing much to do on the day of a game, and lots of time to do it. But most players impose elaborate timetables on themselves, doing things before they need to do them just to stay ahead of time, rushing so as not to rush, so that they control time rather than have time control them. Hurry up and wait.

The Forum gets ready. Workmen stand on portable platforms with their buckets and squeegees giving shine to the arena's protective glass. They mop up aisles never quite free of sole-sticking gum and grime, sponge down the expensive red-coloured seats and stick new billboard ads in place of scarcely cut or discoloured others on the gleaming white boards that ring the ice. The Forum looks like a dinner party just before the guests arrive: a touch up, a few last minute details – and out in the kitchen, the usual frenzy. Thousands of hot dog rolls must be cut, the dough for hundreds of pizzas must be pummeled and stretched and twirled into shape. The day is beginning to pick up steam.

At 4:35 p.m. the phone rings in Kevin Lowe's room. It is his wake-up call. Time's up. The hours that in morning seemed so endless, in afternoon so compressed, are running out. There's nothing ahead but the game.

Lowe turns on his TV set to the football game and gets dressed, briskly brushing his hair into place. It is like any weekday morning scene, a young executive getting ready to catch the 7:36 train on his way to work – except his feet are tapping and his hands clench and unclench to some unheard rhythm. It is the rhythm of the game.

Kevin Lowe tries always to find some time to himself on a day in Montreal; away from teammates, away from family, some time alone when he can think about his late father, and about what it means to have grown up near here and to have dreamed so long about the NHL and playing in the Forum. His dream was realized ten seasons ago, but Lowe wants never to forget how much the dream matters to him. So each time he is here, he arrives at the Forum before his teammates and, as if reaffirming some vows, he finds a private hour to sit and think about where he is and what is taking place in his life.

He still remembers driving by the Forum and being afraid to imagine he might one day be playing there, let alone as a Stanley Cup champion. He still recalls, now with embarrassed good humour, his first game in the Forum as an Oiler and how before the game his teammates had taken down his sweater and talked the trainers into telling him that he wouldn't be playing because Sather was worried he'd be too nervous. He still remembers how crushed he'd been until, finally, they told him it was all a joke.

Around the Forum, the city seems caught up in the game. Restaurant operators, bartenders, souvenir-shop clerks, pizza and hot dog sellers, taxi drivers, tow-truck drivers who await their hockey night bonanza of hastily parked, illegally parked cars, autograph seekers – everyone is getting ready. Time picks up speed. Everything becomes more urgent. Trainers hurry about in their dressing rooms, scalpers shout louder and, like loose dogs, chase after cars that slow as they pass by the Forum. And players, tied to their unforgiving timetables, race to keep up. A game cannot be put off until tomorrow like a meeting can. The show must go on.

Once the players are inside the dressing room, the game becomes inescapable. Gainey arrives early, and so does Lowe. Both rooms vibrate to the pounding beat of rock music, music that imitates the rhythm of the game and the life they live. Like martial music, it blanks the mind and drives the body. The Oilers have a rule. Before five o'clock the dressing room belongs to the trainers and they choose the music that gets played. After five, it is the players' and Lowe is their disc jockey.

But again, the players have more time than things to do. Hurry up and wait. Many leave little things undone from earlier in the day just to keep busy. Like Charlie Huddy and Greg Adams, they half dress in their underwear and sit waiting or work on their sticks, bullying magic and goals into wood that, untampered, would surely let them down. In the hall outside the Canadiens' dressing room, Guy Carbonneau works on his stick with an electric paint stripper, shaping his curve as fastidiously as a teenaged girl works on her curls. Gainey and Russ Courtnall read newspapers. Some talk quietly, some read mail, some gently stretch, some ride exercise bikes – something, anything, to blank their minds, to leave them no space for doubts or fears.

"The energy builds," says Kevin Lowe, "and I just let it take me over. I let the adrenaline high take command."

Burns brings in his players to watch the tapes he has selected for them. They watch with all the detachment of a housewife ironing in front of a day's worth of game shows. Their eyes watch the images, but their minds are in and out of the room, caught on the coattails of the game. A few minutes later they return to the dressing room.

At 6:40 the ghetto blaster in the Oilers' dressing room clicks off. The silence shocks the players into instant chatter.

"One loss in our last *seven* on the road – keep it going, boys!"

"Courtnall'll try to go through the whole team. Gotta watch him!"

"Good feeling in here, boys! *Good feeling* in here!"

The equipment, like a checklist, goes on by the clock: *7:09 p.m.*, socks and leg pads; *7:13 p.m.*, wrists taped; *7:16 p.m.*, skates. Finally, sweaters are pulled over heads and bodies twisted and flexed into comfort. The players are ready. They go out onto the ice for every pre-game warmup, for every period of every game, in an order known only to them, a strange, silly order that means nothing, of course, yet one to which they keep. Messier knows only that he goes behind Anderson, Jimmy Carson behind Charlie Huddy; Kurri waits and looks for Steve Smith, who must go ahead of him. And Lowe, since Dave Semenko was traded two years ago, must wait for them all. He is last – every time. Don't change the luck.

In the Canadiens' dressing room, Carbonneau watches the clock and waits. There are few words, and no music, just the steady *slam, slam, slam* that comes from the seat nearest the door where goaltender Patrick Roy sits bouncing a puck between his legs, catching it, bouncing it, catching it, bouncing it . . . Mike Keene sits with a towel over his head, finding a private moment when none seems possible.

One minute to go. The Canadiens take their positions. Carbonneau stands like a sentinel, his eyes fixed on the clock. Finally Roy stands up, Carbonneau turns and taps the metal clothes rack above him with his stick, then the bench in front of him, and the Canadiens' ritual begins. Every word, every stick tap, every punch and slap is part of the routine they need to win. The final trigger is Roy. He moves toward the door, stops, crouches, and Brian Skrudland slams both his pads hard with his stick. Backup goaltender, Brian Hayward, moves up into Roy's position, crouches, and Skrudland does the same to him. The whole team now moves into action. The players file by each other with taps and slaps and punches, in different patterns for different people. Like the inner works of some intricate machine, gears turn and interlock with other gears, trip switches . . . Everyone has his place, everyone has a role to play. Then the machine grinds to a halt. Naslund is next but Naslund has his sweater half off; his gloves and stick and helmet lie on the floor in front of him. Three of his teammates stand and wait. Naslund quickly gathers

**Backstage:
Eddy Palchak.**

CLUB DE HOCKEY CANADIEN

15 BOBBY SMITH · 23 BOB GAINEY

SMITH 15

GAINEY 23

HIBAUDE 29

he dressing room.

THE CAST

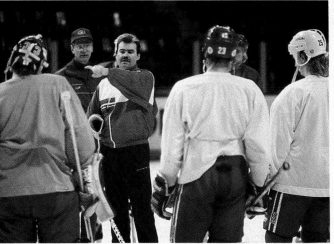

The rookie coach:
Pat Burns.

Craig Ludwig
and twin sons.

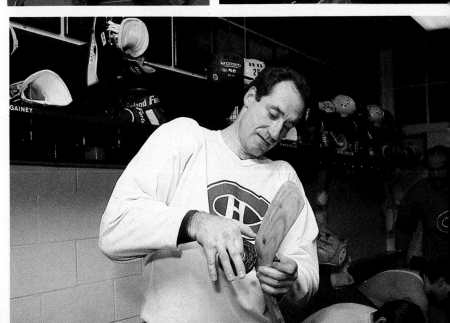

The veteran:
Bob Gainey.

Star struck:
Cameron Lowe (red cap)
and Mark Messier.

Out of
the gate.

DENIS BRODEUR

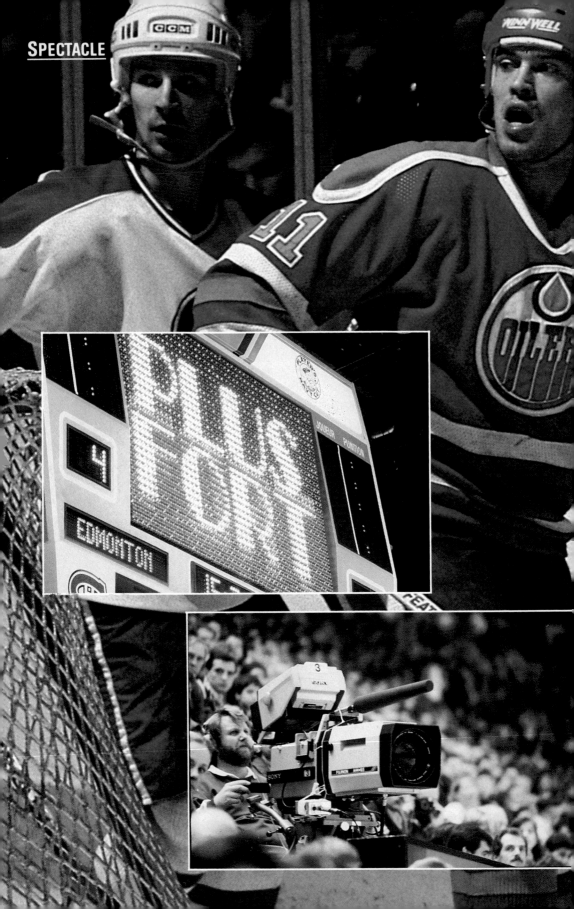

BRODEUR

Claude
Lemieux.

DENIS BRODEUR

CURTAIN CALL

Mats
Naslund

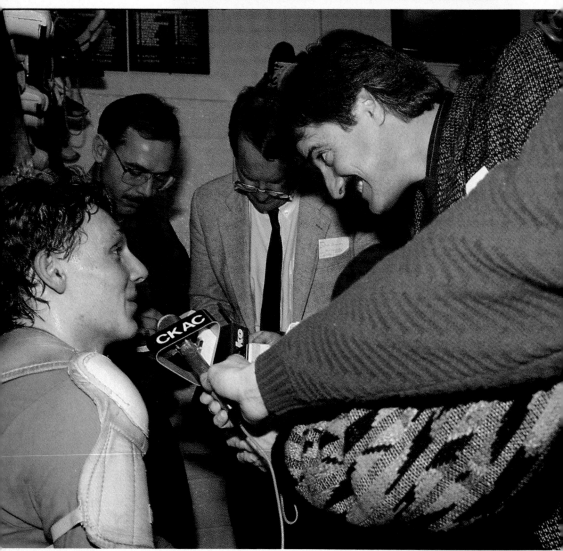

Jyrki Lumme.

up his things to finish getting dressed on the ice. The machine cranks up again. Carbonneau slips into line behind Naslund, then Rick Green. Ludwig, like Lowe, is last.

Out onto the ice they go. Same ice, different world from the morning. The lights are brighter, the colours deeper, the sense of importance undeniable. The music, "La Bamba," blares from above. The players skate differently now, each aware as cats that they are being watched and, like cats, unwilling to acknowledge it. For Kevin Lowe, this is the moment when the game begins. The adrenaline begins to surge; he tries to bring it under control, afraid that if he doesn't once the game begins he will have spent it all.

Around and around they skate, the helmeted Canadiens, the easier-to-be-seen-and-recognized helmetless Oilers, each team sticking to its own side of centre ice. Several players on both teams stop along one length of boards and drop to their knees for stretching, inches from the centre line, inches from each other, yet they look straight ahead. No looks, no words are exchanged.

"To me," Cameron Lowe said at the morning skate, "it's *amazing* how you can skate on ice." He is only eight but it is an astonishment that never seems to leave those who come to watch the very best. Camil Desroches, who has spent forty-two of his seventy-four years as a Forum employee, still feels it. So does "Doc" Serchuck, who for thirty-three years has served behind the visiting team's bench as an assistant trainer. At Doc's level, during the pre-game warmup, the amazement has its own peculiar texture, the sound of skates sizzling on still-wet ice, the same blades crunching into a sharp turn, the surprising feel of sharp breeze as bodies blur past the bench at a speed that is beyond the measurement of the camera.

There is a magic realism to this pause before the game really begins. The seats seem to fill up as if fans are being placed there by wand, and noise is everywhere. What was as quiet as a secret beach a few hours ago has become a Bangkok market: the organ, the shouts of program sellers, and the smells of pizza, popcorn, hot dogs, beer, people. Before this night is through, the more than 17,000 Forum fans will have consumed 7,500 hot dogs, 12,000 bottles of beer, 700 cups of coffee, 7,500 drinks of pop, and 2,400 ice cream bars.

Even to a trained eye, it is hard to see in a warm-up who is ready and who is not. Sometimes Messier's skates feel like broken galoshes; sometimes they feel like Mercury's wings, and he doesn't know why. It has nothing to do with their sharpening, tightening, the make of the skates, or his health and attitude. It is simply true. Yet a warm-up is just the preliminaries. It shouldn't matter – but it does. During the warm-up a shooter doesn't need to score on every shot. A goalie doesn't need to make every save. But each must score and save enough so that they don't begin to wonder if something is wrong and interrupt the feeling of the game that is building within them.

Warm and loose, the players return to their dressing rooms. The energy of the moment explodes out in their words, then subsides. It is time to rest, their engines idle. Eleven minutes before the buzzer sounds that will take the Oilers to the ice, Glen Sather strides into the room and makes his way to a large chalkboard with the message "GET IT UP BOYS" already chalked on it. "Okay, look at the board for a second," he says, then he draws on it the outline of a hockey rink.

"A couple of places we're having problems," he says. And with that Sather begins to write his script for the game, the script he wants his players to act out. He knows, of course, that the Canadiens will get in the way and new improvisational scripts must be written. That is what distinguishes sport from theatre. Still, for every team, there is something a team calls "our game" and "their game," a style of play that suits you both best. And there are no surprises. What Sather is telling them now, what in so many words he tells them before every game, is that if we play *our* game, to our script, we will win.

One big problem, as he sees it, is the way his team is reacting when an opponent dumps the puck into the Oilers' corners from the centre zone. "Where we've been getting in trouble," Sather tells his players in a calm, teacher's voice, "is our forwards go here" – he marks an "X" next to the boards by the face-off circle – "our defence *there*" – another "X" back of the net and in the corner – "and you end up with your ass against the glass all the time. This puck should be the forward's puck, not the defenceman's puck."

A forward is already in motion and can carry and control the puck, especially if the defenceman acts as a blocker to give him some time. A defenceman, by himself, can do little else but shoot the puck uncontrollably around the boards. The Oilers' game is puck control and skating. They must not let the game get jammed up in the corners.

"The other thing is that little pisspot, he comes across the blueline and makes a little turn in here and tries to hit someone going for the net." Sather pauses. He sees some puzzled faces. Not everyone, it seems, knows who he means. "Naslund," he says. "So if he pulls up, and he's hard to stop, you gotta make sure the backchecker picks up the other guy. Courtnall will try to do the same thing." One thing trips another in Sather's mind. "And their defence likes to come up. What's the Finnish guy's name?" he asks.

Kurri, who is sitting next to him, quietly says, "Lumme."

Sather mishears him: "Louie? Louie Luau?" The players laugh.

Another Finn, Esa Tikkanen, who sits beside Kurri, booms out his name, "Loo-may." They laugh again.

"*Loo*-may comes up," Sather says, this time even getting the accent right. "You gotta watch him."

Sather walks away from the board and says nothing more. His script is clear. On defence, watch Naslund, watch Courtnall and Lumme. We must play the Canadiens tonight the way we always have. Tight checking, low scoring – their game – and with our better scorers – our game – we will win it at the end.

The room goes quiet. Messier starts rocking back and forth, clapping his thick hands together rhythmically. "Gotta get the lead and go from there guys," he shouts. "Real tight game . . . let's just be patient out there. Work hard, be patient . . . We can outlast these guys. Let's play their game and beat 'em at it."

Across the ice in the Canadiens' dressing room Pat Burns reads his own script, less sure than Sather, from small slips of paper in his hands. Burns scans the room for defenceman Chris

Chelios but doesn't see him, and, curiously saying nothing, decides to begin without him.

"Okay guys, a couple of points here," he says quietly. "Fuhr, you're not going to score on him from a big long shot. The guy's quick and fast. You get up close on him, fake him, he goes down a lot, put it through his legs. You get a second shot, he's down a lot, so put it upstairs."

The players continue to get dressed as he talks. "Forecheck two guys, the third guy hang back. Don't get overcrowded in there. Don't get overanxious. We're gonna score goals. I'm not worried about that. The worry's how many they're gonna score. So be patient. Make sure you don't overforecheck. Don't get caught three guys in deep. Don't get beat by a pass."

Burns stands in the middle of the room. The trainer walks by. Burns asks him where Chelios is. A moment later, Chelios appears and crosses the room to sit down. "Make our plays at the net," Burns tells them. "Let's go to the net. Let's pick up a rebound." He reads out the Oilers' lineup and his. "Carb, you're starting. Luds and Cheli." The Carbonneau line – Carbonneau, Gainey, and Ryan Walter – with Craig Ludwig and Chelios on defence will start the game against Mark Messier's line.

Eight minutes to show time.

Pat Burns's script is a defensive one. He isn't worried about scoring goals, he says, because a home team's law of averages means that he will get three or four. But he must worry about how many the explosive Oilers will score. So don't overcommit, don't get outnumbered, don't take chances. Keep the score down, forget the pretty plays, go to the net for rebounds and remember, when Fuhr goes down, as he will, put it over him. He will start his best checkers against the Oilers' best scorers, the Messier line.

The energy of each room implodes in silence, then explodes in sound and muscle-clenched bodies. The buzzer goes, the rituals begin again. In the Canadiens' room, everything is the same. Carbonneau taps high and low, Skrudland slams Roy's pads, then Hayward's, every punch and slap just like before. Naslund is dressed this time but still he keeps them waiting: Carbonneau, then Green, then Ludwig is last.

In the Oilers' dressing room, the players bunch toward the door. Shouting like a drill sergeant, Sather calls out the two starting lineups:

"Roy."

"Boo!" the team shouts out together.

"Walter!"

"Boo!"

"Ludwig!"

"Boo!"

"Carbonneau!"

"Boo!"

"Gainey!"

"Boo!"

"Chelios!"

"Boo!"

He pauses a moment . . .

"Fuhr!"

"Yay!"

"Smith!"

"Yay!"

"Anderson!"

"Yay!"

"Simpson!"

"Yay!"

"Gregg!"

"Yay!"

"Messier!"

"Yay!"

It's a ritual the Oilers began many years ago when they made the playoffs for the first time. "New guys on our team see this and they just can't believe it," says Kevin Lowe. "I mean, we're like a bunch of kids booing the opposition and cheering our team. But to us it's special." Don't change the luck.

Just around the corner from the Oilers' room, another dressing room is now empty. Minutes ago, Don Koharski, a thirty-one-year-old powerful, thick-bodied referee from Burlington, Ontario, finished his stretching exercises, pulled on his black and white jersey, and punched lightly the NHL crests on the jerseys of each linesman, Ray Scapinello and Gerry Gauthier. Then together they shouted *"Let's go!"* and walked to the ice. Now as they skate around awaiting the two teams, Koharski hits with his right hand one goal post of the net at the north end of the rink, and two at the south and, like the players, hopes that the goal-post gods will be with him tonight.

"Et maintenant," the Canadiens' director of public relations, Claude Mouton, shouts in French and English into the penalty-box microphone, his hound-dog cheeks rippling with the effort, *"accueillons nos Canadiens!"*

It is the sound that hits them first, then everything together, the roar of lights, the announcer, the music, the wall of people. The players look like bulls set loose into an arena. Their legs quicken, they push and shove their way through the opening in the boards and onto the ice. Sickness, injury, fatigue – gone. Doubts and fears – gone.

Patrick Roy, his long neck bobbing, moves to his net and begins roughing the crease area. His teammates mill around, at random it seems. Yet just as in the dressing room, for every period and every game, every move is orchestrated. Carbonneau and Ludwig stand along the goal line just outside the goal post to Roy's right, Larry Robinson to his left. With Roy they form a receiving line. Players move in and out of the scene, tapping sticks and shin pads, punching in their own personal way. For Lumme – who is about to play his first game, who has spent years of his life in skating, passing, and shooting drills preparing for this moment, who listened carefully to Burns and his team-mates as they set up the game so he would know what to do, who moments ago thought he was finally ready – this is a night-mare. He skates around, lost, just trying to stay out of the way. Naslund comes late, as usual, and stands about fifteen feet in front of the net facing Roy. From Roy's right, Chelios and Shane Corson enter the receiving line. Robinson, to his left, looks around for Green to bump him from behind, which he does, then like a domino, Robinson trips into action. Corson, now through the receiving line from right to left, turns around and joins Robinson, going back through the line. Robinson, finished, turns up ice toward Naslund, who greets him, then swoops in on Roy.

This frees Ludwig from the goal line, then Carbonneau. Carbonneau taps Roy on his leg pads, blocker, and arm and skates up ice. Their demons tamed, the Canadiens can get on with the game.

In the Oilers' end Lowe, Huddy, Kurri, and Messier circle around like hawks in a warm sky, turning one way, then another. They wait for Koharski to blow his whistle. It sounds. Instantly, Lowe makes an intricate turn into the corner, goes behind the net, and stops. Messier cuts in behind him and taps him on his right leg pad, then Charlie Huddy and Jari Kurri do the same. The Oilers are ready.

The starting players line up on the bluelines, the fans rise for Claude Robin Pelletier to sing "O Canada," the first part in French, the last in English. No patriotic formality, an anthem sung by a ringing tenor adds purposeful energy and spectacle to the game. Like a cheerleading announcer, like the organ, it is intended to rouse the rabble, to create the noise that will rouse the game. The players can only vibrate in place, like tuning forks in the rumbles of an earthquake.

"It's the national anthem most of all," says Kevin Lowe. "To stand still for four or five minutes while the anthem is going on and this *huge* energy boost is going through your head – it's like I can't control myself. I'm going to faint, I'm going to fall over. I just *have* to get moving right now!"

As the last chorus dwindles, the tensions of the entire day explode in a cacophony of horns and whistles and stomping feet and throats that will, three hours from now, feel as if they have been stopping pucks themselves.

Patrick Roy, about thirty feet in front of his net, crouches and stares at his goal posts. Every game it's the same – a private word with one, then the other, then he springs toward his net, veering away at the last instant into the corner to his left, then circles back and settles into his crease. He is ready.

The gods all satisfied, they are all ready. Koharski raises both his arms, then like an orchestra conductor, he brings them down, dropping the puck to start the game. It's Carbonneau against Messier, the checker and the scorer, just as the script demands. Messier has already fantasized a complete game with Carbonneau on his back. He knows that Carbonneau will be on him the moment he gets the puck, and often sooner. Tonight, if he can, he will try to come back deeper into the Oilers' zone, dragging Carbonneau with him, giving himself more of the ice to outskate him. And if that doesn't work, and if Carbonneau puts himself in a weak and vulnerable position, "I'm going to try my best to take him out of the game. It's my job to eliminate him."

From their dressing-room words, neither team is seeking a quick knockdown. Burns is hoping to find a cautious, defensive groove. Sather wants time for his team to get comfortable before slowly taking the initiative. Above all, he doesn't want an early goal against that will send a day's worth of plans into a giant spin, and the game out of control. He hopes to subdue the Forum crowd that, early in this game, is holding back, afraid of declaring real hope for fear that the champion Oilers will play with that hope and crush it. The look on Messier's square face tells it all. It is the withering message he wants to deliver to Carbonneau and the Canadiens: *you want to beat us, well maybe you can. But if you try, we will put you through hell first. Every minute, every shift. So how much do you really want to win!*

Then it happens. Barely a minute into the first period, Charlie Huddy presses along the left boards in the Canadiens' end. Hurrying to accept a banked pass back from Messier, he shoots too quickly and has the puck rap off the shinpads of the Canadiens' Carbonneau, who jumps past him as he falls and picks up the loose puck with only open ice in front of him. He skates in alone on Fuhr, dekes once, and scores easily.

In the papers the next morning the feat will appear in six-point agate type and say only "1. Montreal, Carbonneau 7, 1:17": conveying nothing of the sound of the Oilers' skates as they fought to fill the gap between themselves and the scurrying Carbonneau; telling nothing of how Fuhr's eyes sought the puck on Carbonneau's stick as the Montreal checker came in over the blueline and how Fuhr reacted, thinking he had seen something in the drop of a shoulder; saying nothing of how the crowd rose and roared with the might of a dam bursting, none of them quite as startled by the flashing red goal light as the two players most deeply involved, Fuhr and Carbonneau. Nor will it say that, right from the first play of the game, the two master scripts – Sather's and Burns's – went haywire.

It is a game too fast to see, on too many levels to take in. Slow the game down, stop the action, and the game looks different. Carbonneau fights to control the skittering puck, then near the centre line he looks up. His brain takes in everything. He knows an Oiler is behind him and won't catch up, though he doesn't turn to see. He knows the crowd is just beginning to roar, though in the echoing silence of his concentration, he hears nothing. He remembers other games against Fuhr, other chances he has had, Burns's words. He sees where Fuhr is standing. Consciously, he is aware of none of this. Unconsciously, he knows it all. He can feel the moment of climax draw near. He knows that Fuhr can sense it, too. Like *Star Wars* pilots in a dog fight, Fuhr's rhythm and Carbonneau's rhythm jerk out of sync until, finally in each other's sights, they *lock*. Carbonneau moves, Fuhr moves. And then the sound.

From shin pads to red light, 6.9 seconds.

"Never mind," Sather says on the bench. He means it, but he doesn't feel it. It is exactly what Sather and the Oilers did not want. "A goal on the first shot," Sather says, "and the team's confidence crumbles and nothing works. The players break down. The system falls to pieces."

The Canadiens can stick to their game plan: show caution, wait, make sure, and opportunities will present themselves as they have already. The Oilers, on the other hand, must now regroup. You can almost hear the words running through their minds – *still fifty-nine minutes left, plenty of time, be patient, don't try to get the goal back on the next shift, stick with the game plan, play as a team*. But for the Oilers, now up against a louder, more confident crowd, and with the Canadiens throwing haymakers around their ears, it is hard to keep those words in their heads.

"If you see someone get beat," Messier says, "it's up to the next shift to go out there and take the game the other way." This time it is Lowe's turn, and the Oilers find the solid ground they need. Now the long steady slog of the game can begin.

At home in Scarborough, Ontario, Greg Koehler and his brothers, Chris Taylor, and Billy Thompson watch the game.

The game they see is very different from the one the players and fans see in the Forum. Because a hockey puck moves so fast, television's cameras stay back from the action and on the side of the rink. It puts Greg and Chris as viewers the equivalent of several rows back from the ice. What they see at this moment is a Canadiens' player bump an Oilers' player, and McPhee miss an open net. They hear the crowd groan its disappointment. They see the action go one way, then another. They see a scramble around the Canadiens' net. They see more bumping bodychecks. Then, perhaps a minute after that first bump, they see some Canadiens' players go off and others come on.

Mostly what they have seen is action not much different from action earlier in the game, from action they have seen in countless games before. The game they see, the game most Canadians will only see throughout their lives, is slower, with more open spaces, and more time. The game they see is an easier one to play.

But watch from ice level or bring television's cameras near to the ice. Watch a game along the axis of action, from net to net, the offensive players driving toward you, toward the net, the defensive players trying to deflect them away. Forget the puck and keep your eye on just one player. Greg and Chris may not even have noticed that Claude Lemieux was on the ice. But for those same seventy-nine seconds, watch just him.

He stands, coiled, watching, unblinking from the bench, then leaps onto the ice. Immediately he is in the middle of the action. He cuts across the ice with Huddy in his sights, bumps him, and the two of them half fall into the boards. He seems hardly to have broken stride before sprinting up the ice with some unseen teammate, then curls into the corner when nothing comes of it.

It's the size of the players that always surprises: so big and thick, their speed, the confusion. The game goes one way, then another, turning back on itself again and again, without pattern, it seems, a game of fundamental disorder. And the congestion – big bodies everywhere. There's no time, no place to hide, no way to escape. Suddenly, there's an opening, big bodies close in like packs of hounds, and the opening is gone.

Yet it's not a game played on the run. It changes direction so often it rarely hits full speed. Lemieux cruises around, looking, sensing which way the play will go, then bursts ahead of it until it changes again. It's quickness that matters most, not speed.

There's such fury to a game up close – the bumping, the crashing, the racing around. Much is too fast to see, to appreciate, to linger over and admire. It has a terrible beauty that goes straight to the gut. And at ice level it is a game of people. Under the anonymous helmets you can see faces that sweat and snarl and glow. You can see personality, real characters acting out a real drama.

Seventy-nine seconds after Claude Lemieux went over the boards, he takes a long shot that misses the net and leaves the ice. His totals: no goals, no assists, no penalties, no shots on goal. Nothing happened. Yet up close it is like lifting up a rock that was always there and discovering life underneath.

Burns paces up and back behind the Canadiens' bench. There is pain on his face. He winces at each close call around his net and shrieks with whiny anguish at Laperriere when something goes wrong. He can feel the game beginning to turn.

The Canadiens attempt to clear the puck along the boards and out of their zone, but it is blocked at the blueline by Edmonton defenceman Craig Muni. Like a halfback senses a hole that has not yet opened, he winds slowly in, the Canadiens' players being blocked out of his way, until suddenly he is left with a clean run to the net. Shovelling the puck past Roy on an awkward backhand, Muni ties the game.

Sather's expression relaxes a bit. The game is back under control. Then it turns again. Finnish star Jari Kurri, who each season takes only a handful of penalties, hooks down Finnish rookie Jyrki Lumme and the Canadiens go on a power play.

The pain remains on Burns's face, but now it is the pain of anticipation. "Okay, that's it," he yells to himself as the game plays out before him. "Go back to the slot now. Go back to the slot. Good play. Good . . . That's it!!" he shrieks, his arms in the air. "That's the one!" Just as Burns diagrammed with his words, the puck moved back to the slot, then to the net. The goal scorer: Jyrki Lumme.

It was an unlikely goal. The puck was sent back to Lumme, he wound up to shoot. Messier, with too far to go, could only launch himself into a desperate slide toward him, skates first. The puck hit off one of Messier's skates and deflected into the top corner over Fuhr. The mystery of performance, the wonder of fate.

Two objects moving in different directions, Messier's skate, Lumme's puck, colliding at a particular moment and in such a way that three fates are changed. Fuhr had been in perfect position to stop that puck. Messier made an extraordinary effort to block it. Now both are beginning to wonder – what's going on out here? Why is this happening? Why tonight?

As for Lumme, he'll never be the same. He skates back toward the bench looking a little embarrassed, and thrilled to death. There, he is hugged by Larry Robinson, playing in his 1,152nd NHL game. For Lumme it is hard to tell whether the goal or the hug means more.

The first period ends with the Canadiens in front 3–1 following a tap-in goal by Mats Naslund. Again, the Oilers had taken a penalty. Again, Messier is on the ice for a goal against. The game is not going at all according to plan.

The Oilers return to their dressing room, furious and streaming obscenities. An early goal, two power-play goals against – it is exactly the way *not* to play the Montreal Canadiens at the Forum. The Oilers are embarrassed, in front of the crowd and the television cameras, but mostly in front of each other. Captain Mark Messier, like his teammates, sees a game as a series of personal one-on-one battles. No one will ever win them all. But whoever wins the most will win the war, and everyone in the room knows the score. This period, the Oilers and Messier lost more than they won.

The anger soon passes, the rebuilding of wounded psyches begins. "We'll go out there hummin', boys." "We'll turn it around."

On the other side of the ice, Naslund, the goal scorer, enters the room first, like Huck Finn, whistling and one foot bare. His right skate is being resharpened. The rest of the team soon follows.

"Good period, boys!" someone shouts.

"Great goal, Mats," says another.

They feel an underdog's happiness, too much, too soon. Gainey can sense it. "Can't live on that period, guys," he grumbles, and the mood changes.

An intermission is time to wind down and rest, and to wind back up again. And in the course of fifteen short minutes, each team can sense the mood of the game change. The Oilers, down and angry, begin to feel the initiative. The Canadiens, ahead, are now back on their psychological heels. It's hard to feel enough desperate drive to turn a two-goal lead into three. But desperation comes easily when you are behind. The teams are like old-fashioned armies, each taking turns running at the other. It will be the Oilers' turn next, and the Canadiens know it.

This is the time when the great player makes such a difference. Strong enough to fight the prevailing winds, he can break these rhythms with a goal or a big save. But who will do it? Roy? Naslund? Lemieux? The Canadiens' turn will come again.

The two goalies skate out to their positions and face each other 180 feet apart. The game may well turn on what they do in the next several minutes. It is their usual responsibility. And from the way they move their bodies, they make clear once again that a goalie can never really put aside the vulnerability of his position. Fuhr does well masking his insecurities with bounce and effervescence, but they are there. Roy wears his. His head bobs around like a car ornament on a bumpy road, his body moves when there is nothing to move for. He reaches for his goal posts, his stick like an insect's feeler, just to touch them, to know they are no wider apart than the last time. But when the puck comes near to Roy or Fuhr, their minds go blank and their insecurities disappear, the bouncing and bobbing stop, and their bodies become like rock, unmoving, unfeeling, ready. It is when the puck stops that the insecurities return.

Fuhr paces his crease and just can't shake the first period from his mind. Every goal seemed like a hard shot – still, three goals. And now he doesn't remember anymore whether they were hard shots or not. Is it simply one of those nights, he wonders, for the team, for me? But maybe not. Maybe if he can get through these next few minutes, then the next, he can change the pattern around and still make something of this game. But everything's fragile now – Fuhr's confidence, the confidence of his teammates and coaches in him. And every next goal will only bring back the memory of every goal before.

The Oilers come back from their dressing room certain this period will be different from the last. Fuhr thinks, I must not break that spirit. Breakaways, deflections, it doesn't matter – no excuses. I must not let in a goal until we score at least one ourselves.

As for Roy, it is his job to frustrate the Oiler surge until it runs its course and his teammates can come back. He knows he must give his team what it needs, when it needs it, countering every rhythm of the game, being strong when the rest are weak. The Canadiens didn't need him much in the first period. They need him now.

The people in the Forum this night see many different games being played, for the game looks different from every place you see it. Time moves slowly from the press box, from the corporate boxes, from the distance of standing room. From there every move seems possible, every mistake avoidable. The heat of the moment cannot spread its passion that far. It offers no excuse. The game has to get up close to hook you. Hockey is furious action and speed, but mostly it is characters. It is having favourite teams and hated teams, heroes and villains. Carbonneau's goal means little to a channel flipper. But if you know Carbonneau has been benched or hurt, if he is a nice guy, like a familiar character on a TV soap you pull for him, you feel for him. And when he scores, a part of you scores, too.

This is why league expansions hit older fans hard. Older fans have less time than kids to keep up with a season's personal dramas. For them the creation of new teams means needing to know new characters and seeing old friends or enemies on old teams less often, until they seem only acquaintances. And how much can you really feel for an acquaintance? How interesting is a movie or a play that has 100 or 500 main characters? Hockey may have some inherent visual and aural appeal, but it is hockey's people that keep you in your seats and your thumb off the channel flipper. It is their personal dramas – the distinguished veteran who struggles with time, the kid who comes from nowhere, the star who has his world turned upside down – played out before you that keep you tuning in week after week. Drama works best with a few characters you can get to know. That is why stars are so important. It is what makes rivalries so necessary.

From high above the ice, *Hockey Night in Canada*'s announcers recreate the electricity of the action. More than fifty years ago Foster Hewitt began spinning tales to a nation, of the Toronto Maple Leafs, Primeau, Conacher, and Jackson. Only a few thousand people in Toronto and Montreal really ever saw them play, ever knew for sure they really existed. To the millions of others, they were like characters on any radio drama.

Hockey Night in Canada's tradition continues. Week after week, year after year, we watch kids break in, we watch them grow up. "Boy wonder" becomes "emerging star" becomes "middle-age problem" becomes "aging veteran." On our TV screens, we see them literally live out their lives. These characters grow old. These characters fail. *Hockey Night in Canada* is Canada's longest running drama series.

Roy makes several acrobatic saves, Fuhr holds up his now less tested end, and the game continues on, 3–1. Still, the Oilers push harder. "We're all over 'em. We're all over 'em," shout voices on the Oilers' bench. "What is he doin' on the boards?!" screams Burns. Lemieux has drifted out of position, Laperriere tries to explain, but Burns's anguish has little to do with Lemieux. Burns can feel the game slip away.

Bob Gainey carries the puck over centre, ducks a shoulder, and tries to skirt the Oilers' defence with the kind of stickhandling play that worked so well this morning when he went down this same ice surface entirely alone. But this time the puck rolls off his stick and is taken back the other way by the Oilers. No coach could tell Gainey to grab the puck in his own end, race up over centre, and deke his way around the defence. Gainey's rush is not a set play, as football and baseball allow. The play happens so fast, however, so instinctively – and fate is such a superstar in this game – that the fumbled puck does not strike anyone as an error or a miscalculation, simply another turnover in the hundreds that will take place in the hour that it takes to play the game.

Moments later, three Oilers break up ice with only the two Montreal defencemen back. With the puck, Jari Kurri slides easily over centre ice, Esa Tikkanen behind him. Jimmy Carson, who came to the Oilers in the trade for Gretzky, hurries to catch up to his linemates. Kurri crosses the Canadiens' blueline, shifts his shoulder, and then neatly tucks the puck back alongside his right skate blade so it lands, perfectly, on the stick of Tikkanen. Tikkanen also fakes, but it does not work. He loses the puck, but then – again the fates intervene – Chelios hits his own man with a clearing sweep, the puck changes direction and bounces to Carson, who quickly puts it in behind Roy.

The irresistible has happened. There is a near sense of relief on the Canadiens' bench. Sure, the Oilers will keep pressing, but now that they're back in the game their desperation will subside. The worst seems over, at least for now. In a hockey game, one goal rarely matters much. It is when snakes become ladders, when a single and a walk turn into a big inning, when one goal becomes two or three, that games are lost. The next few minutes will be critical. Burns's team must hold steady and get the game back under control.

Then, only sixteen seconds after the Carson goal, Brian Skrudland gets a penalty. Although he argues and shouts at Koharski, the referee, his anger is mostly for himself. His timing could not have been worse, and he knows it. Burns sends Gainey out to try and put order back in the game. A few rows above the Canadiens' bench, his wife, Cathy, and eight-year-old daughter, Laura, sit up a little straighter to watch. "He's going to kill the penalty now," Cathy explains.

"Who is?" Laura asks, straining to see.

"Daddy."

Cathy explains what a penalty is. "Daddy and Guy Carbonneau usually kill the penalty," she adds, "because they're strong players and can try to stop the five when there is four of us."

Laura looks at her mother, not following at all. On the ice,

Carbonneau and Messier are head-to-head once more. All night they have been hitting and jabbing and testing each other. This time Messier is with the man advantage. Carbonneau wins the face-off but Gainey's clearing backhand is stopped by Huddy at the blueline. Huddy trips and from his knees shoots the puck around the boards, past Robinson who is trying to chase it down, to Messier behind the net. A quick pass in front to an open Glenn Anderson and it is 3–3.

"Whoops!" Cathy Gainey exclaims.

"What happened?" asks Laura.

"They scored," Cathy says, then remembering what she has just said, she starts to giggle. "The worst thing happened, hon. See Daddy's face!"

It took ten seconds from the face-off. If Huddy hadn't slipped, his pass would not have been so slow and Robinson wouldn't have thought he could intercept it; he wouldn't have left the front of the net; Anderson wouldn't have been open; the goal wouldn't have been scored. The wonder of fate.

The game has turned again. This time, for the Canadiens, it is serious. As they sit on their bench, the ghosts of too many Oilers' games in the past are now beginning to appear, games where solid leads and hopes suddenly vanished.

"Daddy's tired," Laura concludes.

The crowd goes quiet, as quiet as it ever gets in the Forum. The fans fear what the players are fearing. The home crowd that worried Sather has been subdued. Suddenly, the Forum's organ blares, and an animated horse and rider appear in flashing red-white-and-blue lights, riding as if out of the innards of the Forum's giant message board. The rider is a hockey player, with helmet and stick, his skates and padded legs flying up into the air with each pounding stride of his trusted mount. "CHARGE!!!" the organ and message board scream.

Like a rock show, like *Cats* or *Phantom of the Opera*, hockey is now a spectacle of sound and lights to involve the audience even if sometimes the game does not. But now this spectacle has a more urgent purpose. The Canadiens need help. They might get it from Burns or Naslund or Roy. They might get it from the right mix of sound and light that sets the home crowd roaring. The organist has become their seventh player.

The game slams on its breaks and heads back the other way. Naslund scores his second goal. Then, as Claude Mouton finishes announcing to the arena that only one minute is left in the second period, Skrudland picks up a loose puck close to Fuhr and shoots. Fuhr makes the save but goes down as Burns said he would, and McPhee lifts the puck over him. Once again, at 5–3, the game has gone out of control.

The Oilers began the period two goals down, they caught up, and now they are two goals down again. Before this period, they had set for themselves the task of making up some ground so that the third period would be easier. Now they have given ground back again. They had wanted to go to their second-period dressing room knowing, and knowing the Canadiens knew, that the tide had swung their way.

Burns sends out Carbonneau, Gainey, and Walter, his best defensive forwards, to bring the period to its end. It is Messier against Carbonneau, Carbonneau against Messier, once more the scorer and the checker. This time it is Messier's turn, and in the midst of Mouton's announcement of the McPhee goal, the Oilers score.

As the period ends, Sather, still behind the bench, turns to his co-coach, John Muckler. "Pull him?" he asks. Muckler says nothing, but the twist of his smile says otherwise. "He's down all the time," Sather mutters. It doesn't matter anymore whether Fuhr should have stayed up on his skates, or whether each scoring chance dictated what he did. Five goals have been scored, and that is enough.

Sather walks into the room. "All right, Billy's going in for the next period," he announces to the team and to the goalies. The players go silent. "Good job, Grant." "Let's go, Billy." The words come back to back – "The King is dead. Long live the King."

Bill Ranford will play goal for the Oilers in the third period. He and Fuhr are teammates and competitors, but only one can play at a time. They hope for each other; they hope harder for themselves. Ranford gets up and does some gentle stretching to get himself ready. He looks nervous; Fuhr looks relaxed, but he is puzzled. He knows he has been going down too much, but he doesn't know why. He is not sick or tired or injured, so why tonight, he wonders? Why me? What has gone wrong with my game?

The mood in the Oilers' room is much different than it was a period ago. The tightly controlled, low-scoring script they wrote for themselves has not happened. Still, the game is close and, with their better scorers, they know they can win it at the end, as they planned.

The third period begins. For both teams it feels like the beginning of the game again. They drone the same message to themselves round and round in their minds – *plenty of time to go, no need to win it in the first minute, just get in a groove, play our game and everything will come our way.*

Once more the game turns on its ear. Messier comes back and gets the puck from Ranford. He circles his net and with no Canadiens in sight, he moves up ice in an unconcerned way. Suddenly, Carbonneau appears. Messier swerves to his right and with Gretzky-like finesse flips the puck toward the opening in Carbonneau's legs. Instead, the puck strikes Carbonneau's skate and bounces clear. From fifteen feet, Carbonneau snaps a shot through Ranford's legs. For the Oilers, for Messier, it is disaster again.

The game continues on. The Canadiens break up an Oiler rush and from deep in their own zone break back and only four Ranford saves from close in keep the score from mounting higher. Early in a game it takes only seconds for a team to recover from a goal. But this goal was a kick in the stomach that will take minutes to get over, and not many minutes remain. Bill Ranford made four saves, but the only one that matters is the one he didn't make moments ago.

Sather leans over the back of his young centre Jimmy Carson, obtained in the Gretzky trade from Los Angeles, and talks loud into his ear to make himself heard. He has noticed something. "Play the puck to the boards," Sather says in his most patient voice.

"Okay."

"And then you get the puck, pass it to the defence and 'bing.' "

Carson seems confused. "How do I get the puck if I throw it to the boards?"

"You pass it to the boards," Sather says, still patient, "and as soon as you shoot it there, you go over and get it."

Carson's eyes light up: "Oh! You mean like Gretzky always does!"

"Yeah!"

Tonight, Gretzky is in Calgary with his Los Angeles Kings – he's the guy who isn't here but who's everywhere. He was the temperament and personality of the Oilers. He set their free-wheeling style of play. Everyone was made to fit in around him, and the fit was so good few could see he was the life-energy that bound the team together. Now missing Gretzky, good goal scorers must score more often but they get fewer chances. Missing Gretzky, good leaders must lead, but their burden is greater. The absent Gretzky has become their crutch, their excuse. When they lose, Sather and the players can blame someone else, the man who made the trade. And so they lose more often.

At ice level there are no big player contracts. What moves the player and the viewer is elemental: winning the next face-off; a goal; a save; winning the next personal battle; winning the game that can still be won. This is not art. The game will not wait for the endlessly rehearsed, perfectly crafted move. The spotlight moves. It has to be earned and fought for. The player must simply do the best with what he's got.

The best players create time and moments of order from it. They sense where a game is going and get there first. Quickness gives them a head start, strength and skills open the gap. Success brings confidence and concentration. The crowd disappears. The players play in a huge echoing silence, undisturbed, undistracted by sticks and bodies and fear that all make time go faster.

Fundamentally, every game is about time. Time is endless; time is running out. The glass that is half full is always half empty – it depends on how you see it. For Wayne Gretzky on a hockey rink, time is endless. He creates time, practising movements over and over to do them faster, learning a game's shortcuts from experience. Like the greats in other sports – Joe Montana, Larry Bird – he waits that extra beat of time undistracted by thoughts and fears, holding back until the last moment, until *he* is ready and every option is clear and his teammates are where they need to be.

For the average player, time is always running out. He seems always a beat behind, in a race to catch up, going too fast to keep control, always at a panic point, yet not using the time he has. Others keep telling him, he keeps telling himself – take your time; be patient – but he doesn't listen. He does everything before he needs to, before he is ready, only ensuring that for the next thing he does, he will have less time and feel more panic, until the awkward predictable end.

Yet everyone, even Gretzky, has his panic point, a moment when time goes too fast, when he fumbles at shoelaces and does stupid things. And so a game is about creating time and, for an opponent, taking time away. Those who cope best with time, who respect it and sense its urgency yet make time seem not to matter, who blank their minds through a game's long uneventful day and short frenzied night, those players do best.

To unlock the mysteries of performance we slow down time. Game replays in slow motion make everything look sensible and possible. We can skate like Messier if we move our skates *this way*; we can score like Gretzky if we position ourselves *here* and shoot *there*. But the mystery remains. We have only fooled ourselves, putting illusion in its place, the illusion that we can do all those things if only we do *this* and *that*. The mystery *is* time. It is players doing what they do at twenty-five miles per hour with two 200-pound defencemen bearing down on them, a forward hacking at their arms from behind, with the Forum crowd screaming and their vision panicking from peripheral distractions. Regular time restores mystery to its proper place.

Late in the game, the score 6–4, for the Canadiens time is endless. For the Oilers, time is running out.

In hockey, practices belong to the coaches, games belong to the players. There is not much a coach can do when he feels a game slip away. Sather can change his lines more often, pick an argument with the referee, anything to interrupt the game's fatal rhythm. He can put out his tough guy against theirs, knowing what will happen, and hope his guy wins and makes his team feel like winners. But there is not much else.

The players have their little tricks as well. While killing a penalty, Esa Tikkanen positions himself where a distracted Naslund can bump into him, whereupon Tikkanen falls over in a heap and Naslund gets a penalty. This may be the Oilers' last best chance.

The Oilers put the pressure on the Canadiens but nothing comes of it. Just as Naslund comes out of the penalty box, a long shot that goes wide of Roy rings around the glass straight to Naslund near his blueline. He goes one on one with Tikkanen, brings him to the inside, then quickly outside – and has him beaten. It is now the shooter and the goalie. Naslund, angling over on his skates, keeps his balance and sweeps in front of the net. Ranford intercepts his rhythm and makes his move, but Naslund, like all good scorers, finds a rhythm of his own and keeps on going. Ranford, now locked into place, can make only an awkward dive, and while he's in the air the puck has time to slide under him and find the net.

In the past few decades a hockey fan would have witnessed the introduction of masks, slapshots, organs and animated scoreboards, million-dollar contracts, and goal-scoring goalies. Each pushes at the imagination, but, like Cameron Lowe, age eight, it may be that nothing stretches it the way skating does, as Naslund just did. Speeding around on long metal blades as if riding on some electrified track, staying upright when you're halfway on your side – that is magic.

Sather looks at the clock – eleven minutes to go – and he looks at his team. When they are winning their bodies swell, their chests puff out. They yell at the other team as it skates by. Now they are shrivelling up. Everything can still turn around. They have come from further behind before. But little tricks only work when a big play follows. And the guy who might make it is the guy who isn't here.

Then the gods intervene – a goal comes from nowhere. An Oiler skates through the crease and knocks Roy over – 7–5 – and for the Oilers, hope returns.

"It's not over yet," Sather exhorts, and his players respond. The law of sports is the law of *momentum*, and players and coaches abide by it. If something happens, then something else can happen, then something else, and the impossible becomes possible. But it isn't easy. The next moment doesn't have to be the same as the last, yet it usually is. Something extraordinary must be done to change the fates. With about a minute remaining, Sather calls a timeout.

He charts out an intricate play. The face-off will be outside the Canadiens' blueline. Carson is to get the face-off back to Huddy, who will shoot the puck into the Canadiens' right-hand corner. Kurri will block out the Canadiens' defender allowing Tikkanen to get the puck first. He is to shoot it behind the net to Messier who will then pass to Carson in front for the goal.

Get the face-off, score a quick goal. We'll be up; the Canadiens will panic. We can get another . . . and . . . and to the Oilers and Canadiens, it makes absolute sense.

The players take their positions. Carson loses the face-off – it's over.

For the Oilers, it is just one more game out of eighty, but it isn't. Nothing counts until the playoffs, but it does. They are the champions and want everyone to know it. They want to feel it themselves. Can they win again this year without Gretzky? Sure. But again tonight they did not prove it.

It was a good night for Burns and his players. They saw last year's champion and beat him. They saw each other under fire and each came through. For the first time this season they think maybe this is the year.

Before the game Sather and Burns wrote almost the same script – tight checking, patient, opportunistic, low scoring – but nothing worked the way they expected. Watch Naslund, watch Courtnall and Lumme, Sather warned. Naslund scored three goals and Lumme one. Carbonneau, the checker, outscored

Messier, the scorer. And at the end of the second period, the league's best goalie was yanked from the game. It is the nature of hockey, the randomness of fate.

Baseball is America's game. It is planned and orderly, the action starts and stops, and every next moment seems a brand new chance. Effort matters; skill matters more. Time is slow – you only move when you are ready. The game goes on until a winner is declared. Time is infinite. The game could go on forever. Hockey is messy and confused. Its action rarely stops. One moment runs into the next, and its past lives on in its present and future. Skill matters, effort matters as much, time matters more. Time is finite. A game must end. Time is short and beyond control. Baseball is a game of the imagination, a mythical game. It is a demonstration of life as we might wish it to be. Hockey is real life.

In the Oilers' dressing room the players quietly shower and dress and move on. Across the ice, the Canadiens' room is a swirl of media. Reporters thrust notepads, cameras, and microphones into the faces of Naslund, Carbonneau, and Burns. Also pinned to his seat is Lumme: his first NHL game, his first goal, his first media scrum – he looks overwhelmed.

A few minutes later, when the room is mostly cleared, Bobby Smith, the giant Canadiens' centre, walks over to Lumme, "Good start there, buddy," he says, and shakes his hand.

Jyrki Lumme, from Tampere, Finland, has just lived a day he will never forget.

CHAPTER FOUR

THE BIG MONEY GAME

THE FANS COUNT DOWN THE FINAL SECONDS. ON THE BENCH OF THE Edmonton Oilers, the players, all standing, hug and laugh and pump their arms in the air. The Stanley Cup is won.

It is for the fourth time in five years. But after living through a season of doubts, when to others and sometimes even to themselves they seemed no longer the best, this 1988 Stanley Cup may be for them the sweetest. It is as plain on their dead-white faces as in their incandescent eyes. They have gone through much to get here, and now they feel all the world's relief, release, and pleasure at having made it. And so do their fans. As the clock melts away, they sing down louder and louder each joyous number.

Wayne Gretzky, their leader, accepts the Stanley Cup, and with a child's enormous grin he raises it above his head. The fans roar once more. His teammates join round and together they begin their many laps of honour. Like prehistoric men back from the hunt, they display their shimmering prize, passing it from outstretched arms to outstretched arms, sharing it happily, generously, with each other and with their fans.

It is the pinnacle moment for any team. When they came together eight months ago they had one goal – to win a Stanley Cup. They placed themselves in the powerful, yet vulnerable

137

hands of each other. They worked hard and played hard. Sometimes they were weak and selfish. Many times, they forgot the team and went out in search of their own rewards. But only one thing was going to leave them happy. And eight months later, they got it.

They are probably too young to know how rare it is to set out after something and achieve it. Still, in the way they contort their bodies, acting out the feeling that is too big to keep inside, they know they are part of something special.

It is the only moment in a season when there is more than enough for everyone to share, when there is no temptation to pull on the blanket to take more for yourself. Gretzky hands over the prize to Mark Messier, and Messier to Kevin Lowe, and on and on, each new person greeting the Cup with a whoop and a holler to the true delight of the rest. Everyone gives, everyone shares. It is the best of moments.

Oilers' owner Peter Pocklington works down closer to the ice. From this series he will earn many hundreds of thousands of dollars. Gretzky himself will earn thousands more from NHL and team bonuses. Oilers' fans have paid higher ticket prices to watch these playoff games, but in return they have seen their remarkable team win. Everyone has given as good as he's got. There is no resentment, no bitterness, no other agenda. At this one moment, the business of sport does not exist. Anything other than the game has evaporated.

The players gather near centre ice for a team picture to capture the moment. Some go down on their knees, others stand in behind, leaning on those in front of them, arms hanging on each other's shoulders. The Cup sits in their midst front and centre in the place of honour, Gretzky beside it. Gretzky looks around. He searches into the crowd and anxiously motions someone to join them. He gets up and skates to the boards. Oilers' coach Glen Sather, his assistants John Muckler and Ted Green, and the team's trainers rush happily into the picture. Gretzky returns with the proud and smiling Pocklington on his arm, and together they take their places around the Cup. They are all finally there. *The team* – the players, the owner, and, still standing and cheering in the back, the fans of Edmonton.

There is nowhere in their minds a memory of yesterday, a thought of tomorrow. Yet in a way that would surprise even those who are closest to the action, events are moving forward at a pace and in a direction that is almost irresistible. This team, for months, has been breaking apart.

Gretzky and Pocklington have been negotiating contracts for more than a decade. But this time there is trouble. Pocklington has had offers for Gretzky in the past, but only now he has begun to listen. And the word is spreading: if the price is right, *Gretzky might be available*. Gretzky has heard these stories, too, and now his friends around the league have told him they are true. Only a few sleepless hours from now, Gretzky will tell his disbelieving linemate and friend, Jari Kurri, that he thinks he will be traded. A few hours after that, when their Stanley Cup parade through the adoring streets of Edmonton has ended, Pocklington will tell Gretzky that they must discuss his contract and that if they cannot agree on a longer one he will have to trade him.

The team's celebrations go on loud and long, louder and longer, it seems, than any other year. For Gretzky and Pocklington know that when the party stops, when they allow it to stop, this one perfect moment of *team-ness* will end.

It is the business of sport.

Business and sport seem a contradictory mix. Sport is pure and guileless, at least in our collective imagination. It is play and childhood and cold winter days on frozen pastoral ponds. It has its own code of behaviour, one that is higher and more idealistic than real life expects. Sport seems specifically intended to exist separate from the rough and tumble of life where business is so squarely situated. The fact is, of course, without business, sport would still be on sandlots, in backyards, and on ponds, with very few players and even fewer spectators. It is business that has promoted and popularized sport and created its mass appeal.

One can imagine a scene nearly a century ago. There is a river in the middle of a town and on it a hockey game is being played. The snow has been pushed back to form a rectangular snowbank; players in all manner of clothes and equipment grunt and shriek the pleasures of the game. A man walking home from town cuts across the ice with his daily provisions. He sees the game, stops and watches. A few minutes later, another person does the same. Then another. Still others, attracted by the sight of the growing crowd, gather to see what it is seeing.

They are quickly drawn to the action: the speed, the sense of danger, the look of exhilaration on the faces of the players, the fun they are having. They see among the players someone they know. They watch with a friend's, then a fan's, interest, wishing good things, silently cheering every move. Random players begin to take on the look of teams, random action a game. A goal or a save by one side or the other seems to matter. The drama builds.

The watchers, sensing the interest of those beside them, begin to be heard. There are cheers for one team, and for the other.

The game goes on. One watcher disappears for a few minutes and returns with a pot of coffee. He shares it with chilled, grateful, similarly cheering fans around him. Another finds a tree trunk to rest against, another a wooden crate to sit on. Several others turn toward each other, dicker, and place bets on the game's outcome.

In their midst, one face volleys from side to side apparently as interested in the action around him as in the game in front. He sees boisterous, lively faces, arguing, laughing, cheering. He sees the coffee, the wooden crate, the money changing hands. He sees people having fun.

He has an idea.

He thinks he can sell this game.

That hypothetical river scene resides not very far from the Stanley Cup victory at Edmonton's Northlands Coliseum. The elements of sport's future are all there. Cathedral-like arenas filled with thousands of people, radio, TV, electronic message boards and multi-media spectacle are each only the next predictable step, the latest application of technology and salesmanship to something with immense public appeal. The fundamental point is that hockey is exciting enough to attract players and an audience to watch it be played. Corporations, governments, charitable organizations – anyone with something to sell needs an audience. The ability to attract an audience makes sport an important instrument of selling, itself and other things, and a valuable commodity to own.

The more valuable it becomes, the more sport comes to look like a business and the more it acts like one. If a company is worth $30 million in one community and $50 million in another, it is likely to be moved. So why not a football team? Vice-presidents change companies when their contracts are up, so why not hockey players? If sport is really distinct from business, different rules and regulations and expectations should apply. But if it is not so decisively distinct, gradually sport will function like a business according to business rules and expectations. And sport will become part of life's mainstream, not separate or distinct, not *other*, no longer just "play."

This, in fact, is what has occurred in recent years. Sport has become part of the economic and ethical and behavioural mainstream. More may still be expected of those in sport, as old standards and expectations die slowly and reluctantly. To most, it still does not seem right that players earn so much money for playing a game and can move from team to team at *their* discretion. It does not seem right that owners can abandon one set of fans for another in a different city. But as it is with other businessmen, the law says they can.

The result is a fundamental power realignment within sport. The individual elements that comprise a team – the players, fans, and owner – are set against each other, each competing for a piece of the far more lucrative sports pie. The owner threatens to move to more lucrative, "greener" pastures, just as he moves his other companies. Players seek finally to own themselves as free agents, to sell themselves to competing bidders and go where they want to go. Fans, through various inducements, seek to keep what they have or acquire something new from expansion or from someone else. The stakes are large, and getting larger; the fighting is therefore more intense. This is the present – and the future of professional sport. Its franchises are owned by three parties – the titled owners, the fans, and the players. It is a partnership, a *team*. The closer a sport, a league, and a team are to recognizing this, as in basketball and baseball, the fewer their future problems. For the others, hockey included, those awkward battles are ahead. The issues of sport that so often seem to crowd the games themselves from our sports pages have mostly to do with this realignment of power and the difficulty people have in coming to grips with it. For just as there are good partners and good team players, there are bad ones as well.

"Maybe it began when I first bought Wayne back in 1978," Peter Pocklington says, as he muses about the origins of *the trade*. He "bought" Gretzky from his friend and soulmate, Nelson Skalbania, owner of the Indianapolis Racers of the World Hockey Association. Pocklington then signed Gretzky to a personal services contract rather than a standard league contract, making him literally an asset in his personal portfolio, so that any subsequent dealings would be between the two of them directly, not with any general manager as intermediary. The result, a year later, was a new twenty-one-year contract, signed on Gretzky's eighteenth birthday, that allowed Gretzky to renegotiate after the contract's ninth and fifteenth years. A mature kid from a working-class family, Gretzky got what he was looking for: security and a working-class kid's chance to improve himself, if he produced.

He produced so spectacularly in the following years that existing contracts became unconscionable and renegotiations more frequent. He earned more money, his contracts grew shorter, yet trapped as he was within the lengthy bounds of his early agreements, his contracts remained long by others' standards. Superstars in other sports routinely played out their contracts for a chance at free agency's motherlode, but Gretzky had no such option. No future outside Edmonton seemed possible or, indeed, desirable. He was happy in Edmonton. The team was winning, and both he and the Oilers were at the top of the hockey world.

Then two critical things happened. Needing money, Pocklington decided to take the Oilers public. The air had gone out of the western Canadian economy at the beginning of the 1980s and Pocklington's real estate magic evaporated with it. Patrician Land Corp., his land development company, went bankrupt, bringing down with it his Fidelity Trust Company, producing losses of $200 million. Though deposits were covered by a federal insurance plan, his troubles snowballed with the result that his oil company and car dealership were both forced into receivership. A fierce public champion of private enterprise, he had turned frequently to the Alberta government for financial rescue. He also needed to sell off certain more personal assets, including his extensive art collection. In February, 1987, Pocklington got permission from the NHL's Board of Governors to make the Oilers a publicly traded company.

He had received permission for a more broad-based form of financing once before, early in the 1980s, when he sought to turn the Oilers into a limited partnership. He wanted to sell off a 40 per cent interest in the team which, in pre-Stanley Cup days, he believed was worth $20-25 million. But Pocklington could not sell the minimum number of partnership units he needed, and the plan died. But when the Boston Celtics basketball club went public in December, 1986, its publicly traded value soaring past what its value had been on the private market, Pocklington decided to try again. This time claiming the franchise was worth nearly $100 million, he sought to raise $40 million by selling publicly 45 per cent of the shares of the team. (He had paid $6.503 million for 100 per cent of the team in 1976.) Issuing shares would allow Pocklington to take some of his money out of the team and seek other opportunities with it while still retaining control of the Oilers. First, however, he needed to secure his hold on his principal asset, Gretzky, to satisfy any prospective public investor. The problem, however, was Gretzky's personal services contract. Gretzky would need to agree to tear up his contract with Pocklington and sign a new one with the Oilers, so that the contract could be transferred with the team's other assets to the new public company. Pocklington met with Gretzky to discuss the matter.

Gretzky had heard speculation about the public issue and how much Pocklington might realize from the sale of the team. He knew that he was a major reason why the team's value had soared in recent years. He also knew how important he was to any public sale. "I had a little bit of an upper hand," he remembers, and he decided to use it. He agreed to redo his contract to conform to Pocklington's needs, but he had a price – his career-long twenty-one-year contract, which had been renegotiated back to nine years, was to be reduced further to five years, at which point he would become a free agent *without compensation*. Pocklington understood the implications. "This, of course, spelled tough things for the Edmonton Oilers. To lose someone like Wayne at the end of five years with nothing in return would be disastrous for the team. I said to him at the time, 'Wayne, don't put us under the gun. Don't do that.'" Then Pocklington shrugged. "Unfortunately, his bargaining was better than mine." Still, any pressing problem for Pocklington was at least five years away, at the end of Gretzky's contract when Gretzky would be thirty-one years old and past the peak of his career. At that point Gretzky would also have spent fourteen years in Edmonton (thirteen in the NHL), making a decision to leave the Oilers more difficult and therefore less likely. At that moment, it was doubtful that Gretzky intended to use free agency as anything other than a lever to a better future contract with the Oilers. It seemed likely he would remain in Edmonton. Reluctantly, Pocklington agreed to Gretzky's demands. The first domino had fallen. The next ones would fall more easily.

The second critical factor occurred as a result of the first. Gretzky and Pocklington began to feel older. Though only twenty-seven, Gretzky was beginning to see a long and lengthening trail behind him. He had reached the point of his hockey life where he was setting, or threatening to set, NHL career records held by players many years older when they had set them, to be sure, still as each mark fell, Gretzky couldn't help but be reminded of his age. The long Stanley Cup seasons, the Canada Cups, the now more frequent injuries had also left him tired. He speculated out loud about how much longer he wanted to play. He had always been young enough that the future was always now. There seemed no other time. Now he thought of marriage and children, a place for a family to live and grow up – all that was ahead of him. Like every other player before him, he was beginning to see the end.

His present had always been under control – his performance

ensured it. But when his focus began to shift from present to future, a future about to be filled with a wife and family, control seemed more fragile. So control came to matter more. Perhaps more than anything, Gretzky believed that his decade of unprecedented achievement had earned him some real control over his life. He had been tied up for a whole playing career, and likely more, when he was only eighteen years old, tied not even to a team but to a person, Peter Pocklington. It had also come to bother him that he might not even be able to quit when he wanted but might be compelled to play on even if his joy and fire had gone, perhaps to be embarrassed by skills no longer there, all because of that contract. "I always had this in my mind, you know," Gretzky said, "that if I retire, they can come after me and say, 'No, you have to play.' I didn't want that hanging over me." Before more money or free agency, "that retirement clause was the first thing I asked for from Mr. Pocklington in the new contract."

With agreement on that, it seemed everything had been set straight. His contract would end in five years, and at that point *he* could decide where to play his last years, or if he would continue at all. "It wasn't really the money," Gretzky said of his new contract. "I always wanted to control my destiny. I went from a seven-year deal to twenty-one years to nine years and now to a five-year contract. I kept negotiating down. It was kind of funny getting there. But I finally got it to where I wanted it to be." The situation was clear. If his need for control became threatened in any way, Gretzky would fight back.

When you are young and a Yankee, nothing will ever end. No one will grow old. The winning will never stop. As a man of wealth, Peter Pocklington is indistinguishable from hundreds, maybe thousands, of other Canadians. As owner of the Edmonton Oilers, he is *somebody*. "No one pays attention to a shipbuilder," shipbuilder and New York Yankees' owner George Steinbrenner once put it. But a sports team can put you on the front pages. It can be an instrument of personal ego and a way to sell yourself. And Pocklington used it just those ways, capitalizing on his new-found sports celebrity in business and politics, even seeking the leadership of the federal Progressive Conservative Party (he was easily defeated).

But now the bloom had faded. The public had grown increasingly tired of Pocklington, and he of them. For years, the Oilers could give him a fan's pleasure and still make him an owner's money. But the factory gets old and the equipment wears out, and what then? With each Stanley Cup, the Oilers were coming one year closer to the end. The New York Islanders had won four straight Stanley Cups, but age and injury had driven their great players – Mike Bossy, Bryan Trottier, Denis Potvin – into retirement or mediocrity and the team into a free fall toward the bottom of the league. The Islanders decided its rare winning tradition had to be set in stone to inspire future Islanders' players and fans, to make future winning more likely. Those that embodied that tradition, therefore, Bossy, Trottier, Potvin, could never be traded. But a winning tradition means little – no one sees it or cares about it – if the winning doesn't continue. It is the difference between the Montreal Canadiens and the Toronto Maple Leafs.

But how can winning continue if a team rides its players into the ground and in the end gets nothing for them when they leave the scene? Will 17,312 fans keep coming to see the *former* great, now bottom-dwelling Edmonton Oilers, Pocklington wondered? That nightmare might still be years away, but if a twenty-one-year personal services contract never ends, a five-year free agency contract certainly does. More so, it focuses the mind on the future and makes one think.

A year earlier, Pocklington had had a long conversation with Jerry Buss, then owner of the Los Angeles Kings, then as now owner of the Los Angeles Lakers of the National Basketball Association. Pocklington had come away greatly affected. Buss had wanted to get Gretzky for his Kings. He knew how unsuccessful others had been in trying to raise the issue with Pocklington, so he decided on a different approach. "I wanted to raise the matter as an economic issue," recalls Buss, "because as an emotional issue, I knew there was no way he could discuss it. So I said, 'Peter, you probably feel that you made three to four million dollars on hockey this year.' He said, 'Yes, I did.' I said, 'No, you actually didn't.' I said, 'You forgot to factor in the depreciation on your most valuable asset, Wayne Gretzky.' He said, 'Whaddaya mean?' I said, 'Well look, he's only going to be around another five, six, seven years. If he's worth $15 million, if you put in the depreciation, you probably only broke even.' "

Buss had started Pocklington thinking. He pressed on, "So I pointed out that not only is your asset depreciating, which means that you're not making the profit you think, but in terms of realizing the value of that asset, there's probably only one team in the United States to whom he would be worth $15 million. Because if you have a filled arena, you can't refill it. But if you have an arena with four to five thousand empty seats, you have a chance." That meant Los Angeles, Washington, or Minnesota, but given the size of the investment and the rapid depreciation of the asset, return on investment would need to be fast. According to Buss, that left only L.A. "The only city where a star would have that immediate impact would be 'Stardomland,' Hollywood," Buss smiled. "So I said to Peter, 'I just want to point out two things. Your asset is depreciating, and secondly, your only customer is Los Angeles.' "

The two men talked about it for a while, then emotion returned. "I said, 'No Jerry, he's not for sale,' " Pocklington recalls. " 'Things are going too well. Besides, I'd be hung if I did such a thing.' "

But the conversation didn't end there. Over the next few months, Buss called Pocklington several times. "Jerry would phone and say, 'Have you thought about my proposition?' " Then Pocklington grew thoughtful, "I guess after a while the emotion comes out of it and you start to look at it objectively. But at that point, emotion overruled objectivity. I was too much of a fan. I truly believed that Wayne would go on for seven or eight or nine years or whatever. He was a legend and probably would become even greater."

But Buss had succeeded in opening Pocklington's mind. And now that it was open, Pocklington became more sensitive to everything he saw and heard. In the German magazine, *Der Spiegel*, Gretzky was quoted as saying that while he played for the love of the game, money mattered, and when his contract expired he intended to sign with the highest bidder. Whether Gretzky had said it, or meant it, did not matter. Pocklington heard what he was needing to hear. Consciously or unconsciously, he was building a rationale he would need to persuade himself, then others, that a trade from which he might personally benefit was for the good of the Oilers and the Edmonton fans.

He could see Gretzky going through a life change. Gretzky was thinking of getting married and having a family. Pocklington began wondering just how long he would want to get up in the morning and still make hockey his life. He might even retire soon, he thought, or, distracted by the rest of his life, play on without the relentless drive that made him a star. Either way, Pocklington would get nothing in return. The trigger for these doubts, of course, was the free agency contract that would end in five years and allow Gretzky to move on and leave Pocklington with nothing but a gaping, unfillable hole. Pocklington's case was growing.

And the clock was ticking. Like Bossy and Trottier, Gretzky *was* a depreciating asset. Gretzky was wearing out, losing value every day. And because he could become a free agent *without compensation*, Pocklington realized he no longer owned him, he only leased him. And as a lease grows short, as a contract winds down, its value plummets. Even if Gretzky wanted to stay in Edmonton, making his market value irrelevant, Pocklington knew he was in a bind. Gretzky had held the upper hand in signing this new contract, and five years from now his hand would be even stronger. Pocklington would have to re-sign him at an open market price, but without the money bonanza he had once counted on from taking the team public. The stock market had crashed a few months before and with it any immediate hopes Pocklington had of selling the team publicly. Moreover, he had heard from his money people before the crash that the franchise's value was much less than he wanted to believe. Edmonton was too small a market; its television revenues now and in the future were too limited.

Gretzky had been Pocklington's meal ticket in establishing the franchise and making it a success, and he would have been his meal ticket in taking the team public – the pitch was to be "own a piece of Gretzky." But now that these routes were maximized or gone, Gretzky could be his meal ticket only one other way. To get the most out of his investment in Gretzky, Pocklington was now convinced he had to sell him. He decided that after all these years, financially he would be better off without him.

Pocklington's decision to take the team public had set everything in motion. The irony, of course, is that the triggering event never happened, and his decision need not have been made. The irony, however, is illusion. Pocklington was always looking to realize the greatest return on his investment. At some point, then or later, that could only mean selling Gretzky.

Pocklington's talk with Buss and Gretzky's free agency contract had made the unthinkable thinkable. It was as yet still not *doable*. Both Gretzky and Pocklington could at any moment easily back away from the brink. Indeed, both of them likely believed the other would do just that. They were involved in a high-stakes game of "chicken." The closer they brought themselves to the brink the more likely something would happen to shake them from their destructive course. *Something will happen.* Some alternative solution will be found, they were sure – Gretzky signing a new longer-term, no-trade contract for more money, perhaps – to ensure that he would remain in Edmonton the rest of his career and be paid what he is worth. Or just plain cold feet would stop them.

Instead, it worked the other way. The closer they got to the brink, the more steps each took toward some other reality – *he's shopping me around* (Gretzky); *the guy won't sign a new contract. He's determined to leave when his contract's up* (Pocklington) – the angrier they got with each other, the more rash they became, the less unthinkable and undoable it all seemed, and the more certain was the final break.

Gretzky, Pocklington, and Oilers' president and coach Glen Sather had experienced enormous success. With it, they had acquired, as most do, the attitude and sense of impunity of the champion. *No one can make me do this*, the champion sneers. *If he thinks he can pull that* . . . Sather once mused about how players change during their careers. "When they're younger," he said, "they really don't know anything. Then you bring them through this phase where they learn how to dress, and play, and they become very self-confident and aggressive in their own lives and become experts on everything. Not just hockey, but travel, the government, cars. It's a 'superstar syndrome.'" Though Sather was speaking of hockey players, his words apply equally to Pocklington and to him. The situation had reached the stage where all of them – Gretzky, Pocklington, Sather – emotionally, rashly, had come to want to live without each other, just to show *them*, each having his own "them," that *I am so powerful and special, I am so much my own man, I can do what I want. And if you don't think so, just watch me.* They were like cowboys looking for a fight.

After the Stanley Cup celebrations ended, Gretzky and Pocklington met. "We never even got to dollars and cents," Gretzky recalls, "because in all the years we negotiated that was never a major factor. I said I'd sign for six, seven, eight years, that wasn't a problem." What Gretzky wanted, in return, was a no-trade contract. He knew that agreeing to sign for the longer term, he was really giving up forever his right to become a free agent, for when his contract ended his career would likely be over. Gretzky was telling Pocklington what Pocklington said he needed to know, that Wayne Gretzky was willing to stay in Edmonton until he retired. "I really loved Edmonton," Gretzky said later. "I didn't want to leave. We had a dynasty here. Why move?"

But if he was willing to make that choice, Gretzky wanted assurance from Pocklington that he would indeed stay in Edmonton and not be traded. He believed that if he was willing to give up his control to choose a future *outside* Edmonton, he should be able to control his future *in* Edmonton.

Here the negotiations broke down. Wayne Gretzky was depreciating. He was still of great value to the Edmonton Oilers, but then and always he might be more valuable to someone else. If he became a free agent, Pocklington would get nothing for him. If he played on and got old and retired, he would get from Gretzky those years of service, then nothing. A longer-term contract that would keep Gretzky in Edmonton, even a free agency contract *with* compensation, was not Pocklington's answer. He needed a Wayne Gretzky that would not grow old and depreciate, or one that could be exchanged for someone else before he lost his value altogether. Gretzky's free agency contract without compensation was a red herring. It helped determine the timing; it was an important building block in Pocklington's rationale – nothing more. Buss had finally succeeded. For Pocklington the selling of Gretzky had become an economic issue.

Pocklington rejected a no-trade contract. To Gretzky the message was clear – *he wants me here so that at any moment he chooses he can trade me to build the next generation of Edmonton Oilers. For him, it is just business. Maybe it always was. Maybe we were both so young and starry-eyed and were winning so often that we didn't notice. But if this is business, it's business for me, too. I will keep my free agent's contract and control my own fate.*

They did not know it at the time, but their negotiations effectively were at an end.

A few days later, at the NHL meetings in June, 1988, Pocklington talked to the New York Rangers and Detroit Red Wings about Gretzky. He also spoke again with Bruce McNall, the new owner of the L.A. Kings. McNall and Pocklington had met for the first time at an NHL Board of Governors meeting the year before, where McNall had followed up on Jerry Buss's inquiries about a Gretzky trade to L.A. "[Pocklington] didn't exactly dismiss it out of hand," remembers McNall, "which I guess led me to think there might be something possible." At the June meetings he brought up the subject again. Pocklington "indicated to me that he might have an interest in moving Gretzky, but he wouldn't do it this year. I told him I really wasn't interested in next year. Again, I didn't get any real positive response."

Pocklington seemed more interested in an offer that involved the Vancouver Canucks. Pocklington had talked for months with his old friend Nelson Skalbania, the Vancouver real estate entrepreneur who had been acting as middleman in discussions between Pocklington and the Griffiths family, principal owners of the Canucks. According to Pocklington, Skalbania offered him $22.5 million (Canadian) for Gretzky. Pocklington turned down the offer, he says, because he told Skalbania he needed hockey players to regenerate the Oilers, not just money. Yet though several offers had been rejected, talks between Pocklington and Skalbania were continuing.

Early in July, McNall heard rumours of these talks and again called Pocklington. This time their negotiations intensified. Still, however, it seemed to McNall that Pocklington was considering a trade for Gretzky only the following year.

At this same time, other events were beginning to take precedence. Less than two months after they had celebrated on the ice at Northlands Coliseum, the team was together again for the wedding of Wayne Gretzky and Janet Jones. The day before the wedding, the players got together with other close friends of the couple for a picture on a runway at the city's airport. This time with a World War One bi-plane as their prop, they dressed up in costume party military uniforms, Walter Gretzky, the groom's father, in a bomber jacket and Buck Rogers helmet he chose not to wear, Kevin Lowe in a Prussian spiked helmet, Jari Kurri in Mr. Magoo goggles and ceremonial headgear beyond description. It was a beautiful sunny day; spirits were high. They laughed at each other and at themselves. It was the team "acting stupid together" one more time. One last time.

The wedding had been previewed in the weeks before as a near royal event. Instead, it had the warm, intimate feeling of a small-town wedding that grew. The soloist sang Beethoven's "Ode to Joy"; the people of Edmonton crowded sidewalks outside St. Joseph's Basilica to catch a glimpse of the couple; they honked their horns as the local boy drove away with his bride.

Pocklington was there, and so were the players and fans. The business of sports was far away. It was a day that reminded them of all the good things they shared, a day that might make Pocklington and Gretzky wonder: *Why am I even thinking of this? Life is good. These are my friends. We've gone through a lot together. How often does anyone have the chance to be a part of something so special? Why change a thing?* Trades aren't made on a day like this. The emotion that Jerry Buss feared acts as a roadblock to the logic of the bottom line. But a day like this must end some time, and when it does the team hats go back on the shelf and the business hats are put on again.

"I think there are basically three 'Wayne Gretzkys,'" Gretzky once said. "There's the one that gets upset and that's moody and the one that gets annoyed and the one that can complain and lean on people. It's the one my friends see, my teammates, my coaches, my parents, my wife, and I try to keep that one within. I try to leave that one at home the best I can.

"Then there's the business one. When we're negotiating – whether it be hockey or commercials – for 'Wayne Gretzky' the person or the image. Negotiations can be very tough. But I don't think that's anyone else's business. That's between me and the people I'm negotiating with and against. No one else sees that 'Wayne Gretzky.'

"Then, I think, there's the third 'Wayne Gretzky,' which is like the one I grew up watching on TV, and that is the hockey player. You see him on the ice, you see him score goals. You see him get knocked down and you see him happy, then the game's over and that's all you see. That's how I grew up thinking of Gordie Howe. This man, all he did was play hockey. He doesn't watch movies. He doesn't go to weddings or out for dinner. He's a hockey player, and that's all he does."

The first and third Wayne Gretzkys, the ones driven to be the best, know what it is like to play with others who insist on the same, and they would never leave Edmonton. Similarly, "Peter Pocklington, the hockey fan," who acts and needs to feel like a winner, who loves to be treated as a winner, would never trade Wayne Gretzky. But there is another Wayne Gretzky and another Peter Pocklington, and when the wedding ended and *the team* went its separate ways, there was nothing left to stop the trade.

For the team – the players, owner, and fans of Edmonton – the wedding was their last hurrah. Two days later, on the first day of business after the wedding, Pocklington phoned McNall and told him if he still wanted to do something this year, they should talk.

Bruce McNall had made his initial fortune buying and selling coins. Later he branched out into movies and horse racing and had become a minority partner in the Dallas Mavericks of the National Basketball Association and in the L.A. Kings when Jerry Buss was the principal owner. In February, 1988, he decided to buy out Buss and take over the Kings. The Kings were competitively moribund and hemorrhaging financially, and in L.A. they were a nearly invisible franchise, of no interest to someone as ambitious and wealthy as McNall unless he intended to do something dramatic with them. After twenty years of franchise failure, he would need to give the Kings a kick-start. He knew the only real way to do it and let the fans know he meant business was to get Gretzky.

McNall's negotiations with Pocklington moved quickly. After a deal began to seem possible, McNall and Gretzky needed to meet to see for themselves if they could work together. McNall had to hear in Gretzky's voice, more importantly he had to see in his eyes, that Gretzky *really* wanted to play in L.A. and would be happy there. He had to be certain that Gretzky didn't want to get out of Edmonton only until he was gone, then spend the rest of his life looking whinily over his shoulder at what had once been. If so, Gretzky's performance would fall off, the Kings would quickly be as bad as usual, attendance would go up then abruptly fall, Gretzky would leave in spirit, or by trade or retirement, and McNall would be left holding a very expensive bag.

In turn, Gretzky had to see in McNall's eyes the desire to win a Stanley Cup. He had to be certain McNall understood that the worse Gretzky's supporting cast, the worse he would perform, the worse the Kings' chance of winning the Cup, the more unhappy Gretzky would be, the worse he would perform. He needed to know that McNall realized the only real way to sell hockey in Los Angeles was with a winner, that one great star was not enough. He had to know that McNall would take further steps, and spend more money if necessary, to give them both a real chance.

With their wives, they met for dinner. McNall and Gretzky saw what they needed to see.

By this time, Gretzky's career in Edmonton was over. Once he knew that Pocklington was "shopping him around," he decided he would never go back. "I was reading I was going to Detroit, to New York," said Gretzky. "I was saying to myself, 'you know that's not right. I deserve better than that.' I told Mr. Pocklington that. I said I felt I was one of your most loyal players. I played in every league game. I played hard in every playoff game. I attended every function that I was ever asked to go to. I never missed one exhibition game. I did everything the organization ever asked of me – and I felt they didn't treat me the way they should have. That was the last conversation I had with him. That's when I said, 'Look, it's best now if you move me to where I want to go.' "

And that was to Los Angeles. If Gretzky was losing control over his Edmonton future, he still held some important cards. At any moment, he could make the trade story public. He could incite the wrath that came down on Pocklington after the trade before it ever happened, making any trade more difficult, putting in jeopardy Pocklington's chance to maximize his investment. If Pocklington traded Gretzky to a team other than L.A., Gretzky could go kicking and screaming, his immense popularity inciting public outrage and putting at risk of consumer boycott Pocklington's other businesses, especially Gainers Inc. and Palm Dairies. A conciliatory Gretzky, traded to where he wanted to go, might go quietly. He might even agree to tell the story of the trade publicly in a light more favourable to Pocklington, who personally and corporately would be left behind to live in its fallout. Los Angeles it would be.

And if L.A. was to be his new playing home, Gretzky wanted to do all he could to make that new home a success. As Pocklington and McNall talked almost daily for two weeks trying to agree on the right package of players, draft picks, and money, Gretzky acted as McNall's adviser, wielding unprecedented power for a player, suggesting names that might also be included in *his* trade to make the Kings a better team. If he was to be a pawn in this game, Gretzky would be an aggressive one.

McNall tried to renegotiate the $15-million price with Pocklington, first proposed by Jerry Buss more than a year earlier, but Pocklington's mind was set. McNall then had to determine whether he could earn the $15 million back. But time was short.

He talked to Prime Ticket, the Kings' cable TV broadcaster. He talked to the Forum concessionaire and to the merchandiser of Kings' souvenirs. With Gretzky, McNall could attract bigger arena and television audiences and to those audiences more of everything could be sold. His associates would benefit greatly; would they ensure McNall higher revenues and help him make the trade possible? They told him they would. Still, McNall had no guarantees. No contracts could be finalized in time.

"There's a point in business," says McNall, "when you can't be certain of anything. We'd done projections of all sorts – how many fans would come, what television revenues could be increased to, advertising, merchandising, and so forth. But we never really could come up with a solid answer to give us the certainty that the trade was going to be successful economically. Finally, I decided that I'd done a lot of things in Los Angeles, I'd always lived there, I loved the sport of hockey, and I thought even if I'm wrong and the economics don't work out, that I'll have fun watching Gretzky here in Los Angeles and a lot of my friends will, too, and that I could afford the luxury. So I decided to make the move."

Pocklington and McNall talked right up to the day before the trade, and finally reached an agreement.

All of them – Gretzky, Pocklington, McNall, even Sather – could have stopped the trade if they had really wanted. None did.

Half a world away, at almost the same time, Marcel Aubut, president of the Quebec Nordiques, had just arrived in Scotland with his wife and young children for a long-delayed vacation. Not since Aubut had become president of the Nordiques ten years before, at the age of thirty, had the family spent more than a few consecutive days together. This was their chance. The telephone in their hotel room rang. Aubut answered. Someone had made an offer to buy the Nordiques, he was told, someone from *outside* Quebec. Aubut, leaving his wife and children, rushed back to Canada.

The owner of the Nordiques, Carling O'Keefe Breweries of Canada Ltd., had itself been purchased in 1987 by Elder's IXL

Ltd. of Australia, a large worldwide brewery best known as the maker of Foster's Ale. Elder's had originally been a jam company, the curious "IXL" in its name a shortened acronym for the personal slogan of Henry Jones, the company's founder – "I excel in all the products I make. It is my motto." But by 1988, Elder's had decided it wanted to make only one product – beer. When it acquired another company, as it frequently did, it kept only those parts directly associated with the making and selling of beer and looked to sell off the rest. And so when it bought Carling O'Keefe, Elder's decided to sell its two North American sports franchises, the Nordiques and the Toronto Argonauts of the Canadian Football League.

Until then, Carling O'Keefe and the players and fans of the Nordiques had made a good team. The brewery had once dominated the Quebec City market and in the mid-1960s had a 53 per cent market share. But after a health scare involving one of its brands, that share had dropped precipitously. By 1971, when the Nordiques began to play in the World Hockey Association with Carling O'Keefe as the principal sponsor, the brewery's portion of the market had fallen to 32 per cent. Five years later, when the brewery bought the financially troubled team, its share had increased to 43 per cent.

Things only got better in the years that followed, for both Carling O'Keefe and the Nordiques. The four-team surviving rump of the WHA, which included the Nordiques, merged with the NHL and the great Canadiens-Nordiques rivalry was born. Nordiques' management, including Aubut, recognizing the need for the team to become competitive fast, spirited two Stastny brothers, Peter and Anton, out of their home country of Czechoslovakia, through Austria, to Canada and the Nordiques. A third brother, Marion, joined them soon after. The team made the playoffs the Stastnys' first season, and the next year won the coveted, passionately contested "Battle of Quebec," upsetting the Canadiens in the playoffs. The Nordiques did the same three years later, in 1984-85, all the while playing in front of joyous and raucous sell-out crowds at the Colisée for nearly every league and playoff game. The people of Quebec did not forget their benefactors and Carling O'Keefe's market share in Quebec

City rose in gratitude, reaching its peak at 58 per cent when the brewery introduced Miller beers into Quebec, then settling solidly in at more than 50 per cent. In October, 1988, its market share in Quebec City was 51 per cent, nearly twenty points higher than when the brewery began its association with the Nordiques in 1971 and almost 20 points higher than its 1988 share in the province in general. And to the brewery, each percentage point in Quebec City means about $10 million in annual revenues.

Not all of this rise in fortunes had to do with the Carling O'Keefe-Nordiques connection. And little of what can be attributed, Carling O'Keefe would argue, had to do with the brewery's ownership, as distinct from its sponsorship, of the team. Still, the correlation is clear – if the Nordiques did not generate large revenues themselves, they *did* sell beer. "It was a very nice association," Ed Prévost, then president and CEO of O'Keefe Breweries in Quebec, recalls. "We had a very good share of the market in Quebec City. Everybody seemed happy. The company owning the team wasn't harming anyone, so what the heck." Then he smiled, "What's the expression in English – if it ain't broke, don't fix it."

But Elder's, when it purchased Carling O'Keefe, decided to fix it. "They have a more rigorous business philosophy," Prévost explains, "that requires us to evaluate each of our assets annually. We have to make sure that these assets are in fact generating a return for our shareholders. So when Elder's began to review what they had acquired, they asked themselves: what is this worth, what are we getting out of it, can we get just as much out of it without owning the asset? And the answer was yes." According to Prévost, "It's the promotion and advertising rights that breweries are really after."

Beer drinkers watch sports; sports watchers drink beer. It is the same around the world. Beer companies spend more than $600 million annually on sports advertising in the U.S. "Breweries have always been associated with sports," Peter Bartels, Melbourne-based chief executive of the Elder's Brewing Group explains. "A large proportion of our consumers are sports fanatics. It's true of Australia, and true of Canada." Just as Saturday morning TV cartoons exist to sell toys, television sports run on beer. But to Elder's, that means the sponsorship of sporting events, not the ownership of teams. "Owning a franchise is not our cup of tea," echoes Prévost. "I mean, we don't know how to run a hockey team. We don't know anything about hockey. Our vocation in life is to make beer and sell it to as many people as who want to buy it. That's what we know best. Dealing with superstars and the fickleness of players, fans, media, and what have you, it's a horrendous job."

Elder's believed it could have it both ways. It could "fix it" by selling off the asset, the team, but still keep the promotional rights to it. Elder's saw no good reason to tie up its money in ownership when it already controlled the team's promotional rights. "It's like owning a retail premises," Bartels explains. "Once upon a time a storekeeper owned his shop. Like many storekeepers today, they lease their shop and use their capital for something else. So we wanted to take our capital out of the Nordiques and use that in other parts of our brewing business to create more sales." To a brewery, buying a franchise had been like paying a cover charge to gain access to what it really wanted – the promotion rights. "In the past, you had to own a team to control the rights," Bartels says. "Now you don't."

After seventeen years of sponsorship and twelve years of ownership, Carling O'Keefe had secured in the minds of Quebecers the connection between its brands of beer and the Nordiques. To sustain this good will that sold beer, it felt it needed only to remind the public periodically, through advertising and promotion, of the team-brewery connection. Carling O'Keefe had no fear of another brewery stepping into its shoes because it controlled to whom it would sell. Nor did it fear any subsequent sale and buyer. Molson's already owned the Canadiens and was prohibited by NHL by-laws from owning a second team, and the Nordiques were "small potatoes" for the only other large Canadian brewery, Labatt's. If anything, Labatt's was interested in the Toronto Maple Leafs, an historic team in the major southern Ontario market. So at Elder's direction, Carling O'Keefe proceeded with the sale of the team.

According to Prévost, the brewery did not openly solicit

offers. The sale would be orderly and done without urgency. Any urgency would only come later, if at all, when discussions between Molson's, owners of the Canadiens, and Carling O'Keefe, began that would result in the merger of the two breweries in January, 1989. NHL by-laws precluded anyone holding substantial ownership in more than one franchise in the league, so that in the event of a Carling O'Keefe-Molson's merger, one team would need to be sold. But at stake was a $1.5-billion merger. The future of a mere $20-million business in that context could hardly have produced such urgency as to explain what happened next.

The decision of Elder's to sell the Nordiques was little cause for alarm. How Elder's would make the sale and to whom the team would be sold did matter. "That's where we may have slipped somewhat," Prévost admitted later. His was a classic understatement.

Aubut was notified of Elder's desire to sell the team. He had known about it for several months before he received his phone call in Scotland. In fact, he had held meetings with Carling O'Keefe about buying the team himself, proposing to them a deal that appeared to have a purchase price considerably higher than the one subsequently accepted by the brewery in October, 1988, but structured on an earn-out basis, whereby his purchase price would be paid to Carling O'Keefe only out of the team's future earnings, if any. The Nordiques, playing in such a small market, had never been much more than a break-even operation. It was the team's impact on the beer company's bottom line that made it a valuable asset. A deal structured on the health of the Nordiques' own bottom line was not very attractive to Carling O'Keefe. The brewery knew it would likely realize little or nothing from such an arrangement and, in any event, only after many years. It turned down Aubut's proposals.

But if Aubut could make little headway in buying the team himself, he had considerable leverage if someone else was to make an offer. In 1985, in the midst of his own contract negotiations with Carling O'Keefe, Aubut had asked for, and was given, the right to match any offer for the Nordiques from any third party during his lifetime. This right of *préemption* ran for a

**The Team:
the players,
the owner,
the fans.**

Mr. & Mrs. Pocklington.

The Battle of Quebec:
Ed Prévost, Carling O'Keefe (top);
Marcel Aubut (second from left),
and the new Nordiques partners.

MOLSON IS CANADIAN BEER.

MOLSON GOLDEN
AVAILABLE AT BEERS OF THE WORLD

ruce McNall
nd Michael J. Fox.

DELIVERANCE

period of thirty days, commencing the moment Aubut was notified of any offer the brewery had accepted. "At the time,"
Aubut explains, "I was worried about the Arabs buying everything. I said to myself, maybe they would buy Carling O'Keefe
and wouldn't care about hockey and move the team or sell it to
somebody. . . . I wanted to make sure that the team would
always be owned by Quebecers, run by Quebecers, and that it
would never move from Quebec City. I'd spent too much of my
life building it and creating it to let anyone take it away." Aubut
filed away his *préemption* letter. "I almost threw it into the garbage," he recalls with a storyteller's hyperbole. "I thought I
would never use it in my life." Three years later, that piece of
paper would become very important to him.

There had been "a lot of nibbles" concerning the team in the
early months of 1988, Prévost recalls, people inquiring if it was
for sale, looking for information, but no bona fide offers were
received. Then an offer came. It was in July, and if the speculation is correct, it was for both the Nordiques and the Argonauts.
Aubut insists it was from Harry Ornest, a Canadian-born, Beverly Hills-based businessman who, between 1982 and 1986, had
owned the St. Louis Blues of the NHL. Ornest, a controversial and
prickly character, insists he made no such offer, and Carling
O'Keefe has refused to divulge the proposed buyer's name, citing a confidentiality agreement. It makes no difference. This
much is known: an offer was made; and the offer came from
someone from *outside* Quebec – they are the only two details that
matter.

After only forty-eight hours in Scotland, Aubut was in
Carling O'Keefe's Toronto offices urging them not to accept the
offer. "Quebecers will never forgive you if you sell to anybody
other than Quebecers," he warned. Aubut was in clear conflict
of interest, of course, for he still hoped to buy the team himself.
It was a conflict that did not escape the notice of his Toronto
superiors. Yet Prévost would tell them much the same thing.
Only when Aubut was satisfied that nothing would happen in his
absence did he return to Scotland. The offer to purchase the
Nordiques was rejected.

When Aubut returned to Canada, he and Prévost worked out

guidelines on how best to sell the team and presented them to their superiors in Toronto. Neither of them heard anything more about any sale of the Nordiques, until October.

Then a new offer was made to Carling O'Keefe. Aubut heard about it and contacted Quebec City Mayor Jean Pelletier and Mario Bertrand, chief of staff of Quebec Premier Robert Bourassa. Aubut met with each separately and discussed the implications of a Nordiques sale. Nearly two weeks later, on Friday, October 28, the Quebec City newspaper *Le Soleil* reported that Elder's was on the verge of completing a deal to sell the Nordiques to an unnamed U.S. group that might be interested in moving the team out of Quebec. Aubut denied the story, saying that if any such deal had been made, he would have known about it. That evening, Prévost was advised by Carling O'Keefe's Toronto office that the company had officially accepted the offer to sell the team. He was not told the identity of the new owner. Aubut was similarly notified and informed the company of his right of *préemption*, which gave him thirty days to match the accepted offer. On Sunday, October 30, a copy of the offer was delivered to his home, with only the name of the purchaser deleted.

For Aubut, the clock had begun to tick. Aubut called Prévost and they agreed to say nothing to the media until at least the next day. The following morning Prévost was driving to work and turned on his car radio. "My friend and colleague, Marcel Aubut, is holding a press conference," Prévost recalls, still astonished and angry about it many months later. "That came as a bit of a shock and I might even say, a bit of a slap in the face because I had respected my end and he had chosen to break the ice alone, without consulting me ahead of time about what he was going to do or what he was going to say."

The gloves were off. Carling O'Keefe had wanted a nice, tidy, and quiet deal. *Un P.M.E.*, a very small business, as Prévost describes it, was being sold as scores of others are sold each day in Canada, and life goes on. It is a matter for the lawyers and accountants; no one else need be bothered. But Carling O'Keefe did not understand. Prévost probably did, but his bosses in Toronto, some of whom were Australian and new to Canada, didn't listen to him or to Aubut, or chose not to do so. They knew about sports and beer, about sponsorship and ownership, and they knew it was their company's philosophy to sell off any non-beer entities and that it was their job to do it. They also knew that a team had to matter to its fans, their consumers, or why else would those fans change allegiance and drink their team's beer? Why else would the brewery spend millions of dollars each year forging the team-beer/beer-team connection in the public's mind? Carling O'Keefe just didn't understand how much a team can matter.

"We don't know how to run a hockey team," Prévost had said. "We don't know anything about hockey." For more than ten years, it would have seemed that Prévost was either wrong or being coy. In the end, he was right. Owners of sports franchises like to say that they are not the real owners of a team, that they only hold it in trust for the fans. But that is an exaggeration. They respect the fan as they respect any consumer, but ultimately they treat the asset as their own. The people of Edmonton would not have traded Gretzky; Pocklington did. If it was up to Oakland, Baltimore, and St. Louis fans, the NFL's Raiders, Colts, and Cardinals would still be theirs. Every time the Montreal Canadiens skate onto the ice at the Forum, announcer Claude Mouton exhorts, "Et maintenant, accueillons nos Canadiens! And now, let's welcome our Canadiens!!!" "*Our* Canadiens!" He wants the fans to feel as if they own the team, and the fans want to feel the same. But in the end, it is really "Molson's Canadiens," just as it is "Pocklington's Oilers," "Steinbrenner's Yankees," "Ballard's Maple Leafs," just as it was "Carling O'Keefe's Nordiques."

The people of Quebec would not have sold their hockey team to non-Quebecers; Carling O'Keefe did. In doing so, Carling O'Keefe committed the unpardonable sin of any business – it didn't know its market. The company may have known the market for beer; it didn't know the market for hockey.

It would learn very fast. The response to Aubut's press conference was electrifying. Even Prévost, a Quebecer and a hockey fan, was surprised by its magnitude. "I was absolutely flabbergasted," he recalls. "I couldn't believe it. I couldn't believe what was happening. We were getting reactions from all over the place. It's not that the media weren't busy covering other things – we were in the middle of national election campaigns in Canada and the U.S. – but somehow or other they decided that this was *the* story. And everybody got into the act. I mean the mayor of Quebec got into the act, the Prime Minister [of Quebec], they got to him and he said, you know, he expressed a great deal of concern should the team be called to move somewhere else. And other politicians said as much, at whatever level – federal, provincial, municipal. It was the subject of open lines all over the country. I wasn't just surprised, I couldn't believe what was happening. And at the same time, I could."

Quebecers were reacting as historically they always react when something that matters to them is threatened. "Everybody in this province has played hockey at one point or another," muses Prévost. "But beyond that, we've created two professional teams, both of which have had their share of success. The Canadiens, the dynasty, the legend, are known worldwide. The Nordiques are young and yet to be well known even on the North American continent. But to French Canadians, hockey is their window on the world. It's the thing that allows them to brag, to show themselves off, to take their suspenders and say, 'I'm good, I'm professional, I can play with the biggies. I can beat you.' Hockey has nationalistic roots. The French Canadian gets satisfaction here, he develops self-confidence, which historically he hasn't had to the same degree as other North Americans. He projects himself through these hockey players, and gets from them a tremendous amount of pride and new-found confidence in himself." If Prévost's characterization is exaggerated, it only serves to make the point. Hockey matters to people in this province.

And at the very moment Ed Prévost was winding his way through traffic to his Montreal office, Marcel Aubut was in Quebec City telling the media, and through them the people of the province, that part of their hockey life was in jeopardy. The Nordiques were being sold, the new buyer, *le fantôme*, was unknown, but was from *outside* Quebec. He, Aubut, had a thirty-day right of *préemption*, which now had twenty-nine days to run, and he was looking to find investors to help him save the team and keep it in Quebec. He knew, as everyone did, that the Nordiques had come into the NHL only on the coattails of a merger. This had been their one chance. If the Nordiques left, Quebec City would never get another NHL team.

News of the sale pinballed around the province, instantly, instinctively, translated into a code that Quebecers understand. An outside buyer meant a buyer without loyalty to the province, who at first opportunity would abandon Quebec for richer, bigger markets in the U.S. or English Canada. This was a matter of survival. We must fight back, they thought.

There were two ways to do it – to attack Carling O'Keefe, punishing it for what it had done and/or pressuring it to change its mind; and to generate a competing offer to buy the team from *within* Quebec. Leading the fight was Aubut. He was perfectly scripted for the role: handsome, quick smiling, fast talking, a man of enormous appetites – ambition, attention, wealth, energy, spirit, talk, good will, good deeds – occasionally ballooning to a Falstaffian near 300 pounds, a character bigger than life. He was also a street-fighter, tough and opportunistic. He had fought for eight years the classic underdog's fight – *little guy* Quebec City/Nordiques/Carling O'Keefe against cosmopolitan, establishment *big guy* Montreal/Canadiens/Molson's. Aubut never backed off; he never felt sorry for himself. He attacked at every opportunity, attempting to make his team more Québécois, drafting and trading players as he could for French Canadians, luring away former Montreal players to tweak the Canadiens' noses, with some success making the Canadiens seem Quebec's "Anglo" team.

Now he was up against a multinational corporate giant. The press conference was his chance. He was an employee of Carling O'Keefe, but he would act contrary to its interests. He would inflame public opinion against the company and raise the spectre of a public boycott of its beer, every businessman's nightmare. He would wrap himself in the nationalist's flag and jerk the knees of Quebecers and their instinct for threat and survival. He would get them mad enough and afraid enough to put their money behind him so he could match the accepted offer and take over the team. And in this kind of battle, all was fair. Aubut was out to save the Nordiques for Quebecers, and for himself. At first the causes seemed one and the same. For Aubut, this was perfect.

"Marcel's a guy who absolutely gets his jollies from any opportunity that will give him tremendous coverage," Prévost says, now feeling the mixture of admiration, bitterness, grudging respect, and hard-earned distrust that comes after one has emerged from a public street brawl with Marcel Aubut. "He's a show-business person. I mean, here was an unusual opportunity to get front-page news. He's Mister Quebec. I mean, after the Prime Minister [of Quebec], the Archbishop, who else is there in Quebec. There's Marcel Aubut. He's well above Jean Pelletier and [Montreal mayor] Jean Doré for sure. He's the biggest mover and shaker in this town. Or so he believes. That's why, in jest perhaps, some call him not Marcel Aubut but Marcel 'Imbue.' But I mean, he's like [former Montreal mayor] Johnny Drapeau. You have to take him with all of his qualities and all of his faults."

Why did Aubut play up the external threat at his press conference and bring his employer into disrepute? "I think Marcel was fighting for survival," Prévost explains. "He was fighting for his job, number one, because clearly the mysterious buyer had as one of his conditions that Marcel would no longer be part of the team. And several of his senior managers would also be liquidated in the process. He knew that he had to fight for his job and for security for his family. So that's fair. But I think that in his unconscious mind he probably had come to the point where he believed the asset and himself were one and the same. He had fallen in love with the asset. He had come to believe that *he* was the Nordiques. And he had come to believe, legitimately or not, that there was a threat of the franchise moving somewhere else, when in fact that was never even suggested or whispered."

But no suggestion or whisper was necessary. The threat was either real or plausible, and either was enough. Consider the details that were known: an unnamed purchaser who could not be named and who was from *outside* Quebec; a deal that had been hidden from the public, made known by its opponents and only after the deal had been consummated; a deal that contained no specific provision guaranteeing that the Nordiques would remain in Quebec (the explanation given was that such a guarantee would hamstring the future owner in negotiations with the Colisée over arena rental for the team which, again the explanation goes, was already much higher than most teams paid). Add to those the well-earned cultural fears, insecurities, and long historical record of grievances that go with life as a minority, and what conclusions would any Quebecer draw?

Right after the press conference, radio phone-in shows were filled with threats of boycott of Carling O'Keefe beers. By the next day stories began circulating, apocryphal or not, of small-town corner grocery stores and Carling O'Keefe beer trucks pulling up to them. "What'll it be today?" the truck drivers in these stories called out, just as they had each day that they passed. "Nothing," they were told. "Nothing." "Nothing." "Nothing." Again and again the same word echoed around the province. It was a word the drivers had not heard before. Prévost insists these scenes never happened. But it doesn't matter. The mood was such that they *could* have happened, something even Prévost is unlikely to deny. And if not today, maybe tomorrow. Prévost and Carling O'Keefe had a huge problem. They had to do something fast or see their Nordiques-assisted rise in market share turn into a Nordiques-induced collapse.

Prévost was highly critical of the media. "The media clearly played a monstrous role in this thing. They played on the emotions and Marcel, because it served his own purpose, used the media and the emotions to his advantage." Prévost complained of "half truths and mistruths" that were circulated, especially as they related to the possibility of the team leaving Quebec. "That was never *intended*," he argued. "It was never written in the contract by anyone, including that mysterious buyer with whom the company had signed the deal. And yet that was the major point around which all of the media coverage focused." The media, he believed, "did not play their normal objective, journalistic role. They took sides, clearly."

But he could have expected nothing else. Under the deal that Carling O'Keefe accepted, the team could leave Quebec. That may not have been *intended* by the brewery, but once the sale was finalized and Carling O'Keefe had become "former" owner, it could not prevent a move from happening. Moreover, Carling O'Keefe had agreed to a sale to someone who had an arguable reason to move the team – he was a non-Quebecer. Carling O'Keefe, itself, could have moved the team out of Quebec. Aubut or any subsequent owner could do the same. But the people knew them, they knew their ties to Quebec. And mostly, they knew that if any of them ever tried to move the team, the cost to Carling O'Keefe in lost beer sales, to Aubut and his partners in lost reputation and business, would be so great as likely not to be worth it. But what about an unknown buyer, and a non-Quebecer at that? What hold did they have on him? What power over him could they exercise? No one knew, so everyone was afraid.

These matters were the real focus of the media coverage and the public reaction that ensued. They were easily predictable and not over-wrought. Carling O'Keefe may have saved the Nordiques from going bankrupt in 1976, it may have financed the team through its merger into the NHL and to competitive respectability, but it put the team's future in Quebec at risk by selling the team in the way and to whom it did. The people understood. Carling O'Keefe got the reaction it deserved.

It was Prévost's job to try to gain some control over public opinion and turn it around. He told anyone who would listen – "Given the importance of the Nordiques as an institution in Quebec City, and their importance to O'Keefe as a promotional vehicle, why would O'Keefe, in its right mind, ever consider selling to someone who one year from now or three years from now would take the team and move it to Binghamton or wherever? It doesn't make any sense. We don't sell beer in Binghamton." His logic was impeccable, but so was that of his listeners. "Why did you sell the team to non-Quebecers?" they wanted to know.

Meanwhile, Marcel Aubut and his followers, operating out of their self-described "war room," went out in search of the money they needed to match the accepted offer. Much of it just found them. Telegrams, faxes, phone calls, big amounts, small amounts, personal money as well as corporate money, the pledges came in. Few questions were asked – if you need it, you've got it. A threat existed, survival was at issue, and Quebecers responded. "I could have raised $500 million at that point," Aubut recalls with a storyteller's wonder. Twenty-eight days and counting, but for Aubut things were beginning to look good.

On Wednesday morning, two days after Aubut's press conference, Lise Bacon, deputy premier and member of the Quebec National Assembly, announced that while the provincial government would not buy the team, it would intervene in any transaction that might endanger the future of the Nordiques in Quebec. More importantly, that same day Ed Prévost announced that the "mysterious purchaser" had withdrawn his offer and henceforth Carling O'Keefe would sell the team only to Quebecers. He explained that the new buyer had quickly come to realize in the few days since Aubut's press conference that things would not be easy for him. He could see himself arriving on the scene "being booed by the town, being criticized, being boycotted at the Colisée," as Prévost put it. "The value of the franchise overnight had gone down tremendously from what he had agreed to pay for it and he probably came to the conclusion that there was no future for him in Quebec. And that if he had any insidious plan to move the franchise, it would be much more difficult to accomplish it under the circumstances."

Others, including Aubut, explained the withdrawal differently. They believe that Carling O'Keefe, to save its Nordiques-enhanced market share in the province, paid the "mysterious purchaser" to withdraw his offer. No matter. Seventy-two hours after it had begun, the drama was over. The team was saved. The Nordiques would stay in Quebec. But for Aubut, the drama was just beginning.

If there was no offer, no clock was ticking. No right of *préemption* was in motion nor would it be until the next offer came in. Aubut's inside track was gone. He was now in competition for the Nordiques with every other Quebecer and now with no ceiling price to match. He would have to compete on an open market that might push the price of the team beyond his means.

Moreover, if there was no *external* threat, if survival was no longer at issue, the telegrams, faxes, and phone calls would, and did, stop coming in. He had helped save the team for Quebec, but now he would need to save it for himself. He feared that task might be even tougher.

Aubut was afraid that Carling O'Keefe would pay him back for his disloyalty (after years of loyalty) in the way that would hurt him the most – by selling the team, his team, to someone else. Instead, Carling O'Keefe, tired and bloodied, had lost its stomach for the fight and, without much prodding, gave him a period of exclusivity to put together his financing and make his offer. On November 29, the sale of the Nordiques was announced. The new owners were *Quebecers*, led by Marcel Aubut. Also on November 29, Carling O'Keefe announced that the Toronto Argonauts of the Canadian Football League had been sold to – guess who? – Harry Ornest.

The new owners of the Nordiques include: La Mutuelle des Fonctionnaires du Québec (MFQ) through their subsidiary, La Capitale Compagne d'Assurance, an insurance company; a large supermarket chain, La Groupe Métro-Richelieu; Les Fonds de Solidarité des Travailleurs du Québec (FTQ), the venture capital arm of the Quebec Federation of Labour, a labour union; Dai-showa Inc., a Japanese pulp and paper company which had recently acquired Reed International Paper, Quebec City's largest private-sector employer; and Société Autil, a partnership created specifically for this venture by Aubut and Quebec businessman Marcel Dutil. Each of the partners contributed about $3 million to the purchase price. Carling O'Keefe retained 5 per cent ownership of the team and promotional rights, including options, for a period of up to sixteen years.

The partners knew they would realize little *directly* from their investment in the Nordiques. Instead, each got involved because each had a stake in the Quebec City community and because, like Carling O'Keefe, each had something else to sell. Beer drinkers watch hockey and so do unionized workers. Les Fonds de Solidarité needs more of its workers to invest more of their money in its venture capital fund. It thinks an association with the Nordiques can help. Provigo, Métro-Richelieu's biggest supermarket competitor, had been the Nordiques' largest sponsor. Now as one of the owners, Métro-Richelieu can make the Nordiques *their* promotional tool. The company is already strong in the eastern part of the province. As Marcel Guertin, chairman of Métro-Richelieu, puts it, "If we were to acquire, as we believe very strongly we will, a few points of market share in the east of the province, that would be more than satisfactory for us. This would mean an additional many millions of dollars in sales. And if we were only to protect what we already have, it would almost be an achievement because today in our business, it's a struggle for life." Is buying a part of the Nordiques a good deal, he was asked? "It is surely a good deal."

For La Capitale, its new association with the Nordiques probably will not sell much insurance, but it does help to protect the company's investments in Quebec City. "The Quebec area is a very strong market in which we're pretty successful," says Jacques Labreque, president of La Capitale. "We believe the team brings important economic benefits and helps to keep the economy of the area growing."

About forty years ago, Anglo-Canadian Pulp and Paper Mills Ltd. launched the Quebec Aces, the city's top hockey team, and employed many of its players. (The name, "Aces," in fact was an acronym for "Anglo-Canadian Employees.") Later, the company was acquired by Reed Paper, which came to play a major role in Quebec City's economy until it in turn was bought by Daishowa only a short time before. Daishowa had an image problem. As Aubut explains, "People see the Japanese buying everything, and they get scared. The Japanese control so much." Daishowa needed a way to show a friendly and human face to the Quebec community and let its varied publics – government officials, other businesses, and its own employees – know that it intended to continue to be involved in the Quebec community. Daishowa was buying image. And as Aubut put it, "There's no way it could afford to buy it in any other way in so short a time."

The price for each new owner was not great, and using the available favourable tax schemes it cost them even less. As for Société Autil, the other partners got involved because of Aubut. If he wasn't going to put some of his money into the venture, neither were they. He did it, with partner Marcel Dutil, through Société Autil.

"I made a hell of a deal," Marcel Aubut said, grinning one of his full-bodied grins. The unknown purchaser from outside Quebec, Carling O'Keefe's secrecy, the "revolution of Quebecers," as Aubut likes to describe it, the threat of loss of market share – "that's why we got the team for peanuts compared to its real value. I would say today that any NHL franchise is worth more than $25 million Canadian, and that includes Quebec. We just made a good deal." Then swapping his nationalist's cloak for his more neatly tailored businessman's garb, his smile grows even wider. "It's not a bad thing to make a good deal," he laughs.

When Ed Prévost thinks back on the experience, one lesson comes to mind. "I think we have to be honest with the people," he says. "We can't do things in cloak and dagger. I mean, we're a brewery, we're very high profile, particularly in this province. We're involved in every facet of people's lives through community events, sports, and what have you. We have to play it very open, very transparently with people all the time. If the company, for its own reasons, which we could very easily justify, desired to dispose of 95 per cent of the Nordiques, then we should have come out publicly and said so, not come out in the way we did and create a stir and a surprise that we were selling the team, because the fans and people of Quebec at large have as much at stake in the team, if not a bigger stake in the team, than we do. We would not have had the population in a rage at what was happening and it could have been a very open, democratic deal and no one would have been hurt in the process. As it happens, the end result gave us the equivalent of that, but we could have easily done without the preliminaries."

"When you own something," Aubut said, "it's easy to say, 'Hey, I'm the boss. I'll sell what I want.' But in a small place like Quebec, people all feel they own this team, and when you own something, you take care of it. That's what Carling forgot. They treated the Nordiques like any other asset they might sell. They didn't realize they owned it but they didn't at the same time. The people owned it, too. They were only sharing ownership. I'll tell you, it's tough to learn that."

Carling O'Keefe forgot that today's sports franchise is a part-nership, a *team*. After being a good partner and team player for more than a decade, it treated the Nordiques as if it was its sole owner, selling to whomever it chose without any consultation with its partners. But it paid a price only because enough fans cared enough, because Carling O'Keefe, unlike most titled owners, was vulnerable to counterattack on its other assets, because the team was not yet gone, as Gretzky was, and because Quebecers know how to fight. But in the business of sport, no team is forever secure.

Together, Aubut and his partners paid about $15 million Canadian for the Nordiques, less than Bruce McNall was about to pay for just one player.

A few weeks before the trade, Mark Messier began to hear rumours. "I just laughed at them," he said, "because in my mind, well everybody thought there was no way it could ever happen." So he called Gretzky. Gretzky told him that a trade was possible. "I said to myself, 'Wow, this is pretty serious,'" he recalls, "but still I didn't think it would ever happen. I mean, it's unbelievable."

Messier called Gretzky again the day before the trade. Gretzky wasn't in, and Messier left a message for him to call. He said it was important. Gretzky recalls, "I remember my wife saying, 'You should call Mark. I think you owe it to him.' And I told her, 'If I call him back, then I won't be able to go through with it. Because everything I'd talk to Mark about, all the memories, all the thoughts I've ever had, all the good things, will come to the surface, and all the reasons, all the bad things that are in my mind right now, why I want to go through with the trade, will be wiped out.' So I never called him back."

On August 8, at about midnight, McNall called Gretzky. "I said, 'Wayne, we're done. Let's go to Edmonton.'"

They left the next morning at seven o'clock. When they landed in Edmonton, the first place Gretzky went was Messier's house. "He was pretty shaken up," Messier remembers. "He had a tough time dealing with, well, the whole Edmonton thing and what we had here. You don't forget those things. Very rarely in a lifetime are you part of something like we were. There are players that will play the rest of their lives, and thousands more who'll play after us and never even come close to the feelings we've had – as a team, as an organization, as friends. I mean, you just don't get those chances. And Wayne had a hard time dealing with that, the friendships, the city, just everything. At that point, I don't think he really knew whether the trade was going to happen or not."

Gretzky called some other of his teammates to let them know, and to explain. Later, he met with Pocklington and Sather. They asked him one more time if he was certain this is what he wanted, that the whole thing could still be called off. "But as I said to them," Gretzky recalls, "I said, 'It's like the Polish fellow who swims halfway across the lake and says I'm tired, and swims back. What am I supposed to do now?' I mean, it was a kind of funny situation – 'We've traded you for $15 million but you don't have to do this.' I said, 'This doesn't make a lot of sense to me.'"

A few minutes later, McNall called him aside and asked him the same thing. "Obviously from my standpoint," McNall explains, "Wayne's happiness, both from a business perspective and a personal one, was paramount."

" 'You have a great tradition here,' " Gretzky remembers McNall saying. " 'Great history, good friendships. If you don't want to come to L.A., I'll understand. I'll back out right now. I want you to be happy.' "

Then Gretzky took a deep breath. "That's when I looked at him and said, 'That's why I want to go to L.A.'"

Rumours swirled around Edmonton all day. Gretzky had been traded, a press conference had been called. But few would believe it. It defied every sense, every logic. It was like telling a caveman that the world is round. The stretch of imagination was too great; only seeing would be believing. In this case, only the words from Gretzky's lips would make it true.

It was true.

Pocklington spoke first. "It is with mixed emotions and a heavy heart for our community and our hockey club, but . . . with delight and sincere best wishes for Wayne Gretzky, that I

announce . . . that the Edmonton Oilers have agreed to trade
Wayne Gretzky to the Los Angeles Kings." With that, Pocklington officially ended the most successful association in NHL history. He went on to explain the reasons for the trade. "As all of
you are aware, Wayne was married this summer to a very
special young woman. Anyone involved in a committed relationship who wants to have a family knows that changes are brought
about by marriage. This is why, despite a tremendous amount of
trepidation, I truly understood when Wayne approached me and
asked that he be traded to the Los Angeles Kings.

"He wants to spend more time with Janet and begin their
family life under one roof, in one city, and be able to call it
home. Let's face it, despite the obvious pluses, it is not the easiest
thing to be Mr. and Mrs. Wayne Gretzky.

"The best comparisons I can draw to this situation are these:
what to do when an outstanding, loyal employee approaches you
as an employer and asks for an opportunity to move along for
logical and understandable reasons. In an emotional sense, you
know you don't want to lose him. But at the same time, you
don't want to stop him from pursuing his dreams and achieving
his goals. Wayne has given so much to our hockey club and to
this city for the last decade, I believe he has earned the right to
determine his own destiny in the National Hockey League.

"The situation also might be compared to a son or daughter
advising their parents of the desire to leave the house, to go to
university or to take a job. Your heart says 'no,' but at the same
time, your head understands and says 'yes.' "

And so, Pocklington concluded, "I put aside my emotions and
out of deep personal respect for Wayne, I made a decision based
more on Wayne the person than Wayne the hockey player."

His tone was soft and sympathetic, almost grandfatherly.
When he finished, it was as if he turned instantly to stone. His
face grew tight and, though finding a seat next to the microphone where he had just been, his being retreated into the
shadows and out of that room as far away from the people there
as he could go. He had said his piece. As owner of the team, it
was a right that could not be denied him. He had said all he
wanted to say in just the way he wanted to say it. Yet he knew

that few believed him. He could sense that those present were only marking time, taping him, jotting down notes later to trap him with the truth when it came out, as it surely would. The mood in the room said: *It is just Pocklington saying what Pocklington would say. Now let's get on with it.*

Gretzky then moved forward to the bank of microphones. "I approached Mr. Pocklington about the possibility of playing with another hockey club. I was still young enough and capable enough of helping a new franchise win the Stanley Cup. Mr. Pocklington met my request and let Mr. McNall chat with me directly and, after spending some time with him, [I] decided that for the benefit of Wayne Gretzky, my new wife, and our expected child in the new year, that it would be beneficial for everyone involved to let me play with the Los Angeles Kings. I'm disappointed about having to leave Edmonton. I truly admire all the fans and respect everyone over the years, but . . ." With that, Gretzky began to break down. For several seconds, he fought to regain control. "It's coming back . . ." he assured his audience. "So, as I said," he began again. Again, he broke down. Finally, he said, "I promised Mess I wouldn't do this." He tried again. "But as I said, there comes a time . . ." He couldn't finish. Moments later, he got up and left the microphones. The assembled journalists applauded.

Sather moved in front of the microphones, a different Glen Sather than most had ever seen before. Gone was his chippy self-assurance. He tried only once to put a smirky smile on things – "and I know that in a couple of days I'm gonna work my hardest to try to find a way of beating the hell out of the Los Angeles Kings." But he did not have the heart to keep it up; he was sombre and serious. Gretzky continued to dab at his eyes. Pocklington had gone rigid. The immensity of what they had done had hit home; they didn't look like cowboys anymore.

A few hours later, Gretzky had to do it all over again at a press conference in Los Angeles. It had been "very quiet" on the plane ride down, McNall remembers. But by the time they landed, Gretzky's mood had picked up. It was important to both of them that Gretzky face the Los Angeles media with the look of excitement and challenge in his eyes. He had to seem happy, it had to seem a joyous occasion, for the people of Los Angeles and for Kings' fans. After all, this was the pivotal moment in the transformation of the Kings that both Gretzky and McNall were trying to achieve. At no other time would they have such attention. They had to make the best of it.

And Gretzky pulled it off, as Gretzky does. It was a remarkable achievement. In the space of a few hours he had to get across to two very differently interested parties his deep ambivalence about the trade. He had to allow the mood of each place to be his mood, to be appropriately sad in Edmonton, leaving behind friends and loyal fans, leaving behind a special team of players, leaving behind a time of his life he can never repeat. In Los Angeles, he had to be appropriately excited, for this was now his new life. He could manage it so well because he was expressing his real feelings.

It had been a "sad to go . . . great to be here" day. And many hours after it had begun, it finally was over. The selling of Gretzky in Los Angeles had begun.

The reaction to the trade in Canada was predictable, but the reaction in the U.S. was not. It was front-page news even in New Orleans, where George Bush was accepting the Republican nomination for president of the United States. The U.S. media knew the Gretzky name, they knew *he* was important, and so they treated his story the way other stories about identifiably important people get treated. He became water-cooler conversation for people who had never seen him play, who until one day before had paid him no interest. And for those in Los Angeles, he became a reason to look at the Kings one more time, to give them one last chance.

Back in Canada, the visible public response brought few surprises. There were front-page banner headlines in most of the major newspapers and comments made by government figures. There were death threats for Pocklington and threats of public boycott of products made by other Pocklington companies. The word "treason" was heard. People felt so strongly they seemed to be searching for some context in which to understand what had happened. To some, it was just another example of Canadian natural resources moving south to the U.S. Many saw the Gretzky trade as a galvanizing symbol for the anti-free trade side in the Canadian debate then being waged over trade with the U.S. It would have no such impact.

In the end, when Canadians had time to catch up with their feelings, mostly, it seemed, they just felt sad. It is the feeling of loss one gets when one's illusions have taken a pummelling. The trade may be explainable, it may even be understandable – it's just not right.

Perhaps, one single image put best for Canadians the emotion and dimensions of the trade. In the *Edmonton Sun*, the day after the trade, the front page showed a close-up picture of Gretzky dabbing one eye with a tissue, and over the picture in huge letters was the caption, "99 TEARS!" Across the bottom of the page, the newspaper previewed its own coverage of the story in its inside pages: "Pages: 2, 3, 4, 5, 6, 10, 18, 19, 23, 30, 36, 37, 38, 39, 40, 41, 42, 43, 46 and 47."

The team, the Edmonton partnership that had brought Stanley Cup success and fortune, had broken up. It did not need to happen. Indeed, what makes its story so compelling is that at almost every step, all that was going on could have been turned on its ear and another story, just as plausible and with a far different ending, could have been written in its place. This was not a bad marriage. Neither party had to get out physically or psychologically to save itself. There were powerful reasons for things to go on almost as they had been. Even if each detail of breakdown took on a logic of its own, in its bigger picture, the whole thing, as Messier put it, seemed "unbelievable."

Yet really it was a case of two classic, well-matched antagonists, the archetypal owner and the archetypal modern player, engaged in the dance of contemporary sports. Who owns? Who controls? In this age of spiralling money, how do the titled owner, the player, and fan live with each other? Only the dimensions of one of its characters, Gretzky, only the sports backdrop, made this drama different from countless others, made it more than a routine business deal.

The owner-player-fans relationship is evolving. Depending on the sport, the country, and the titled owner, it moves slowly or occasionally a little faster. But by law, equity, expectation, and the reality of entertainment/sports and the power of the star, it is moving in the direction of the professional sports franchise as a partnership, as *the team*. For those sports such as hockey, where players have little control over their careers, the cards remain mostly in the hands of owners more adept at resisting than accommodating. Faced with changing circumstances, few of them adapt well.

Though Gretzky had the NHL's custom and structure against him, he had come to own himself through the power of his own performance. He negotiated a free agency contract *without* compensation from Pocklington. If he had been unable to prevent his own trade, at least he was able to intervene and determine to whom he would be traded and, to some extent, with and for whom he was traded. He could go to a team that needed him so desperately, and needed him to be content, that he could sell himself at a dramatically higher price.

In return, he had to be *professional*. He had to put aside life's disruptions, leaving behind old teammates and friends, exchanging one home for another, and overcome the distractions of life-securing money and memories of a past that cannot be recovered. And he had to produce – like a lawyer or doctor or any hired hand, to give a day's work for a day's pay, no matter the circumstances. No excuses. He didn't have to be above emotion, but he had to control it. He would need to feel loyalty toward new teammates and coaches but not be dependent on them. Above all, he had to be loyal to himself, to his own reputation, standards, and legacy. Few people can do it; few free agents have ever pulled it off. Gretzky did.

The rest is detail. Wayne Gretzky moved south to Los Angeles and his magic went with him. It was far from clear that it would. Gretzky was used to having star players around him, people who shared his need to do things right and all the time, who found real satisfaction in the achievement of only one goal – a Stanley Cup. How would he react to the rutted mediocrity of the Kings? He needed to make every one of their players better. Instead, wouldn't the sheer weight of twenty other players make him worse? "I knew I wouldn't let myself down," he said, with quiet steel in his voice, "because I knew I'd push everybody else. I was going to bust my rear end and I knew I'd make everyone else do the same. And I knew that on paper there were some talented people there." His eyes brightened, "And I loved the thought of the situation, of the pressure, going down to L.A. where people said hockey won't go."

And how did Gretzky react to Los Angeles? Since he was six or seven years old, a spotlight had always followed him. In Brantford, Sault Ste. Marie, and Edmonton, he had been the centre of his own world. He was the biggest act in town. In L.A. it would be different, with the Dodgers, the Lakers, the Rams and Raiders, USC, UCLA, Magic Johnson, Kareem Abdul Jabbar, Orel Hershiser, all the big names of movies and music. L.A.'s centre stage was a glut of stars. What light was left for him? A great star needs a great ego. He needs to feel important. In Los Angeles Gretzky might wither and die.

The Kings needed Gretzky to become important in L.A. The trade made front-page news and put him on Johnny Carson's *Tonight Show*, but no one in L.A. can remain in that kind of spotlight day after day. What would keep Gretzky talked about and current, in people's minds if not always on their screens? For as with other great stars, that is far more telling.

The answer was simple enough – winning. Great stars must make great movies. No one survives too many bad ones.

Gretzky found he could compete for the attention of centre stage. He also found a measure of control and normalcy in L.A. that had been missing from his life for more than a decade. In Canada, he said, "Open a newspaper, and it's all about hockey. Go to the back page and you learn about every other team in the NHL, their injuries or their problems. It's all hockey. Turn on the TV, half-hour sports shows, it's all hockey. Open your window, kids are on the streets, they're playing hockey. And it's like this ten months a year, which is great. But now it's different to get the newspaper and be able to come up to the house, set it on the table, and not see my name on the front page. It's nice. And yet I can open the paper and see hockey in there, but it's not thrown in your face constantly. In Canada, I always felt like people were watching me, you know, staring. It's nice to be able to sit down at a table in a restaurant and know that no one has a clue who I am or what I'm doing. It's funny, because one of the reasons I moved away from home at fourteen was because the pressure and the focus on me in Brantford got to be so enormous. I didn't move to Toronto to become a hockey player. I moved to Toronto to become another person, to become a grade nine student like everyone else was. My two years in Toronto were two of the happiest years of my life because, for the first year, no one had any idea I was a hockey player. And I just wanted to see what it was like to be like everyone else. Coming down here was very similar to that. I left the city where there was an enormous amount of pressure, a tremendous spotlight, and have come to a bigger city where I can kind of blend in and be one of the crowd." He still craves attention as all great stars do, yet now, it seems, he has it both ways. At L.A.'s Great Western Forum and wherever he goes on the road, the spotlight of importance is on him. But the rest of the time in L.A., with its size and busy-ness and glut of stars, he has his refuge.

With each year that passes, with the self-assurance that one more year of success brings, Gretzky is earning control of his life. No longer is he "Canada's natural resource" but his own. And now he has an owner, Bruce McNall, who treats him as a partner, not as Peter Pocklington did, as an imaginary son.

In L.A., he is also beginning to spread his wings. As player, motivator, inspirational leader and symbol, partner of and adviser to the owner, salesman for the game of hockey in southern California, the western half of the United States, and the U.S. in general. He now sees what he never had to see, isolated in Canada's hockey heartland. He now senses far better the state of the game in the U.S., not just its gate receipts and sold-out arenas, but how it plays on Mainstreet. And he has changed his mind.

"We always talk about people who come to the games to see the fighting. And I was one of the ones who believed that. I live in California now. I live in Los Angeles and I'm telling you I get tired of turning on the TV and hearing an announcer say – 'I was at a football game and a hockey game broke out' – where you see two guys wrestling around on the ground. We have such a poor image in California and the United States just because we allow fighting. We don't need it anymore. They talk about people coming to games because of the fighting, I wonder if they've ever done an analysis on how many people *don't* come just because of fighting. People who don't want their kids to see it. I know, in California, there's a lot. The people who come to their first game – and I know a lot have seen their first game this year – they come up to me after a game and say, 'Boy, this is the most exciting, the greatest sporting event I've ever seen,' and have gone right up and bought season tickets. Just like that. Because before they'd been led astray, the image and all. They thought the game was totally different, just from hearsay on the streets, and on TV and in the papers. We gotta get rid of fighting, simple as that."

To Gretzky, fighting is not a psychological or sociological question. It is not a matter of understanding human nature and human behaviour. Fighting in hockey has nothing to do with whether violence releases the drive for further violence (and so fighting means less stick swinging and is therefore constructive), or whether violence only breeds more violence. The endless argument of whether fighting is in the nature of hockey – in its speed, enclosed ice surface, the sticks players carry, the collisions – or in its culture is irrelevant. To the NHL, now to Gretzky, fighting is an economic issue pure and simple. Does it fill seats or not?

For more than a decade, the NHL fought financial wars triggered by competition from the once rival WHA. Several franchises found themselves on shaky ground; the league sought stability and security. Now, the words "expansion" and "growth" are being heard again. "Opportunity," not stability, is the new vision. What Gretzky is saying in so many words is that people will continue to fill arena seats just as they always have, whether fighting continues or not. The real opportunity is "Mainstreet," the extended fan. The challenge is to fill *living-room* seats all over the U.S., to get channel flippers, who for years at the sight of hockey have flipped on by as fast as they could, to stop and look again. To give hockey another chance. Cable television, "pay per view" – that's where the real financial opportunity lies. But how do you fight the image that has triggered a nation of impatient thumbs? You don't do it with the subtleties of minor rule changes that only "discourage" fighting. You get rid of fighting, "simple as that." Then you have something to sell.

Then the atmosphere that surrounds and pervades the NHL can change. For years the league has operated as if burdened by a deep dark secret it cannot shed, that will not go away. And the secret is deep enough and dark enough that if the league ventures into the light of day, the secret will be found out. So it hides and hopes the world will go away. Games are not a problem; the NHL owns the image that reaches into the living room. Newspaper game stories are also fine. They come and go and, with so many things to cover and so little space and time, little can hit the mark. It is the U.S. big-city columnists and commentators that the league fears, that deal with hockey only on occasion, that need and look for some excuse and find it, always it seems, in bad news, pandering to the image that is already there. These commentators affect public opinion. Their bad news is bad enough; worse is the airless sails they leave behind. The NBA is out there selling; major-league baseball, the NFL, the World Wrestling Federation, and so on and so on, they are all selling hard, but the moment the NHL starts to sell, it gets a two-hander from some sacrosanct columnist and retreats back into its deep, dark, comfortable offices to lick its wounds.

Gretzky is saying that isn't good enough any more. Shut out the secret, go and hide, but the world will just lie in waiting. It is time to come out of closeting offices and into the light, literally and psychologically. It is time to sell. But for selling you need an audience, and for opportunity you need access to the non-hockey fans. Those audiences will pay hockey no more attention until fighting is abolished. Only then will columnists, commentators, and channel flippers stop and look again.

Gretzky knows he has a huge stake in the state of hockey. In so many words, he told Peter Pocklington and he has worked out with Bruce McNall – I am a partner in this game. Whatever decisions you make affect me. Fighting in hockey keeps U.S. living-room watchers from watching. Living-room watchers buy T-shirts and posters and commercial products I might endorse. Everyone who doesn't watch hockey means money out of my pocket and an opportunity lost. Fighting *is* an economic issue, just as you have always said, but not just for you, the league and its owners, but for the players as well. And now, if ever, it makes no sense.

In L.A., Gretzky pushed his teammates and made them better; the Kings won games; the people of L.A. came out to watch them play; more watched them on television as well. They bought more hot dogs and beer, more sweatshirts and T-shirts, more key rings, posters, and pennants, and they had more fun doing it. Gretzky earned more money; McNall came close to paying off his $15-million gamble in *one* year, not four or five. Did the fans feel bitter, resentful, envious at the good fortune of Gretzky and McNall? *Good for them*, they said. *More power to them. They had produced*. That's what mattered, that's all that mattered.

Never has L.A. hockey done so much business. Never has business seemed to matter less. Together Gretzky and McNall made the business of sports work.

If *the team* is alive and well in Los Angeles, in Edmonton it is not. After the trade, sad and frustrated Oilers fans looked for a way to fight back. A few turned in their season tickets but most could not bring themselves to stay away from the games. It would mean hurting themselves again, in trying to hurt Pocklington, and they loved the team too much. But one brand of meat or dairy product, like one brand of beer, is pretty much like every other. They hit back instead at Gainer's Inc. and Palm Dairies, two of Pocklington's other businesses. Yet, unlike the fearsome threat of boycott that built up in Quebec, this one never really picked up steam. Perhaps Albertans lack the survivalist's instincts and fighting experience of Quebecers. Perhaps they just lost heart, for Gretzky was gone and, unlike the Nordiques, no matter how much they punished Pocklington, nothing would bring him back.

There was talk of the players staging a strike or boycott themselves, but nothing seemed to come of it. Ahead, though, was a messy, joyless season. Their bodies filled out their orange-blue-and-white uniforms, they moved up and down the ice much the same way, but emotionally and psychologically it was as if they boycotted the season. The players felt betrayed.

"We definitely had a chance to go on winning for quite a few more years," the Oilers' new captain, Mark Messier, said midway through the season, the frustration in his voice just starting to build. "I mean, when you've got the energy and the chemistry and have everything it takes to do it," he stops himself. He can't quite find the words that sound like what he feels. "I mean, there've been only three teams in the last thirteen years that have won the Stanley Cup. Why? Because very rarely, very, very rarely do you get the right chemistry at the right time, the right players, just the right *everything* to win the championship. When you got it, you don't get rid of it." His voice had grown softer, more intent, more confused and wistful and sad and disbelieving.

A player has only a few years to be a player. He gets no second chance. When the trade comes to pay off for Peter Pocklington, if it ever does, it will be a few years from now when Jimmy Carson and Martin Gelinas are at the peaks of their careers and when L.A.'s first-round draft picks arrive to make their mark. By then Messier will be gone, and so will Lowe and Fuhr and Kurri and Glenn Anderson, or they all will be in the lingering years of their careers. At best, in trading Gretzky, Pocklington made a pact to secure the future of the Edmonton Oilers. But Messier knows that is somebody else's Oilers.

In Messier's chilling-to-the-bone stare, there is hurt. *We could've been the best of all time*, it says. *Four Stanley Cups in five years, who knows how many more we could have won. Better than the Canadiens, better than the Islanders and Leafs. The best.* In ten or fifteen years a player's career is gone, over. The memories, the past achievements, take its place. No one can take those away.

But Pocklington did, and the players never forgave him. Many of them had started together, almost grown up together: Messier, Lowe, Fuhr, Kurri, Huddy, Anderson, Randy Gregg, Gretzky. They got excited together as young and promising kids, getting better, winning more often, making personal breakthroughs, feeling "specialness" come closer and closer.

They got frustrated together when, on the verge of greatness, they fell just short and began to wonder if their time would ever come. Then they became the best together. They thought of themselves as a team like no other – ever. "There are players that will play the rest of their lives, and thousands more who'll play after us and never even come close to the feelings we've had." Messier's words echo and re-echo. The players had a bond that Sather encouraged. It made them strong. In a very real sense, they developed a "cult of team." "We spent ten years," Gretzky recalls, "all of us, in our contract negotiations, saying 'Okay, I'll take a little less just to keep the tradition and dynasty going.' We weren't greedy. We wanted to stay together."

It all blew apart with the Gretzky trade. The bond was to an idea, to a feeling they had about themselves and what they represented. But when Gretzky left and Pocklington got his money, it was over, done, gone. They felt stupid, like all of those years hadn't been what they had seemed, like they had all been taken in. And to an extent that surprised them, they discovered just how central Gretzky was to that bond. He was the cypher. The interrelationships seemed always to come from him, to him, winding in and around him, like a thread in a sweater, just one of many, but the only one that wends its way from the waist to the neck to the shoulders and wrists. At a casual glance it may look only a little more important than the others. Remove it, and everything unravels.

In 1988-89, the group collapsed. Their skills remained, so frustratingly they looked the same, but psychologically they had come apart. Jari Kurri had spent his NHL career the beneficiary of Gretzky's genius. He is from Finland and between seasons he returns to his native country. Whether because of language, culture, custom, or personality, he had always remained a little separate from his teammates and their "cult of team." Interestingly, in 1988-89, less dependent psychologically on the team, Kurri coped best.

Peter Pocklington likes to describe himself as an entrepreneur and self-made man. There is something quite solitary about him that is clear in his instincts and drives. He is Tom Wolfe's "single combat warrior," the guy who needs the freedom to act alone, unconstrained by governments, structures, rules and regulations, and other people. He does not understand interrelationships and group dynamics. To him, they seem only to slow him down, hold him back, complicate his life. He doesn't understand the nature and feeling of working together. He doesn't understand a team. He thought he could trade Gretzky and, for the players and fans, if not quite the same, everything would be fine. He doesn't understand *the team*.

In return for Gretzky, Marty McSorley, and Mike Krushelnyski, Pocklington received Jimmy Carson, Martin Gelinas, Craig Redmond, the Kings' first draft picks in 1989, 1991, and 1993, and $15 million U.S. He argued that the trade was made to accommodate Gretzky and to secure the future of the Oilers. There were some, at the time, who agreed with what he had done. But what happened to the $15 million? "Well, a lot of it is still in the Edmonton Oilers," says Pocklington. "There's a war chest there that if there's ever an opportunity, believe me, it will be used for the team." Pocklington also says, "Obviously, the amount of money I received in the trade goes into other situations, creating other jobs, creating other wealth in Alberta. You know, I'm an entrepreneur. I love to create wealth. I love not only to play the game of hockey, but to watch other businesses grow. And it hasn't gone into bonds. It's gone into business. It's gone into where it's going to do a lot of people a lot of good."

If Pocklington had used the $15 million to buy other players or draft picks for the team instead of acting as the bad partner and stripping the money off for other purposes, the Gretzky trade would be only a trade, good or bad, endlessly arguable, and nothing more. But today, the Edmonton Oilers, the partnership, *the team*, is $15 million poorer than it was August 8, 1988, the day before the trade was made. This is Pocklington's smoking gun.

The North American economies are fuelled by selling, which requires an audience, and sport is able to attract that audience. The business of sport develops from there. North Americans also have a seemingly quenchless desire for entertainment. Movies, theatre, music, sports, TV – it doesn't matter if a person can sing or act or catch a ball himself, if the entertainment is good, if the setting is right, people will pay money and watch. And so hockey can sell in Los Angeles and ballet in Winnipeg. Never mind that hockey is a Canadian winter game that few Americans have ever played. If the Kings win, culture and climate don't matter much. The people will watch. And if the game is bad, turn up the lights and music and bring on the mascots and dancing girls. Add spectacle to sport to keep the fan in his seat, your seat. The entertainment competition is fierce. More and more people expect a guarantee of entertainment for their valuable time and money. If a game is unpredictable by nature, mediate it with fun and spectacle and maybe people will come back.

Sport as business began by selling itself, attracting ticket-buying fans to arenas and playing fields. Later, to the far greater audience that radio and TV brought, sports came to sell other products, consumer products mostly – beer, cars, gasoline – but also social values – good sportsmanship, good education, drug-free lives. Cities learned to sell themselves through sports. A major-league team, a new cathedral-like arena, a unique sporting event can gain a city priceless attention and sell the city to a national and international audience. It can mean thousands more vacationers and conventioneers, new businesses, and millions of outside dollars coming into a local economy.

Late in the nineteenth century, an aristocratic Frenchman, Pierre de Coubertin, brought back the ancient Greek pageant of the Olympic Games. He wanted, as he put it, to "rebronze" a French nation demoralized by war and decadence, to sell the French people a different set of values. Since then, Olympic host cities and countries every four years have bought the world's attention to offer their own messages. For Los Angeles in 1984 it was a chance to tell more than a billion TV viewers that "America/Capitalism Works." Calgary's message to the world during the 1988 Winter Olympics was that Canada, like the Games' mascots Heidi and Howdy, was "friendly and nice." For Seoul in 1988, the Olympics was a coming-out party – economically, now athletically, "Korea has arrived," the Games proclaimed.

Where is the next great opportunity for the business of

sports? If arenas cannot get too much bigger, nor much more filled; if the fan is close to the limits of what he will pay for his ticket; if TV audiences are more fragmented because of more channels, and each viewer's eyeballs are no more valuable to an advertiser than they were before – what next? The circle may close. The new focus of opportunity may be the old focus – the fan. How great the opportunity and how soon depends on new TV technologies and when they reach the average home. The operative terms are "pay per view" and "the extended arena."

The TV sports fan has traditionally watched for free the same game for which an arena fan may have paid $25. Disregarding middlemen along the way, the commercial transaction is essentially one between the owner of the event and the advertiser. The advertiser pays the event owner for access to the TV fan who will watch the event. The TV fan pays the advertiser's costs, passed along to him in the form of higher product prices, not for the game itself. "Pay per view" presupposes that the TV fan's "free" ride would be over. Like the arena fan, the TV fan would pay directly for every game watched.

The notion of "pay per view" has been around for many years, propelled by the logic of incredible financial opportunity, but has had little impact. TV viewing customs and expectations have been too hard to break. Only special events, notably boxing's championship fights, many special enough never to have been encompassed by free TV's customs, have found public acceptance on "pay per view." The question for every event owner is how to break that custom.

Many fans believe that slow-motion and replay cameras have made the TV game superior to watching the live game. Yet "pay per view" has gained no ground. The answer may be in new TV technologies – big screens, high-definition image, stereo sound, and such interactive possibilities as viewers being able to choose from a range of images what they want to see. These technologies, in turn, would transform the way sports are covered and presented: multiple split screens big enough to see, the narrative of the game on one screen, favourite players, personal dramas played out moment by moment on the others. The result would be a very different viewing experience, engaging enough perhaps and with a new enough look to break old customs and expectations and pave the way for "pay per view."

Listen to Bruce McNall, whose business is entertainment, as he talks about the business of sport, the future, and "pay per view." "Funnily enough, I think all sports are in their infancy in terms of exploiting their revenue potential. I can remember in 1979 when I first bought into the Dallas Mavericks of the NBA, the price of the franchise was $12 million and we thought that was the craziest thing we had ever heard in our lives. Now the NBA expansion price is $32.5 million and all the owners I've spoken to say that in hindsight that was way too low. Satellite television has not even begun yet. What happens with international satellite television, increased cable, or pay per view, for example.

"I was involved with Jerry Buss in the television cable rights for the Los Angeles area for the Sugar Ray Leonard-Thomas Hearns fight. It went pay per view and I think they were charging $30 or so for it. The revenues generated were enormous in just that one local area. So if you can imagine having three million subscribers to a cable system and your team reaches the Stanley Cup finals and you know that you can't get a ticket. So you pay $10 to sit and watch at home with your family or friends. It would be a great bargain. And if we penetrated only, say, 20 per cent of that audience of three million people, that's 600,000 homes at $10 a home – $6 million. If you go through, say, twenty-odd games in the playoffs, it's well over $100 million. That's just for television cable rights to the playoffs.

"I think what we're seeing now is that sports is a big business. Nothing is impossible in sports anymore. My God, when Madison Square Garden pays over $500 million to the Yankees for local cable television rights, what does that make a franchise worth today? That's why you're seeing more and more people looking to make more creative deals, not just to win, but for the economics. Who knows if you wouldn't find one day that the television demographics are such that 'x' number of viewers more will watch a team if you get a certain great player, and that might result in a $500-million contract with Madison Square

Garden. If you go out and pay $250 million for that guy, is that a good deal or a bad deal? It's a pretty doggone good deal. So nothing is impossible these days.

"That's why the Gretzky kind of deals are more and more possible. I'm sure one day we'll look back on this deal and say, 'My God, look how cheap he was back then. It's nothing.'" McNall shrugs, and smiles, "It's just now it seems like a lot of money."

Sport has become a big money game. It is big money that builds big arenas, that has taken hockey into our homes and made it a national passion. Big money allows players to work harder and longer to become better athletes and gives to the fans a better show. And big money fuels the instinct for ownership, the temptation to buy and sell, the urge to fight.

Every *thing* is for sale. Every *one* is for sale. Price, it seems, is the only question, be it Wayne Gretzky or the Quebec Nordiques. This is the story of business in motion, moving from smaller opportunity to bigger one, loyalties and traditions trapped in the middle. In our imaginations, sport still seems an idealized world. In our imaginations, we still believe that every *thing*, every *one*, is not for sale. So when sport behaves like real life, when the instinct to sell is stronger than the instinct to be loyal, it hurts. What Bruce McNall's excited eyes and soaring numbers convey is that in this big money game – *you ain't seen nothin' yet!*

CHAPTER FIVE

NO FINAL VICTORIES

I was less than 200 feet away. I remember things from just before and just after, but not then. I remember feeling no fear of losing, no desperation as the clock blinked down to series' end, no resignation over the all-but-certain tie. A year before, from the same distance away, I had seen Henri Richard's Stanley Cup-winning goal seconds before it happened. Clearly, absolutely. From where Esposito and Henderson, Liapkin and Tretiak were standing, from the position of the puck, I remember feeling no sudden rush of hope, no pattern that made me know what would happen next.

Then memory returns. Sprinting, tripping in bulky leg pads, my own whoops shouting in my ears – I remember being somewhere in the middle of Luzhniki's vacant ice dashing to catch the scrum of celebration near the Soviet net. Memory goes away before I reach the pile. It comes back again several seconds later, in the midst of the joyous pummelling. Stop, I hear myself say. Get a hold of yourself. There's still thirty-four seconds to go!

My next memory comes after the game is over. Finding a corner deep inside myself, grinning, burning with twenty-seven days of pleasure, disaster, and relief, I think to myself – wouldn't this have been great to watch at home! Can you believe what it must've been like. I mean, I would've gone crazy.

IT IS ONE OF THE THINGS THAT MAKES US DISTINCTLY CANADIAN, THIS memory. Not of one-room schoolhouses or clear, cool lakes, but where we were on a certain date when a fairly anonymous young man who had no right to be where he was did something unexpected in another country. The date was September 28, 1972. The time of day depended on where you were in Canada's vast stretch of time zones, and few will remember precisely. But all remember there were exactly thirty-four seconds to go. And most Canadians old enough to be aware will remember forever exactly where they were the moment Paul Henderson scored the goal that beat the Russians.

It is rare that a Canadian event has made time stand still, even for Canadians. There has always seemed a shortage of domestic "world-class" happenings – the sort of murders, invasions, crashes, sinkings, and other catastrophic or triumphant moments that cause people to take note of where they were and what they were doing when these happened. Many older Canadians remember where they were when Hitler invaded Poland, when Pearl Harbor was attacked, when the bomb was dropped on Hiroshima. They remember v-e Day, when the war in Europe came to an end. Everyone thirty-five or older remembers precisely where they were – perhaps even what was said – when John Kennedy was shot on November 22, 1963. The news of Kennedy's shooting struck Canada so fast it was possible to be aware not only that he had been shot, but at this very moment may lie dying, and created a personal mental snapshot of time and place.

For Canadians, there is only one wholly Canadian event that has left a similar trail of memory: Henderson's goal in Moscow, for all but 3,000 Canadians and a handful of hockey players, scored to the soaring, chilling accompaniment of Foster Hewitt.

"... *Cournoyer has it on that wing! Here's a shot! Henderson made a wild stab for it and fell. Here's another shot! Right in front! THEY SCORE!!! Henderson has scored for Canada! Henderson right in front of the net and the fans and the team are going wild. Henderson right in front of the Soviet goal with thirty-four seconds left in the game! ..."*

It is hard to explain the power of that memory to Canadians, perhaps now a majority, who are under twenty-five or who in 1972 lived outside Canada. It is hard to explain it even to those who were "there" and felt it at the time. It was just the end moment to a hockey series. Sure, it was the first time our best had played their best. Sure, hockey is part of the living, breathing culture of this country, and the unimaginable pattern of the series ended in an unimaginable way. Still, there must be more. The specifics of memory do not deliver the resonance of the feeling that lingers. Visual records are of little help. They show Canadian players, helmetless, long sideburned, and hairy, more as time-capsule curiosities, no more capable, surely less so, than today's heroes. The passing, quickness, and team play of the Soviets, such a sensation at the time, look routine to eyes accustomed to seventeen years of change. Only one goal, scored by Peter Mahovlich in the second game in Toronto, was of timeless quality and no saves were show-stoppers. Why all the fuss?

Foster Hewitt's voice offers some hint. Momentous, hollow with distance, filled with a sense of threat, it has a war-correspondent-at-the-front sound. It comes at us shouting over the action, over thousands of miles of space, quavering, crackling, breaking up, as it stretched to the limits of its strength and range, straining to be heard, never certain of getting through to the millions at home.

Visual images, but from off the ice, also help. They show 3,000 Canadians in the midst of Moscow's Cold-War grey. Wide ties or no ties at all, long hair, bright, colourful shirts and double-knit jackets, stripes and checks – some were not much different from today's affluent young event-seekers. But most were not much more than average Canadians, from Sarnia and Red Deer and Chicoutimi, banner-making, flag-waving hockey pilgrims in a strange land, just travelling the road to the next town as they had done for much of their lives, to be there with "the boys" when they were needed the most.

There is an innocence to the scene, to the time, that is more than nostalgia. It has to do with being there, watching, as Canada entered the world, jumping in with both feet, with un-Canadian confidence and enthusiasm because of our certainty of smashing, glorious victory, because it was hockey. Then we nearly drowned, but somehow we fought back and gained what had become an improbable victory. It has to do with being there when the Soviets were in full possession of their fantasies, their models, their promise, in full possession of the future. And it is looking back from the future to that moment and seeing where both of us have been and how we got here.

The year 1972 was a coming of age. This drama, the sweep of its story, the immensity of its theatre, makes it a Canadian memory.

The year 1946 was more notable than most in the history of the real world, let alone hockey. Things put on hold by six years of war finally got their chance. Lives had time to be rebuilt and redirected. Plans for the future could look ahead more than one day at a time. The United Nations held its first meeting; Dr. Benjamin Spock published his *Baby and Child Care*; the University of Pennsylvania produced an "electric brain" that would begin the computer revolution. In the not-so-real world, Uncle Remus sang "Zip-a-dee-doo-dah"; and the National Hockey League – thirty years old and down to those teams that would become known eventually as "the Original Six" – introduced player bonuses and synchronized goal lights. Hereafter, games would be officiated by one referee and two linesmen. The Montreal Forum and Maple Leaf Gardens were already state-of-the-art arenas, with cooling systems so sophisticated running beneath the ice that fans, often in the same clothes, were able to sit more comfortably in their Saturday night seats than in their Sunday morning pews. It was the beginning of hockey's modern era. Rocket Richard had already scored fifty goals in fifty games, a record that would survive for nearly forty years. Canadian hockey was entering its golden age.

Five thousand miles away, in that same year, 1946, the first-ever public hockey game was played in the Soviet Union, seventy-one years after Canada's first organized game in Montreal. It took place at Dynamo Stadium in Moscow, not in ice-palace splendour but outdoors on a bandy rink before thousands of standing, shuffling, frozen-footed fans.

Bandy, like field hockey on ice, had been played in the Soviet hinterland for generations. Eleven to a side with no substitutions, players skated over a huge expanse of ice carrying small crook sticks, manipulating a baseball-size ball of twine – painted bright orange, with cork in the centre – stickhandling it, with quick intricate passing plays moving it up ice, with hands together golfing it toward a net about half the size of a soccer goal.

The first Russian hockey game was a curious sight: players with long-bladed sticks and skates, their aviator-like helmets like those worn by "Red Barons" of another time; the wooden nets; bandy's six-inch-high boards over which, with an opponent's gentle nudge, the unsuspecting were tripped and sent sprawling; goalies who served their own penalties and, used to playing with stick-free hands as in bandy, who tossed aside their unwanted anchors to dive after every puck; shooters, accustomed to golfing at a bandy ball, unable to lift the flattened puck. "Zdenek Zikmund sent the puck into the air," a reporter for *Sovietsky Sport* felt compelled to note in an account of the game, so rare was the event.

Eight time zones away were the Rocket, Howe, Maple Leaf Gardens – it seemed an impossible, unbridgeable distance between that game and this. But if one looked more closely, beyond skates and helmets to the Soviet players' strong powerful strides, to their stickhandling and passing, there was a different message. These one-time bandy players had really played this game before.

But their challenge was enormous. It was the same challenge Soviet industry and agriculture had already faced for more than twenty years: how to catch up in a world with a head start many decades long. The Soviets needed a common direction. Having few resources – players, coaches, ice surfaces, equipment – they had to be efficient. Their response, as in industry and agriculture, was to centralize control. While the Soviets could not bring the farms to Moscow for bureaucrats to watch over every planting and harvest, they could bring what few good players and coaches they had to the central city. In Moscow they could test each other, the best athletes and best minds, and begin to close the hockey gap.

The question was how to do it. These hockey pioneers knew much about the game through similar sports, such as bandy and soccer, but they had no reason to know this at the time. And so they looked for teachers. The Czechoslovaks had a long history in hockey and played it well, and so did the Scandinavians, but in 1946 there was really only one hockey country, and that was Canada. Canadians had been the world's teacher and were easily the best players.

"I wanted to go abroad," recalls Anatoli Tarasov, one of the early Soviet players. "I was thirty years old at the time and had seen nothing but the war." A relentless bear of a man, Tarasov later would be coach of the Central Army and Soviet national teams for many years, and was the first Soviet inducted into the Hockey Hall of Fame in Toronto. But at this moment, like most of his hockey friends, he wanted to travel to Canada to learn how hockey should be played. He tells of a fateful conversation he had with a friend and mentor, Mikhail Tovarovsky. "There's nothing for you in Canada," Tovarovsky chided him. "Go your own way. Devise your own style of hockey." Years later, Tarasov could say with the wisdom of experience and success, "To copy is always to be second best," but in 1946, not to copy seemed unthinkable.

The Soviets' first test came less than two years later, in 1948. The Czechoslovakian champion, LTC Prague, visited Moscow for a series of games. On its roster were many of the best players from the country's national team, world champions the year before. The teams played three games. LTC Prague won one, one game was tied, the Soviets won the other. At series end, the Czechoslovak coach took Tarasov aside. "Learn our methods," he suggested. "If necessary, I can come here to work with you for a while." Tarasov recalls, "I wrote in my diary at the time: 'Look, listen, but we must do it our own way.'"

The series proved the psychological turning point in the development of Soviet hockey. It showed Tarasov and his colleagues they were on the right track.

The early Soviet players worked more hours of the day and more months of the year than Canadians had ever deemed necessary – or possible. The country had but one artificial ice rink – a slab of ice, really, in a Moscow children's park. The players built it themselves. Without walls or roof or even boards, it was just twelve metres by ten metres, roughly one-quarter the size of the defensive zone of a normal rink. In summer, they covered the rink with a canvas tent to keep out the ice-melting sun and, in soccer shorts and shin pads, continued to play. As for the country's other rinks, with natural ice they were at the unforgiving whim of the seasons.

So the Soviets took hockey off the ice and did on playing fields and in gymnasiums what they could not do in arenas. They ran, rowed, lifted weights, tumbled. They made themselves better athletes. They learned hockey techniques and strategies by playing other games, doing other drills. Skating and conditioning were the twin foundations of their game. Skating they got from bandy; conditioning was just hard work. Together, they would allow the Soviets to compete until their hockey skills and feel for the game had time to catch up and enable them to win.

It didn't take long. The Soviets put off their initial appearance at the world championship until 1953, then put it off another year when their great player, Vsevolod Bobrov, took ill before the games. But in 1954, at Stockholm, in the deciding game, the Soviets beat Canada 7–2, and won the world championship.

Just one year before, Tarasov had seen the Canadians play for the first time. It had been in Sweden and Switzerland. He had purposely avoided any contact until then, fearful of how he might react, not trusting what he might do. "By that time," he recalls, however, "I was convinced that no one, not even the Canadians, would astound me or throw me off my course. You know," he muses, "we newcomers should not have been allowed to watch too much Canadian hockey. Today, it's okay. Today, it's useful because our coaches and players are experienced. We take only the best, the most necessary, and transform it, strengthen it, to our own purposes. At that time, we would have taken it all just as it was."

The shock that hit Canada in 1954 was not far removed from that felt the night of September 2, 1972, when the Soviets defeated Canada 7–3 in the first game of *the series*. It was at the height of the Cold War. East and West, the world was in a strangle of competition. No symbol was unimportant. The battlefield for the mind was everywhere. Sure, "Canada" was really just the East York Lyndhursts, a Senior "B" team of part-time players and full-time car salesmen, electricians, and such. But on their jerseys it said "Canada." We knew that our best, the best, were playing in the NHL, quarantined away from the world's amateurs. But did *they* know? Did the players and coaches, did the people of the Soviet Union and the rest of Europe know? Being the best in the hockey world had been one of Canada's international claims to fame, one thing we could always be sure of. There was no visible pride to wear for leading the world in pulp or iron ore production. But in hockey . . . What *they* thought mattered to us, a lot.

Canada won the world championship the next year, the Soviets an Olympic gold medal in 1956. In the next six years, Canada won three times, Sweden twice, the U.S. once. It wasn't until 1963 that the Soviets won again. Since then, they have only lost four times, never to Canada.

In 1957, Tarasov made his first visit to Canada. His team was to play a series of games against Canadian amateur teams. Between those games, of far greater interest to Tarasov, he had his chance, finally, to see his mythical NHL teams play. "It had been my dream to see professional players," he recalled years later. Then hurt and pride filled his voice. "You came to my practices and I went to yours, but there was a difference. You watched for five or ten minutes, and laughed at me and my players," he bellowed. "Then everyone left. I sat through your practices bewitched. I've never written so much so fast. It pleased me that you laughed at us. Either you were too smug and didn't care, or you didn't understand what kind of hockey we were playing."

Canadians were curious about the Soviets, just not very interested. After all, what could they teach us. *We were better.* It was through this optic that we saw everything. We shot harder and more often; we rushed the puck solo in great end-to-end dashes; we bodychecked. If they passed more, shot and bodychecked less, it could only mean that they passed *too* much, shot and bodychecked *too* little. Because *we were better.* What interested Canadians about the Soviets was beating them, that's all, and that was getting harder.

Tarasov was obsessed with the NHL. The NHL was his fantasy

place, his ultimate opponent, his bogeyman. It offered him the perfect Soviet Cold War caricature of the West. Built on money, not on the higher standards of sport and society, it was a perversion of what it should have been. NHL owners, driven by greed, lined their pockets at the expense of everyone else. The players, as "professionals," played for money, not for the love of the sport, and they lived an immensely vulnerable, joyless, and pitiable existence. The "workers" in the system, they were far more manipulated by money than motivated by it. Their jobs, their livelihoods, *everything* depended on how they played, on winning, and they were constantly at risk. The owners could cut them off in an instant, ruin them. It was fear, not love of country or dedication to friends and colleagues and their collective task, that drove the professional. For Tarasov, all this explained the NHL's sporting excesses, the professional's instinct, in his words, "to behave absolutely ruthlessly for the sake of victory; to fight and brutalize anyone who gets in the way." In the West's dog-eat-dog world, it was the only way. To Tarasov, this also explained why the professional plays more by himself, less with the team, drawing the crowd's and owner's attention to him, with spectacular rushes, spectacular shots, spectacular fights.

In what he viewed as the weakness of the West, Tarasov saw the weakness of the NHL. This was how his happy, dedicated little collective would reverse the gap. In the late 1940s, Tarasov, in fact, had had no choice but to go his own way. To copy meant not only to be second best, but to adopt a system that was philosophically unacceptable. He would need to win, as every Cold War battle had to be won, but do it another, Soviet, way. His favourite Canadian player was Bobby Hull, then a golden-haired power-skating, slapshooting superstar with the Chicago Black Hawks. Tarasov used Hull as the standard against which he measured the progress of his own team. In speed and strength, in hockey skills, Hull was unmatchable, Tarasov believed. But put five Bobby Hulls on the ice at once, great individual stars, and collectively they would be far less than the sum of their parts. Tarasov believed that if he could put together five lesser players and have them play as a team, he could win.

Tarasov's team was the Central Army Club of Moscow, also

called the "Red Army" or CSKA. It would be his crucible. There, unfettered by the North American professional sports tradition of equalizing drafts and trades, Tarasov would attract the best players, players skilled enough to carry out his vision. They would flock to him, drawn to the team's winning tradition, to the big-city life of Moscow, to the chance to play for the man who also was coach of the national team. But he would not take everyone because his players also needed good opponents to play against.

Yet good league competition was not so crucial in Tarasov's mind as it is to the NHL. Tarasov was a follower of the great Russian actor/director Stanislavsky. He studied with Moiseyev. Tarasov saw sport as a kind of art, himself as choreographer and director, his players as performers. He believed in endless practice, repeating movements again and again to perfect technique from which true artistry could grow. His teams, as all Soviet teams, played fewer games. Instead, his players competed against themselves and each other in practice and, like artists in other fields, against an artistic standard in their teacher's head. As time passed, as the players improved, the standard would rise. The standard, in fact, was unreachable, for Tarasov was the ultimate scorekeeper.

All this time, the Soviets were building an infrastructure for the game. Hockey needed fans to make it seem important. It required masses of young boys, and the best athletes among them, to choose it over soccer or track and field as their sport of passion. It needed competition to improve its level of play and, most of all, glorious international victories to attract more players and fans, more government support and higher priority, to build more arenas and make more equipment, in turn to build stronger and broader roots for Soviet hockey. And gradually, that is what happened. From 1963 to 1972, Tarasov's teams won nine straight world championships and three Olympic gold medals; more than 3 million boys a year came to play the game; Soviet Premier Leonid Brezhnev, a devoted fan, attended games frequently and encouraged national TV to broadcast more of them. Hockey had become the Soviet Union's most popular sport.

In twenty-five short years, the Soviets had moved from bandy to hockey, set out on their own direction, centralized resources, improved rapidly, and become a huge philosophical and on-ice success. They had left the rest of the world behind. Only Canada and the NHL remained.

So evolved the Canada-Russia series of September, 1972: eight games, four in Canada, four in the Soviet Union. Finally, it was our best against their best. Ironically, the series would be played without Tarasov. After coaching the Soviet team to an Olympic gold medal just six months before, he was abruptly replaced by his former star player and rival, Vsevolod Bobrov. Tarasov would never meet his ultimate opponent face to face.

It is hard to believe memories of that time. Most details have been edited away by the years. Only the best of things, the worst, the strangest and funniest – the most memorable – are left behind. Surely they are too exaggerated to be real, the kind of phoney stuff from which legends come. For no series, no game, *nothing* could have meant that much. In 1972, to Canada, it did.

Sports pages, front pages, commentaries from editorial pages confirm this. But more than that, it was the recollected sounds from the streets. The talk all through the summer of 1972 was about *the series*. And because Canada was the best and sure to win, Canadians couldn't wait for the series to begin. It would be a glorious "coming out" party, a celebration of *us*. This gave to it a more fundamental dimension. For though much may be special about Canada, surrounded as it is historically and geographically by countries that are bigger, richer, more powerful, whose specialness seems more obvious, we cling to every symbol. A game is a game. But a symbol is not. *We had to win this series*.

"I remember my brother, Tony, saying 'Why are we going? Why are we doing this? Who are we playing?' And I says, 'I don't know, we're playing the Russians. How good can they be? I mean, they've won world championships, and won the Olympics, but they've never played against the pros. So how good can they be?' "

The words are Phil Esposito's. Seventeen years later, along with three of his Team Canada teammates, Paul Henderson,

Serge Savard, and Bill White, Esposito had travelled to Montreal to recall *the series*.

Bill White, tall, lean, and cobra-bent, was already in 1972 a veteran defenceman for the Chicago Black Hawks. Eschewing the power game, he played with great finesse, using his long arms and stick to break up plays, sending his teammates into open ice with clever, penetrating passes.

Serge Savard had been a Montreal Canadiens' *wunderkind* until a twice-broken leg threatened his career. At the time of the series, he was still rebuilding his body and game and was not expected to be chosen for the team. Strong, with the grace and agility of someone much smaller, he didn't play in games one, four, and five, all of which Team Canada lost.

Paul Henderson was a good, solid, two-way player. Of modest size, he was a darting skater, at his most effective without the puck, checking vigorously, using his speed to create a sudden offensive opening for a quick pass and shot. He proved the exemplar for a well-earned, hard-learned series lesson – all-star teams are not an amalgam of all-star players; every good team requires a mix of skills, strengths, and personalities. A non-star, Henderson scored winning goals in three of Team Canada's four victories.

Phil Esposito was already thirty years old in 1972. If Bobby Orr had been uninjured, if Bobby Hull had not signed a contract with the World Hockey Association, Esposito would likely have been a minor figure in the series. He had scored more single-season goals than Hull, earned more points than defenceman Orr, but they were the greatest stars of the time. They were exciting and dynamic, drawing every eye to them. Esposito was just a goal scorer. Later, Soviet goaltender Vladislav Tretiak would say of him in the series, "He played as if he sang." Henderson scored the legendary goal; Esposito emerged as the series' legendary figure. In 1972, he was the heart and soul and driving force of his team.

They remember their own laughable innocence, how they arrived at their August training camp more ready, more in shape than for any training camp they had ever attended, how they worked harder than they ever had before. Only later would they learn what *real* readiness, *real* shape, *real* hard work were. They remember when the two NHL scouts returned from Moscow with news of the Soviets that only confirmed what little they knew. "We were told that Tretiak couldn't stop anything," Esposito recalls, "that their players could skate, but not that well, and they could shoot but not that hard." He rolls his eyes, "Wow!" he says now, and begins to laugh. They also remember the day Team Canada coach Harry Sinden brought in his films. Once captain of the world champion Whitby Dunlops, Sinden wanted to give his players a sense of the Soviets and international hockey. The lights went out, the room darkened, and onto the screen in grainy black-and-white came a slightly speeded-up version of Whitby's win in an open-air rink in Oslo in 1958. Sinden looked twenty years old, the scene looked a hundred – and everyone laughed hysterically.

But as the first game approached, they remember a feeling building, an urgency, on the streets, in the newspapers, in them, that they had never felt before, that surprised them. "I remember the afternoon of the first game," Esposito says, and as he does, he begins to shake his head. "Somebody called me on the phone. I don't know who it was – a fan. 'Good luck,' he says. 'You're gonna kill these guys.' I mean, I'm trying to sleep and I want to say, please leave me alone, you know. But I couldn't sleep. I never had a problem sleeping. But I couldn't sleep that afternoon."

Esposito had never expected to feel this way. He had been in playoff games; his teams had won two Stanley Cups. It was a feeling that would only build, minute by minute, circumstance by circumstance, game by game, soaring to dangerous, uncontrollable new territory. That night at the Montreal Forum, he skated to centre ice with Soviet forward Vladimir Vikulov for the ceremonial opening face-off. Prime Minister Pierre Trudeau, in the midst of a federal election campaign, his sideburns as long as those of the players, readied himself to drop the puck. Esposito tensed his body. As each memory of that moment returns, his voice pitches higher. "It was only a ceremonial face-off, but I had to win that draw!" he shrieks incredulously. "I mean, I had to win that draw!! This guy didn't even try, and it really aggravated me. I wanted to spear him or something. Try, you know. Try! I remember I drew the puck back and put up my hand like, wow, we won the first face-off!"

At that same moment, sounding a little surprised himself, Foster Hewitt, who had in his lifetime described thousands of games, was telling his nation-wide audience, "I can't recall any game that I've ever been at where you can just feel the tension. And it keeps building up."

We struck with frightening energy. Esposito after thirty seconds; Henderson six minutes later. It was the energy of a decade of losing – revenge, frustration, pride, self-doubt – exploding in celebration. The Soviets didn't know what hit them, and neither did we. Every myth was confirmed, ours of them, theirs of us, ours of ourselves. We were just too good.

But then there came a moment. The players could sense it before the fans could. For Paul Henderson, it was only a few seconds after the opening goal. "My first shift on the ice," Henderson recalls. "I'd worked really hard in training camp. I mean, I had to. I wasn't a superstar. I was just trying to get into the lineup. So you know, I skate into our end, then back into theirs, jostling along the boards, up to centre, and then there's a face-off. By this time, I was really gasping for air. And I look up and this Russian is standing beside me, it's like he's singing – *da dada da da* – not breathing at all. I mean right then and there . . . I just felt sick. I knew we'd been sucked in."

It was an excruciating night. For fifty-three minutes, Team Canada's players, its fans, Canadians, could feel *everything* slip away. Nothing could stop it. By the end of the first period, the score was 2–2; by game's end, 7–3 for the Soviets.

"Soviet amateurs shatter myth of Canadian pros' invincibility." So said Soviet news agency Tass the following morning. Canadian headlines spoke of "shock," "disaster," "disgrace," but really it was more than that. Canadians were *embarrassed*. Our expectations had been so high. We were so sure we would win. Now we felt stupid, taken in by our own macho, prideful selves. It was the perfect squelch.

There was also something in us that made us hate ourselves for feeling this way. After all, it was just a silly game. Why should we get so worked up? Ninety-five per cent of the people in the world didn't even know the game had been played and couldn't have cared less if they did. But we cared. And that, in part, was why we were embarrassed. The Soviets had exposed us utterly. On the same ice surface, they had been our mirror. Playing a different way, they had made us see ourselves, perhaps for the first time. And we didn't like what we saw.

We saw players who were not quite in shape, a little too prosperous and overfed, whose concept of team play was conservative and unambitious, who under stress became disorganized and undisciplined, who by instinct went it alone. We saw a style of play that was rough and unsophisticated, with little system or science to it, a style that seemed out of touch with the times.

We saw ourselves.

Near the end of the game, Team Canada players "gooned" it up with slashes and high sticks. Canadians booed the Canadian players, and cheered the Russians.

Hockey had always been a symbol for Canadians of what we wanted to be. Now it seemed just another symbol of what we really were. Our hockey, built on natural resources – cold and ice – and exported south beyond our control, after a decades' long headstart, had been caught by those who had added human resources, science and system, to make something more advanced. All the stereotypes others held of us, and we held of ourselves, were confirmed. A spasm of self-hatred shook the country.

The players had to pick up the pieces. The emotion that had been building since early in the summer now reached new levels. "I mean, we were shocked," Esposito says, as he remembers the post-game dressing room. "All of us were like, wow! And without saying it, we were thinking – we are in for one tough time. The country's at stake here. I mean, that's what I thought. It's our society against theirs. I think that's when I started . . ." He stopped, and tried again. "It's like that cartoon about the really prim and proper guy but when he gets behind the wheel of a car, he turns into a maniac." He nods, a little embarrassed at his own memory. "That's when I started to become a real maniac."

Team Canada won in Toronto, tied in Winnipeg, then disaster

struck again in Vancouver. The Soviets took an early lead, kept control, and gradually extended their lead. It was all too much for the frustrated fans, who booed frequently, then, near the end of the game, almost constantly. After the game, Phil Esposito was interviewed for Canadian television. He was sad and weary and hurt and angry and every bit of every one of those emotions was there in his face, and in his voice. He was standing before millions of people who in their living rooms had been booing him and his team just as loudly as the fans had done in Vancouver, who were furious that their team, their high-paid superstars, in a series that mattered so much to them, were not trying and did not care. And there stood Esposito, sweat and try and anguish oozing out of him. He looked like he had gone through hell.

"For the people across Canada, we tried. We gave it our best. For the people who booed us, jeez, all of us guys are really disheartened and we're disillusioned and we're disappointed in some of the people. We cannot believe the bad press we've got, the booing we've gotten in our own buildings. If the Russian fans boo their players like some of the Canadian fans – I'm not saying all of them – some of them booed us, then I'll come back and apologize to each and every Canadian. But I don't think they will. I'm really, really, I'm really disappointed. I am completely disappointed, I cannot believe it. Some of our guys are really really down in the dumps. We know – we're trying. What the hell, we're doing the best we can. They've got a good team and let's face facts. But it doesn't mean that we're not giving it our 150 per cent because we certainly are . . .

"We came because we love Canada. And even though we play in the United States and we earn money in the United States, Canada is still our home and that's the only reason we come. And I don't think it's fair that we should be booed."

It was an incredible visual moment. He pleaded, he explained, he lectured, he seemed never less than fair. But it was that sad-eyed, washed-out face, bathed with the sweat of the world, that penetrated those millions of living rooms and hit like a bomb. Anger and disappointment remained, but now there was guilt as well. It was time to pull together.

And they would need to, for the load was now immense and

the grade far steeper. Behind two games to one with one game tied, *at home*, Team Canada now headed for Moscow. This was to be a road trip like no other. There they would find bigger ice surfaces, a hostile crowd, and life on a very different road.

Athletes play under great pressure. A game will not wait until they are psyched up, healthy, happy, and ready to play. They must deliver when the moment demands it. And so they live on an emotional edge. To cope, most develop elaborate routines – when to get up, what to eat, when to leave for the rink – to get them through a day undistracted by the rest of life and ready for the game at hand. At home, they sleep in their own beds, eat meals they are used to eating. They are mostly in control of the environment around them. On the road, it is harder. So teams return to the same big chain hotels trip after trip to achieve a sense of comfortable sameness. No surprises.

When routines get broken, players can go over the emotional edge. Team Canada of 1972 was an experienced, veteran team. The players had seen it all and done it all many times before on the ice and off. But that was in North America, and this was Europe. This was Moscow in 1972.

We were like babes in the world. Until this series, few of the fans, fewer of the players, had ever been outside of North America. In Moscow, there were no Hiltons or Sheratons, no western beef, no Cokes, no queen-sized beds, no TV game shows to help pass the long pre-game afternoons. There were no Mars bars, no Hershey bars, no hamburgers, no morning papers, in short, none of the things that had before never seemed to matter much but that now became fixations. The beds were narrow, the pillows oversized, and the blankets didn't tuck in. The phones rang when they shouldn't; wires ran across ceilings, down walls, disappearing under threadbare rugs – where were they going? what were they for? The meat was like shoe-leather, the toilet paper like sandpaper . . . and as the tension of the series screwed tighter, it became almost too much.

"I don't know about you guys," says Esposito, his face suddenly furrowed and grave, "but I'm convinced we ate horsemeat." He looks around the room and sees smiles, and his face, too, brightens. "I'm convinced of it. I mean, it kept going," and letting his lips go slack, he blows through them, like a horse's whinney, and everyone laughs. "No, no, but I'm convinced we ate horsemeat." He remembers the players' wives and their separate menu, and a puzzled look comes over him, "Wasn't there something with the girls, they ate blackbird or something? Or crow?"

Savard tries to help out. "Black *bread*?"

"No, no, no, not black bread," he laughs. "I don't know –"

"It was the eggs that were green," interrupts Henderson, and they all laugh again. "My wife was served eggs one morning, and I remember this because I went over to see them. No butter in the pan, the bottom of the eggs were absolutely black and the tops were rotten. They were just green."

The little things loomed large: the elevators went *bump-bump* and got you there, but maybe wouldn't; the belligerent-sounding whine of spoken Russian; the hotel "floor ladies," Moscow's first line of defence against Napoleon, Hitler, and any invited fool who tried to enter a hotel room that wasn't his or hers; the "guides" and interpreters, with you to ease your lives, trained in five languages to say, "It is impossible."

One day, Team Canada forward Wayne Cashman threw the hotel room's mirror out his window. "He thought it was bugged," laughs Esposito. "I mean, he literally threw it out the window. I'm sitting here thinking, my God. After that, his wife had to come to our room to put on her make-up."

Canadians had always lived in splendid isolation, separated from the world by two massive oceans and by sheets of ice over which no one would ever come, away from the complications of polyglot languages and cultures and not enough space. We knew little of the world in 1972, but then we had little reason to know more and could not have cared less. As players, coaches, fans, and officials, we were unworldly and inexperienced, uncomfortable anywhere but in our own backyard, and anxious to return to it as soon as we could. In the meantime, we had two choices: we could accept, or ignore, the "little" distractions as part of the reality of "doing business" in the world, or we could take on a bunker-like paranoia – it's us versus them – and let the paranoia charge the atmosphere even higher.

Everything had shifted to the Soviets' favour, except for the most important thing. Fear. It is what the Soviets had felt for twenty-six years, the fear of losing, of being embarrassed – the fear every team must have to win. This fear drove them to work more hours of the day, more months of the year; it drove them through their long, hard summer of preparation; it opened their ears to coaches' theories and ways; and it formed them together *as a team*. "It's the one thing you have to learn in hockey," Savard says. "If you're not scared of losing, you're not going to win. And when we started the series, we didn't have that fear." Now, in Moscow – "We were scared like hell."

The Soviets had lost that elemental fear. They became even more comfortable when, in the third period of the fifth game (the first in Moscow), trailing Team Canada, 3–0, they scored five goals and won the game. The series now stood 3–1–1 for the Soviets. Years later, Soviet goalie Vladislav Tretiak remembered the shifting moods. "When we left Vancouver, we saw for the first time that we were going to win the series. We knew your weak points and strong points and we knew that in Moscow, in our own rink, we could not lose. This was our fatal mistake. If Tarasov had been our coach, he would have noticed our over-confidence. But Bobrov wasn't very experienced as a coach and he didn't see that our team was 'swimming in glory.' We weren't training as hard as before. A few of our players even left our training sessions to visit their wives for a while! That had never happened before."

But fear can also be paralysing. Early in game six, afraid of losing, Canadian fans were quiet. They remained that way even as their team came from a 1–0 deficit and scored three quick goals in the second period. Two nights before, the fans had watched the Soviets come from behind so cruelly. Now too afraid to hope, they held back. Then defenceman Guy Lapointe and Valeri Vasiliev were penalized for roughing. Less than two minutes later, Bobby Clarke was sent off for slashing and given a ten-minute misconduct. Then Dennis Hull also went off for slashing. The Soviets scored to make it 3–2. Forty-four seconds later, Esposito received a five-minute major for high-sticking, Team Canada a two-minute bench minor. All hell had broken loose. By the end of the period, Canada had received twenty-nine minutes in penalties, the Soviets four.

In that last ten minutes of the second period the game, and the series, changed. There had been an ambivalence until then. Canadian fans had been thrilled, and angered, by their own players. They had admired the skills and pluck of the Soviets. No more. The string of penalties seemed to crystallize everything – the food, the elevators, the wires that disappeared, the floor ladies who wouldn't. The game, the series, that fundamental something that hockey meant to Canadians – they weren't being won; they were being taken away.

And so, backed into our final corner, we fought back. "Da Da Ca-na-da, Nyet, Nyet Sov-i-et!!" the Canadian fans chanted and sang. From then on, it was us against them.

"To me, it was war," Esposito said later. He had had seventeen years to try to understand and explain this feeling that shocked and scared him, and he wasn't quite sure he could. "I've said this to a few people, but I've never really said it publicly, but it got to a point with me . . ." He paused and started again. "I've often wondered – like, I've never shot a deer. I've never shot anything in my life. I've never hunted. I'm just not that type of guy. But there's no doubt in my mind that I think I would have killed to win. And that scares me! That really scares me. When I think about it, like right now, I sort of get goose bumps, because I would have killed them to win. I would have done *anything* to win. Absolutely anything. I think in a war, maybe that's what happens."

The maniacs were behind the wheel.

"Here's Dennis Hull getting a chance! He shoots a hot one!!" shrieks Foster Hewitt late in the third period, Canada still clinging to a 3–2 lead. "Petrov and Dennis Hull, now mixing it up again as they spear at each other. This is really the hardest-fought game I think I've seen in years."

His colour commentator was former NHL player Brian Conacher. "Foster, I can't believe it. Down on that ice, it's just sheer war. They're not sparing the lumber. They're not sparing the body . . ." And they never would until the end of the series.

In the next game, Esposito got a penalty for cross-checking

Soviet antagonist/pest Boris Mikhailov. In the penalty box, even
before he sat down, Esposito began an extended, near-comic
pantomime with Mikhailov across the ice on the Soviet bench.
He did it without obvious rancour, simply with matter-of-fact,
universal gestures, easily understood by Mikhailov and by the
tens of millions watching across Canada and the Soviet Union.
Esposito pointed at Mikhailov and, as if Mikhailov, unseen by
the camera, had pointed innocently at himself, Esposito nodded
and, with a slitting motion, twice swept his right forefinger
across his throat. Then, as if he had something more in mind,
Esposito pointed again at Mikhailov and mouthed clearly, "Me
and you." He put his stick down to free his other hand, pointed
at Mikhailov yet again, then at himself, raised his now-clenched
fists, and pretended to box. Then he pointed at Mikhailov and at
himself again and again – *me and you, me and you* – so his intention
would be unmistakable.

In game eight, confirmed pacifist Rod Gilbert fought with the
Soviets' Eugeny Mishakov; mild-mannered Bill White shot the
puck at a referee; Jean-Paul Parise, a quiet, uncomplaining,
workman-like player, angered at being penalized, swooped after
the referee, drew back his stick like a baseball bat, and swung it
forward, stopping it just before making contact; coach Harry
Sinden threw a chair onto the ice; team official Alan Eagleson,
about to be ejected from the arena after a dispute with Soviet
militia, was rescued by the players. He jumped over the boards
to the safety of the ice and was escorted to the Team Canada
bench. The series itself seemed to take control. When it was
over, Paul Henderson recalls, "I told my wife, I will never, ever,
let myself get that emotionally involved in something again."

"Hello Canada! I'm Foster Hewitt and I'll be doing the play-
by-play for tonight's eighth and final game of the series . . ." The game was broadcast on both CBC and CTV. All
other programming came to stop. Canada's population in 1972
was 21.8 million. On this Thursday afternoon, a work day, 7.5
million watched. When the game was repeated a few hours
later, 5 million watched.

Walter Kyliuk dismissed his high school class in Albion, Saskatchewan, and, with his students and those from other classes,

assembled in one room in front of a television set. Alfons Hajt listened on radio to the first period while combining his fields in Radisson, then left his work to watch the rest on TV. Scotty Mundt, in charge of local operations for the province's electrical power company, watched and sweated, hoping there would be no electrical failure for which he would be blamed. Three thousand kilometres to the east, Walter Gretzky was fixing a teletype machine in Brantford, Ontario, listening on radio. Son Wayne, age eleven, with his father's blessing and his mother's resistance, skipped school and watched in his living room.

". . . Each team has won three, tied one, and lost three," Hewitt continued. "So they go into the final game all tied up. The Soviets have scored twenty-seven goals in seven games and Canada has scored twenty-five. So if you've been writing the script, it couldn't have produced a more dramatic and exciting final . . ."

All across Canada, the story was the same: bars and living rooms filled, businesses shut down – there was no business to do. On Ottawa's Sparks Street Mall, scores of people stopped in front of an appliance store window to watch the game's flickering images, if not hear its sounds. In nearby Rockcliffe Park, former Prime Minister John Diefenbaker and his wife, Olive, watched at home as TV cameras watched them. Diefenbaker looked more out of place than his 3,000 countrymen in Moscow. It seemed as if he had never even seen a game before. He cheered like no sports fan cheers; his every reaction came late, as if he needed Hewitt's explanation as his guide. As for Mrs. Diefenbaker, she seemed to take her lead from her husband. Yet they, too, were watching.

". . . the teams and fans are really up for this one. Brian," Hewitt said, addressing his colour commentator, "I wouldn't miss this one for all the tea in China . . ."

At the end of the second period, the Soviets led 5–3.

"I can remember Harry [Sinden] saying, 'Listen, we need to get one early. Don't open it up, but if we get one early, we'll be okay,'" Henderson recalls. "I can tell you the play. I can see it like it was yesterday."

"Some guy once asked me if there was ever a moment in a

game where time seemed just to slow down," Esposito went on. "Well, that was the one – around the net, up that right side, throwing it in, banging with Gusev, the puck coming to me in the air, dropping it down, shooting it once, Tretiak goes down, the puck bounces, I had to shoot it again. It was all in slow motion. It was like – incredible!"

They hadn't seen films of the series for years, but they remembered the fifth and sixth goals with the same detail. One of them starts the story, another continues it, then another as if they are doing a seamless play-by-play. With less than a minute to play, the score is tied 5–5. These are Hewitt's words –

". . . Liapkin rolled one to Savard. Savard cleared the pass to Stapleton. He cleared to the open wing to Cournoyer . . . Cournoyer took a shot. The defenceman fell over, Liapkin. And the – Cournoyer has it on that wing! Here's a shot! Henderson made a wild stab for it and fell. Here's another shot! Right in front! THEY SCORE!!! Henderson has scored for Canada! . . ."

No one was more startled by what happened than Henderson himself. He wasn't even supposed to be on the ice in those critical dying seconds of the game. His position was taken by Peter Mahovlich, who had set up the first goal of that final period and was rested and fresher than Henderson.

"Amazingly," Henderson recalls of that moment, "I really thought I could score a goal and I yelled to Peter to come off the ice. I don't know why. I've never called a player off the ice before and I've never done it since, but I really had a sense that I could score.

"I came charging out and Cournoyer had it at the far point and I yelled at him. He tried to give it to me, but he was behind me, and as I reached back the guy tripped me. As I went down I knew in my mind we probably would have enough time to get down to the other end of the ice and get it back and come back and there would be one more shot. So I got up in a hurry. And I saw Phil get the puck and he just hammered it and Tretiak didn't handle the rebound. And so I got the rebound and tried to slide it right along the ice and Tretiak, well, he got it again – but then he was down and, of course, it was all over."

"I remember the guys on the bench yelling at me, 'Phil!

Phil!' " Esposito says. "There wasn't any way in the world that I was going off. None. It was like, I gotta be in on this because it's gonna happen. It's going to happen! And when he scored –" he searches for the words, "I mean, that's the closest I ever came to really loving another guy."

Henderson, White, and Savard howl with laughter.

"I literally loved him. I think if I had a million dollars, I would have given it to him right there."

"Well, you've got it today," laughs Henderson. "You didn't have it then."

"I don't love you that much anymore," says Esposito, and there is more laughter.

Henderson, the unlikely hero, thinks back on that series, and that goal. "I still talk about that goal 300 days a year," he says. "Every Canadian I meet for the first time will invariably tell me exactly where they were and what they were doing. I mean, it's gotta die, but it's not going to die. I mean, it's just indelibly written in Canadians' hearts. And the thing about it," he says excitedly, "they felt a part of it. They always say, 'We.' They don't say 'You did this.' We as Canadians did it."

When the game ended, Moscow's 3,000 Canadians stood up and sang "O Canada."

"We knew we had the population behind us like never before," says Savard. "I don't think we'll ever see that again. I don't think you could get the country together like that behind one team again."

I played on six Stanley cup winning teams. I've been asked many times my most memorable moment. I used to pretend I didn't know. "The Stanley Cups, the '72 series, they're all special," I'm sure I've said. But really, it's easy. Nothing ever brought me so low; nothing ever took me so high. Nothing meant so much.

The year 1972 didn't end with Henderson's goal. And when the country's celebration ended, the new day looked different. A lot had happened in the twenty-seven days since the first game in Montreal. A symbol, something about us, that we had always taken as self-evident, had been rocked. Our innocence, our confidence and enthusiasm, our urge to jump into the world's deep water – we had changed. We still shot harder and more often; we rushed the puck solo in great end-to-end dashes; we body-checked. But now we had seen another way, more modern and scientific, it seemed, and it had worked. Because *we were better* – our forever explanation and reason to look the other way suddenly rang hollow. Never before had victory felt so much like defeat. We had won the present but lost the future.

We celebrated with excitement and relief, and a new, sober-eyed perspective. Like a celebration on the *Titanic*, the iceberg had been hit, so the party might as well be loud and long because it would likely be our last.

The Soviets had come so far so fast. Time was clearly on their side. Their style of game, based on conditioning and team play, made such good sense. So, too, did their relentless hard work and the systematic rigour with which they approached everything. If they were this good now, after our seventy-one-year headstart, how good would they be in just a few years? And what about us? It was a frightening thought.

History was moving away from us again, Canadians thought, and it came as no surprise. We are a country conditioned to assume that if we're ahead, someone is gaining on us and it won't be long until they catch us and pass us by. We are small, or young, we explain; for too long we were an historical append-age to someplace else. It is the same for all smaller countries, for all former colonies. The centre of the world has been somewhere else for such a long time that an inferiority complex becomes a state of mind, an attitude, a style, and being something less than first becomes an expectation. For so many years, we were at the centre of the hockey world. We were the best and everybody knew it. But destiny caught us, as destiny always had.

Yet, what else could we do? Up against a country more than ten times our size with more than ten times the players to choose from, with a northern climate, a common passion for the game, and an unquenchable desire to be best, we perceived the battle to be unwinnable. Sports is not a mathematical equation, but the situation was too clear. Size and power is destiny. For Canada it always was so.

To Canadians, this seemed a typically Canadian story. But at almost the same time, another country was having its own difficulties in a different field.

The United States had been the car industry's birthplace and developer. It had dominated the industry world-wide for so long that its position was conceded and accepted. Japan had also built cars for a long time but, because of the war, had been forced to begin again almost from scratch in 1946. Japan began modestly, never believing it could one day offer the United States a serious challenge. But the American industry lived in the comfort of its own supremacy. It was the best, therefore it must do things the best, and only, way. To the United States' car companies, their own domestic competition seemed real enough. Each company felt pressured to change this or that to get the necessary edge on its competitors. Each worked hard to succeed. Or so it seemed.

But really, little that it did was new. Its changes were decorative. The product looked better but otherwise was not being improved. The customer bought what the customer had always bought. No one offered anything any different. The companies felt no incentive to innovate. If it ain't broke, don't fix it.

To the American car makers, there also seemed no way someone else could offer something better. American global superiority stemmed from an inherent national specialness, they believed, not historical advantages that in time might be overcome. We make the best because we *are* the best.

Even the Japanese did not disagree. Instead, they worked harder and longer. They tried new methods, had different ideas. And finally they caught up, though neither they nor their American counterparts noticed for some time. By the early 1970s, however, the proof was there for all to see.

Arguably, the car industry is the image of America. Hockey may be its Canadian equivalent. Both stories have to do with the arrogance and complacency of an originator, and with learning the hard way. In the end, the American car manufacturers learned that relative size and power may not be destiny after all. It wasn't until fifteen years after *the series* that Canadians began to feel the same about hockey.

The "Red Army" club, more properly the Central Army Club of Moscow or CSKA, is the sporting home of such chess greats as former world champion Anatoli Karpov, basketball and gymnastic champions, and hockey stars – Tarasov, Makarov, Fetisov. Indeed, CSKA is the world's most successful hockey team. In forty-three Soviet hockey seasons, CSKA has won the national championship an astonishing thirty-one times. But today within its grounds, as in factories and offices all over the Soviet Union, a fundamental struggle is going on. It is over power, history, and, most of all, the rights and place of the individual in Soviet society. Its twin banners are *glasnost* and *perestroika*. And CSKA, an *army* club at the very heart of the Soviet establishment, provides an unlikely stage for this national drama.

The struggle for the most part is not visible. It is a sound, as if for their whole lives the Soviet people have been storing up their thoughts and feelings waiting for a chance to express them. Now, and since Premier Mikhail Gorbachev has made such thoughts and feelings not just possible but an expression of good citizenship, like national psychotherapy, they have come gushing out, passionate, realistic, sometimes cynical. Words that only a few years ago were unimaginable, that care little of philosophical models or the *promise* of what will someday be, that are determined to express what is. They come from Soviet citizens who care less of the glories of space, sport, military adventure, and what the rest of the world thinks. From people who want to know – what about *me*? what about *my* life?

One player who is asking these questions is Vyacheslav Fetisov, once a major in the Soviet army, once captain of CSKA and the Soviet national team, many time world and Olympic champion, recipient of the Order of Lenin, in the 1980s his country's greatest player. On January 16, 1989, Fetisov arrived as usual for his CSKA practice, but instead delivered to assistant coach Boris Mikhailov his stunning news. "I will not play for CSKA anymore," he said. The next night, when his teammates took the ice against their Moscow rival, the Soviet Wings, Fetisov was not with them. The headline in *Moskovsky Komsomalets* that day offered his simple explanation, "I Don't Want to Play on Tikhonov's Team." Viktor Tikhonov had been his CSKA and national team coach since 1977. Their relationship had often been strained, especially in recent years. Finally Fetisov had had enough.

In trying to explain the Fetisov problem to newspaper readers, former CSKA star Anatoli Firsov likened the team to a "sleeping volcano that finally awakened." From the outside, he said, nothing was visible; inside and unseen, there was a poisonous swirl, growing more violent by the day and ready to erupt. Many times, players had come to Tikhonov with their complaints. Many times, they had been rebuffed. But everything had been kept within the team. The intransigent Russian dictum – "Don't bring your garbage out in the room" – had always prevailed.

But no more. With *glasnost* or "openness," the garbage of decades was beginning to be revealed. It had become every citizen's right, even obligation, to see things as they are if *perestroika*, Gorbachev's internal program of social, economic, and attitudinal change, were to work. Except *glasnost* came late in hockey. It wasn't until October, 1988, that its first unavoidable evidence appeared. It came in the Soviet national magazine *Ogonyok*, in the form of an open letter to Tikhonov from CSKA and national team star Igor Larionov. Larionov, nearing thirty, with linemates Sergei Makarov and Vladimir Krutov and defencemen Fetisov and Alexei Kasatonov, had formed the powerful unit of "five" that had dominated Soviet hockey during the 1980s. Only someone of Larionov's stature could gain such a forum and be heard.

His letter offered a fascinating insider's tale. At times, it was gossipy: "On CSKA, we don't even wear the same uniforms. We play in whatever is left from the national team. We came out to play one semifinal playoff game against Dynamo Riga wearing nine different kinds of hockey socks. It was like a masquerade ball." But more often, Larionov hit at something fundamental, and Tikhonov was never far from the centre of what he said. His criticisms of him were often personal, but they were most telling when directed at Tikhonov *the symbol*. In his own world, Tikhonov was the system itself. Distant, cold, distrustful, all-powerful, he controls and monopolizes all favours – money, hard currency, foreign travel, status, cars, apartments, children's nurseries; he has the power to give them or take them back at whim; he has in his hands the tools to manipulate the behaviour he wants. And he has the deeply ingrained instincts never to give those tools up. To do so would allow others some control over their own lives. That might unfetter the human instinct for more and better, which in turn might unfetter Soviet society. These are the essential engines of *perestroika*, but to Tikhonov it is a question of trust and human nature. He sees human weakness; he is blind to human strength. No one can be left to his own devices, he believes; the workers can't be trusted.

Tikhonov is a symbol of the old way, the very enemy of *glasnost* and *perestroika*, the reason they are needed. Larionov is a voice of the new. In *Ogonyok*, Larionov wrote that once in an interview he had said there should be player exchanges between Canada and the Soviet Union. Tikhonov had reprimanded him but would not leave it at that. "After a while, I forgot about it," Larionov wrote. Then he addressed Tikhonov directly, "But you, Viktor Vasilievitch [Tikhonov] did not." A few days before Larionov and his teammates were to leave for games in North America against NHL teams, "I was told I would have certain 'difficulties' in getting my visa." Later, he had the same difficulties before games in Italy and Sweden. He learned after that the team had been told he would be staying at home, but the coaches did not tell him. It wasn't until 8 a.m. on the day the team was to depart for Italy, he writes, "when I stood in front of the mirror knotting my tie, that one of the assistant coaches called to tell me I wasn't going." As for the Swedish trip, he had been told specifically that he would be making the trip. But the night before the team's departure, he opened up a copy of *Pravda*, read the team roster for the games, and couldn't find his name.

Tikhonov was leaving behind little reminders. You, Larionov, can score goals, he was saying. You can contribute to national and world championship teams, but in this life nothing is earned, everything is given, and your income, status, lifestyle, your passion in life, hockey, can be taken away from you *like that*, and that depends on me. Fighting back changes nothing, for no one, least of all me, is listening. Times may be changing, but make no mistake about it. The fear and inertia of the past dies slowly.

"I have had many conflicts with Tikhonov," Larionov wrote. "I saw injustices but kept quiet. But the main problem is a human one. Regrettably, Viktor Vasilievitch doesn't treat his players like men. He doesn't care about our problems. What is important for him is only how we play. You cannot sit down and talk with him heart to heart. You can't talk about something other than hockey. I told him this, but he doesn't agree. So now it's time to talk about it. Before my complaints were only an empty noise. I talked and 'spent my nerves,' but nobody would publish what I said.

"Today they will. It is just my opinion but I hope that some of the players will support me. I'm not trying to force the coach out because he makes us work too hard. I am ready as I've always been to go through any of his drills and discipline on the ice. But he should treat the players like people. People should be believed in, and trusted, especially those who have done so much for him, and trusted not just on the ice."

On the ice, Larionov and the rest of "the five" can mostly escape from Tikhonov's control. There, they have another audience to judge them. They need only to score often enough, and win, to earn the freedom they desire to improvise their own game. But off the ice it is different. Eleven months a year, they are with the team. Six days a week, ten months a year, they live on the outskirts of Moscow in Archangelskoye, in army barracks, upscale by Soviet standards, but a barracks nonetheless, *away from their families*. The barracks has one phone, in the central lobby. It is the players' only regular instrument of contact with their wives and children.

Larionov has a wife and baby daughter. Archangelskoye is surrounded by a beautiful birch forest. It offers space and clean, crisp air, rare privileges for those who live in the Moscow region. The food in the barracks is good, the staff in the kitchen, all women, watch over the players like genial mother hens. "It's very beautiful there," Larionov admits, "but after eight years it gets to you. The people are nice, but I prefer my own mother, and my wife." Larionov remembers back to when he was seventeen and playing in Voskresensk, a town of 50,000 about ninety kilometres south of Moscow. His team was Khimik, also in the top Soviet league, and he lived at home. "My coach trusted me in everything," he writes. "Then I was transferred to CSKA and became many times a world and Olympic champion, and lost that trust."

He cannot understand why his life should be this way. It has to do with the army, he knows, and its traditions. He thinks it may be rooted in the accepted psychological training of the soldier, that free time only leads to unneeded and dangerous thoughts. But he is no soldier, he insists. He is a full-time hockey player, and hockey players in Europe and North America have shown that they can win, yet they live a different way. "I know that living at home you can still practise and play," he writes in *Ogonyok*. "During the summer we have a very demanding schedule. We work out three times a day, about five or six hours altogether, and we live at home. It works." So he formulates arguments to support his case, when really he knows that argument has nothing to do with it. It is power that counts. Many times, he and other senior players on the team have approached Tikhonov. "I used to say to him," Larionov explains, " 'you can't treat people this way. I mean, it's almost as if we are slaves here.' He says to me, 'There were guys like you before who said that. There'll be guys like you after. You're not going to change anything.' "

Trust and control: these are the roots of Larionov's *Ogonyok* message. He wants greater control over his own life. He wants *perestroika* in Soviet hockey. "It's time to speak more pointedly about the style of leadership in our hockey organizations," Larionov sums up emphatically. "What has been created is a personality cult where military discipline and unquestioning subordination are substituted for democracy."

It was a remarkable letter. Just as remarkable was the silence that followed. Soviet fans checked their newspapers each day expecting to find Tikhonov's return salvo. They found nothing. Larionov's teammates, awaiting some official word on the price of his insubordination, also were quiet. But clearly, something was happening. The weight of the system that could so easily and had so often come crashing down, didn't. Tikhonov's many critics were beginning to leave their closets and fight back. If Tikhonov was powerful enough to resist them, they had become powerful enough to resist him. Larionov was their point man. He could say things that needed to be said, and that they could not. It was up to them to use their positions of authority to protect him from the most severe sanctions, so that he and they could go on fighting, so other players and critics would feel secure enough to come forward and do the same.

Larionov broke his ankle in a game shortly after the *Ogonyok* letter appeared, removing himself from the team for more than a month. He worked hard to regain his form and seemed ready to return to regular action just before Christmas, in time for the Izvestia Prize, the Soviet Union's major international tournament. This was Tikhonov's chance. Citing a lack of conditioning brought on by the injury, he left Larionov off the Izvestia team and off CSKA's post-Christmas series of games in North America against NHL teams. For Larionov, it was his Italy–Sweden experience all over again.

Fetisov, Makarov, and Krutov met with Tikhonov, urging him to reinstate Larionov for the games. Tikhonov refused. But this time the matter didn't end. Vyacheslav Koloskov, the chief of Soviet hockey and soccer, intervened and worked out a compromise. Larionov would not play in the Izvestia tournament, but he would play for CSKA against the NHL teams.

Still, three months had passed since the *Ogonyok* letter had been published and nothing fundamental had changed. It was almost a year since the Soviets had won their liberating gold medal at the Calgary Olympics. In the three years before, they had twice lost the world championship, and they had lost the Canada Cup and even their own Izvestia tournament, for the second time, just weeks before the Olympics began. Tikhonov looked increasingly unstable. In Calgary, Koloskov put himself behind the players' bench, nearly invisible among the assistant coaches and trainers, just to be near. More than once, he came up behind an overly angry Tikhonov and gently cupped his elbows with his hands, to steady him.

The Soviets recovered long enough to win again, led by the brilliant and dynamic Fetisov. It was the perfect end to a Soviet hockey era. Tikhonov and Fetisov, who had both won so many national and international victories and who would be too old for the next Olympics, could now leave the scene in a fitting way. They had earned their rewards. Tikhonov would join Tarasov as an influential elder statesman in Soviet hockey. Fetisov, strong, mobile, unbreakably tough physically and mentally, would be the Soviets' perfect pioneer in the NHL.

And they would be free of each other. A watershed in Soviet hockey had been reached. One generation had grown old, a new one would replace it. Soviet hockey's transition into the *perestroika* era would now be easier. A younger man with more contemporary Soviet attitudes would replace Tikhonov. Excited, energized players would respond with even more victories. With no messy unwinnable battles, there would be no losers. Except Tikhonov wouldn't leave.

Fetisov commenced negotiations with the NHL's New Jersey Devils. Lou Lamoriello, the Devils' president and general manager, flew to Moscow to conclude the contract. Fetisov, vacationing on the Black Sea, flew back to Moscow to receive one of his country's highest honours, the Order of Lenin, for his rare contribution to Soviet hockey in a ceremony that would be held the next day; and the same day, ironically, sever his connection to it by signing his precedent-setting NHL contract. As Fetisov was flying in, his Soviet negotiators received a phone call. There is a problem, they were told. It was the same message that General Marushak, chairman of the Sport Committee of the Ministry of Defence, would later tell Fetisov. His release from the army had been delayed, Marushak said, and would not come in time for the next season. Fetisov blamed Tikhonov. Tikhonov said Marushak's decision was beyond his control.

Fetisov was thirty-one. Months passed. Now in the middle of the next season, he was growing more depressed. He could see ahead more fights with Tikhonov, more delays. He had been heartened by Larionov's letter in *Ogonyok*, but when nothing came of it, when Tikhonov tried to keep Larionov out of the

Victory:
Moscow, 1972.

**After the war:
Anatoli Tarasov (top left),
Vsevolod Bobrov
(second from left).**

**The first artificial rink, winter:
Tarasov (far left).**

The patriarch:
Anatoli Tarasov.

The artificial rink, summer,
inside a tent.

MSTISLAV N. BOTASHEV

Inferno:
Game 1, Montreal.

Babes
the wo
Mosco

Maestro: Phil Esposito.

Pilgrimage.

BRIAN PICKELL

The good soldier:
coach Viktor Tikhonov.

The telephone:
Igor Larionov
at Archangelsko

No boundaries:
Igor Larionov's locker.

Vyacheslav
Fetisov.

Father and son:
Sasha Kharlamov, age 13, and
the tomb of Valeri Kharlamov.

**The Rivalry:
CSKA-Dynamo.**

**The new generation:
Luzhniki Arena, Moscow.**

Izvestia tournament and the NHL games, he began to see no end. The system could out-wait him. For him, time was running out.

He raised the stakes. Private words hadn't worked, nor public ones, so he acted. He quit CSKA and the national team. He would no longer play for Tikhonov. He had run out of solutions.

What followed was a national soap opera. The day after Fetisov sat out his first game against Soviet Wings, Tikhonov explained in *Sovietsky Sport* why a few months earlier he had stripped Fetisov of the captaincy of both CSKA and the national team. There had been an incident in Kiev, Tikhonov said. Fetisov, drunk after a game, had punched a hotel worker, an elderly man much decorated in World War Two, fought and used abusive language with militia members summoned to settle him down, militia workers who had worked heroically at Chernobyl after the nuclear plant disaster, offended a nurse at an alcohol rehabilitation centre who said she couldn't believe a sportsman could stoop this low, and made ashamed of him all those who heard him say, as Tikhonov relates, "I am the famous Fetisov. I have received many honours. The NHL paid a million dollars for me. What about you?"

A week later, it was Fetisov's turn in *Sovietsky Sport* to explain why he quit. In the meantime, Soviet readers were told that to keep in shape he had played a game with a pencil factory team. Then the wives got involved. Irina Starikova, wife of Sergei Starikov, a long-time teammate of Fetisov and Larionov, wrote in *Sovietskaya Kultura* that her husband would also resign from CSKA unless Tikhonov was removed. Earlier Tikhonov had suggested that Fetisov's real problem was greed. "The famous Fetisov decided long ago to sell his famous soul," said Tikhonov. The smell of foreign currency had turned his head. Irina Starikova would have none of it. "My husband didn't sign any contract with the NHL so you won't have any chance to accuse him of money-seeking. He is tired of the constant psychological pressure which you created in the club." She cited the cases of two other CSKA players, Mikhail Vasiliev and Alexander Zybin, who had recently left to join other Soviet teams. "Once another player's wife, Alla Babinova, counted that during one season, ten months, her husband spent thirteen evenings at home. But he was lucky to have a wife. Those who didn't weren't allowed to leave Archangelskoye. I feel so sorry for the guys who have to waste their best years so lonely and bored."

Five days later, Tatiana Tikhonova, Tikhonov's wife, defended her man. It was an illuminating interview. She recollected their early years. As a young boy, Viktor had left school at the end of grade seven to play hockey and work. It was only as an adult, going to night school, that he managed to graduate from high school. Then he went on to university, where he graduated as well. It was the same single-mindedness that brought him success in hockey. He sleeps only four or five hours a night, his wife pointed out; for eighteen straight years, Viktor had been apart from her and their son at New Year's, the biggest holiday of the Soviet year, all because of hockey. But asked to comment on Viktor's supposed fanatical devotion to the game, she was unimpressed: "To be successful in anything you have to be fanatically devoted." She remembered the best times in their lives as those when Viktor was coaching in Riga, Latvia. He had been an undistinguished defenceman in the 1950s; he would need to make his name as a coach in the hockey hinterlands. It was in Riga, she recalled, that he felt the real self-confidence that had escaped him all his previous life as a student and player. Even though his greatest success and glory awaited his years in Moscow with CSKA and the national team, she stated that their feelings for Riga should not be surprising. "Every fuzzy-cheeked lieutenant may dream of being a grey-haired general," she explains. "But what does every grey-haired general dream of?"

As for the criticisms of Fetisov and Larionov, she understood their desire to spend more time at home. But if it took living in Archangelskoye's barracks to win, that's the way it had to be.

Late in February, Fetisov was back practising with CSKA. It had taken the intervention of General Marushak himself. If the Tikhonov-Fetisov matter was ever to be resolved, Fetisov would need to be in shape for it to make any difference. And so he must practise. Fetisov wanted none of it; Tikhonov wanted none of him. So their sparring continued. Tikhonov gave instructions that Fetisov be issued a black practice sweater, the sweater of the

"Black Aces," the outcasts. In turn, Fetisov went through the motions of practice. He took part in some of the drills; for others, he just stood by the boards, talking to friends through the mesh netting that surrounded CSKA's practice rink, making sure that when the puck was shot around the boards, he lifted his skates.

This went on for a week. Then one afternoon, Tikhonov and Fetisov met after practice and, when they failed to resolve their differences, Fetisov was released from CSKA. On March 15, ten days later, he received his final paycheque from the army. No longer a player and officer, Fetisov was now a civilian and unemployed.

Meanwhile, Fetisov's CSKA and national team teammates had met and six of them had decided on a course of action. The day after their CSKA season ended, they would have to report to the national team's training camp in Novogorsk to prepare for the world championship. They would tell Tikhonov that if Fetisov was not named to the team, they would refuse to go.

On March 17, 1989, CSKA's final league game ended and Larionov, Makarov, and Krutov went on national television to be interviewed. They told the Soviet people what they had told Tikhonov. Six players, the three of them, plus Valeri Kamensky, Vyacheslav Bykov, and Andrei Khomutov, had issued an ultimatum to Tikhonov. Fetisov plays or we don't play. Tikhonov responded, "We have a lot of good players. We can replace anybody." The next day, the national team met in Novogorsk and voted unanimously for Fetisov's reinstatement. Tikhonov gave in. Fetisov was back on the team.

A few weeks later in Stockholm, with Fetisov, Makarov, and Larionov leading the way, with Tikhonov behind the bench and Koloskov at his elbow, the Soviets won the world championship.

But before the team could leave Stockholm, its young star, Alexander Mogilny, defected. Dancers, writers, and musicians had defected in the past, but never before had a hockey player. A year earlier, after the Calgary Olympics, Tikhonov had summoned Mogilny to his office. He was being promoted to officer rank, Tikhonov told him, as a reward for winning a gold medal. Mogilny related the conversation to Lawrence Martin of the

Globe and Mail. "I said to Tikhonov that I don't want to . . . be a military man." But Tikhonov persisted. "He said that I must sign because he was forming a new first line to replace Makarov, Larionov, and Krutov. He said that if I refused I would not be included in it." Still, Mogilny would not commit himself. "I just don't know yet," he told Tikhonov. "Maybe, maybe not."

Days afterward, the national team flew to Japan for two games as a reward for winning in Calgary. Mogilny was left at home.

Later, Mogilny caved in to Tikhonov's pressure and applied to become an army officer. Tikhonov had won. Once again, he had used his monopoly of rewards and punishments to manipulate the behaviour he wanted. But then Mogilny watched the season-long struggles of his much older teammates with Tikhonov and began to see his own future. Stockholm was his chance. He decided that at twenty years of age he couldn't wait any longer.

For the Soviets, for us, the year 1972 seems unimaginably long ago. Surprisingly perhaps, because they lost, *the series* is almost as cherished a memory for them as it is for Canadians. But in 1972, they were the fuzzy-cheeked lieutenants. Talented, suddenly self-confident and respected, they were full of promise. The future was theirs. They lost *the series* but they won what they had to win.

In many ways what came next was, and is, Tikhonov's story. It is the story of a generation shaped by the patriotism, privation, and mindset of the post-war period. They came to power, and stayed, and ran out of steam, a generation that understood suffering as ethical and good and liberating, that made it a virtue, because they had to. It was the only life open to them. Then, faced with changing times, circumstances, and mindsets, with choice, they could not, and cannot, change. Tikhonov is his generation's good soldier. But Soviet hockey, like Soviet agriculture and industry, has paid the price.

More than forty years ago the Soviets, with few resources and a long headstart to close, centralized everything. They brought to Moscow, eventually to CSKA, the best coaches and players, and the strategy worked. But to keep on working, they needed then to reverse themselves, to decentralize, spreading players and coaches around to other teams in other places, generating competition, stimulating interest, building a bigger, better base of players and coaches. They haven't done it, and Soviet hockey has stagnated. Once the outside world offered the Soviets all the competition they could handle. That changed more than twenty years ago. Now, except for the occasional game against NHL teams, almost always involving the same Soviet players, there is no real outside competition. Inside, it is worse.

CSKA has won thirteen straight championships. In a recent year, it lost only *one* game the entire season. In his entire career, Fetisov never *lost* a single Soviet league title. Vyacheslav Koloskov, the head of Soviet hockey and soccer, admits the obvious. "The major problem with our hockey is that there is virtually no competition in the Soviet league."

The reason has to do with certain Soviet facts of life, among them: centralization gives Moscow more and better of most everything, making it the place of choice for most Soviet citizens and athletes; compulsory military service, for two years at least, brings the best athletes into Army or Dynamo (militia) sports clubs; sports "free agency" allows players to move to their team of choice unconstrained by draft or trade.

Add to these the powerful Soviet instinct to play for the "motherland" and the universal instinct for money, status, and travel that playing for the national team brings. Players on winning teams are chosen more often for the national team, as are winning coaches. Coaches pick the players they know best. Tarasov and Tikhonov, in total, have coached CSKA and the national team for a period of nearly thirty years. Soviet coaches believe in intricate team play. They want their players to play in regular "units," ideally of five, at least of three (forwards) or two (defencemen). Only the best teams have enough good players to form a unit sufficiently strong for national team consideration. Individual stars from weaker teams get overlooked until they move to a better team.

And then there are Tikhonov's own peculiarities. He came to CSKA as the outsider from hockey's hinterland, into the inescapable shadow of Tarasov. CSKA had lost the Soviet championship two of the previous four years, the national team had lost the world championship twice in a row. Insecure by nature, he needed to make his mark quickly and indelibly. He also believed that the national team needed to play at a faster pace. This required better team play, which required greater familiarity between players, which meant playing together more often, which meant playing on the same club team (his). To the stars on weaker teams who somehow didn't get the message, Tikhonov weaved his manipulations. If you don't transfer to CSKA, you'll never see the national team.

Tikhonov stripped the best players from other Soviet teams and lured them to CSKA: Makarov from Chelyabinsk, Kasatonov from Leningrad, Larionov and Kamensky from Voskresensk . . . two-thirds of his current team, more than sixty players in all. He brought CSKA back to the top by making himself too strong and the others too weak. CSKA has never lost again.

This was allowed to happen because it would have taken deliberate, strong-willed, and persistent intervention to keep it from happening and none was forthcoming. Great teams are made up of great players who move on into positions of influence. They take with them pride in their team's past and a stake in its future. Tarnish that future, lose more often, and their memory, and others' of them, is tarnished. They also take with them a powerful reason to underrate or ignore altogether the role their enormous advantages played in their success. They want to see themselves as self-made men. They want their success to reflect back on *them* – their hard work, their discipline, their specialness. Change the rules to weaken CSKA? Let the other teams do as we did and improve themselves, they say.

But mostly, it was allowed to happen because in the Soviet Union the national team takes first priority. What the rest of the world thinks matters to Canadians, but it seems to matter more to the Soviets. In fact, it may be that because the Soviet Union is a far poorer country, it cannot afford to perform to both a world and domestic audience at once and so, unlike rich countries, it must choose: guns instead of butter; space stations instead of automobiles. The world audience doesn't matter more, but the domestic matters less.

Thus, one superteam is created as a foundation to win world championships and Olympic gold medals. It establishes an international reputation for excellence, travels the world as the image of Soviet hockey and Soviet life, and earns much needed hard currency. Except to do so, CSKA must play almost as many games outside the Soviet Union, before foreign audiences, as it does inside, and the Soviet league schedule must accommodate this. But a season is only so long – only so many games can be played. As a result, for each of the nearly forty games CSKA plays abroad, thirteen teams sit home and watch.

The national team causes even greater disruption. The Soviet league season begins the second week of October, then shuts down early in December for six weeks to allow the national team to prepare for the Izvestia tournament and a few club teams to play abroad. Starting up again in mid-January, the league finishes completely by mid-March so the national team can prepare for the world championship. The season lasts only forty games, which poses no problem for the elite few good enough to play many additional games but a big problem for the rest. Yet, this is the bargain the Soviet hockey system has been willing to strike: in the eyes of Soviet officials, a stacked, non-competitive CSKA and a short season are both necessary to the success of the national team. As proof, the national team has won world championships and world attention. As usual, however, those at home pay the price.

Competition is the lifeblood of sport. Sport is not an art. Good players need good opponents to improve; fans need competition for the drama and excitement it brings. Kids need a reason to play hockey and not soccer, basketball, or track and field. Without competition, fan support weakens, fewer kids play hockey, and those who do, and reach the top, grow quickly bored and stagnate and begin to lose. It is what has happened to Soviet hockey.

There are four Moscow teams now in the sixteen-team Soviet league – CSKA, Dynamo, Spartak, and Soviet Wings. Almost every season, CSKA finishes on top, while the others share three of the next four places. When they play each other, usually in the new Luzhniki arena, they do so in front of near-capacity crowds – but fewer than 8,000. When they play non-Moscow teams, the crowds are usually between 2,000 and 3,000 people.

There are many reasons why. Here, in their absence, one can see the power of North American marketing techniques and their importance to sports. Even the most basic information – the date and time and opponents for a game – is unknown to the public until a few days in advance. There are no posters around the city to tell of games, no wallet-size schedules to consult, no newspaper, radio, or TV ads or pre-game stories to inform and promote; there is not even a regular home night for the fans to count on. The intricate, symbiotic, inextricable web of "advertainment" so crucial to entertainment success in North America does not exist in the Soviet Union. It is word-of-mouth – pass it on.

There are no sweaters or hats or T-shirts for fans to buy to identify with their favourite team or player. A few posters of "the five" – Fetisov, Krutov, Makarov, Larionov, Kasatonov – are available and they get gobbled up like Levis during between-period intermissions. But little is done to encourage the fan, to get him and her out of their now larger and more comfortable flats and into a hockey rink. As Yuri Korolev, deputy head of Soviet hockey, relates, "Not long ago, we didn't even let anybody into an arena under the age of sixteen without their parents. Three or four years ago, there was a campaign to suppress hooliganism and the disturbance of public order. It meant that fans had to sit in an arena as you do at an opera, without being able to jump to your feet, shout, or anything. So fans stayed away. Why should they go to an arena and sit like mummies?"

But the ultimate marketing technique is competition, and without it none of the rest matters much. The absence of competition is killing Soviet hockey for the fans, but also for the players and coaches. If you already know who is going to win, why watch? Why play? And the Soviets know. What does it do to a player who knows he is sure to win? "When there's no competition, there's no fight," Fetisov complains. "It's just not interesting to play. You lose your sense of danger, your sense of survival. You lose the energy you really need when you're in trouble. It's the same for the team. You never test yourself. You never push your limits." Says Larionov, "For five years, winning the national championship has brought no joy or interest to me."

What does it do to the coach of a weaker team who loses a star player to CSKA? "It is a tragedy," cries Nikolai Epstein. Now retired, Epstein coached Khimik, from Larionov's hometown of Voskresensk. He saw Alexander Ragulin, Alexander Maltsev, Larionov, Kamensky, and others swallowed up by CSKA. "Imagine, they took Ragulin, they took Eduoard Ivanov from me. They played for CSKA for ten years. They were the best defence pair in the country. What would Khimik have been like if they stayed? At times, you just want to throw in the towel and walk away. It's like you've climbed to the top of the mountain, you have a goal, and boom. Or you've just finished building a snowman. You just have to add the eyes, and the next morning you go back and they've knocked it down. And you've got to build it all over again."

The tragedy is also the players'. Only a few who are taken by CSKA become stars; most fade from view. "They are leaders on their own teams," explains Epstein. "When they come to CSKA, they are intimidated. They see all the great stars around them. It's hard for them to spread their wings and develop what's in them. Makarov and Larionov didn't join CSKA until they were mature players. They were lucky." As for the rest, it is sad. Larionov says, "When kids come to CSKA, they are put into a definite and rigid framework. 'Play according to the plan, do what you are told,' they hear. They can't do anything on their own because if they do, and make a mistake, the coaches will be so rough on them that they'll never try again. As separate personalities, they just cease to exist. They play without any thought or improvisation. On the ice, their job is to get open, receive passes, pass, and that's it."

All around the country, Soviet fans ask, "Where are the new young stars? Who will replace Fetisov, Krutov, Makarov, Larionov? What about the new young coaches? Where did they all go?" They went with the competitive wind, with CSKA's monopoly. Young players need good players around them as teammates to be their inspirations and models. Young coaches need good players on their teams to carry out innovative new strategies, to encourage them to create and dream. If these good players are taken away, young players and coaches never develop, and the system begins to break down. At one time what was good for CSKA was good for Soviet hockey. It is no longer.

Things are now beginning to change. The Soviet sense of inarguable destiny, rightness, and infallibility is fading if not gone. The Soviets, too, are starting to see that there *are* other ways. Advertising now covers the boards that ring Luzhniki's ice surface. The name "Giza," an Italian agricultural company, runs across the chests of Spartak players. Asked if CSKA might ever cover the front of its proud jerseys with McDonald's "golden arches," the Soviet official in charge of negotiating such matters only shrugged. "Why not?!" he said. The war on fan hooliganism seems over; the fans have won. Supporters of opposing teams now sit at opposite ends of the arena and, like English soccer fans, sing and wave their flags and banners to the accompaniment of – an organ! And what does the organ play? Such traditional favourites as: "When the Saints Go Marchin' In," "Hava Nagelah," and, adopted by CSKA as a fight song, "Kiss Him Goodbye" – "Na-na, na-na-na-na, hey-hey, goodbye!" The wonders of *glasnost*.

As for the players, they might be Canadian, American, West European. Fetisov drives around Moscow in his blue Mercedes wearing an ABC-TV Calgary Olympics ski jacket. At Archangelskoye, Krutov and Larionov lounge around reading newspapers, Krutov in a sweatshirt that reads "The 40th NHL All-Star Game Edmonton, Alberta," Larionov in one from Quebec City's "Rendez-vous '87." Kasatonov and several others wear sweatshirts with "ROOTS" across their chests. Others have on New Jersey Devils' and Calgary Flames' baseball hats. Five years ago, their look would have seemed disloyal, but no more. They are contemporary Soviets. They see no boundaries on their horizons. They look outside, not in.

And outside, they now see the NHL. It was Tarasov's fantasy place, his ultimate opponent, his bogeyman. Last year, two NHL games were broadcast on Soviet television. This fall, the Calgary Flames and Washington Capitals held their training camps in the Soviet Union. To Fetisov's father and his generation, NHL players were soulless professionals. They lived vulnerable, joyless, and pitiable lives, manipulated by owners and their money; they played out of fear, not love of sport or country. To Fetisov and his generation, an NHL player is just like them. It is what they want to be.

The Soviet Ice Hockey Federation has decided to cast its lot with the NHL. The Federation is not yet certain how to do it. Like most westward steps taken in this country, each is cautious, waters-testing, and reversible. A few older players, an experimental guard, have been allowed to sign with NHL teams. The Federation will watch carefully. How do they play? How are they treated by teammates, management, fans, opponents? How do they adapt to North American living? Are there embarrassing "incidents," defections, failures? What price are NHL teams willing to pay for them?

And what about back home? How do already long-suffering, star-starved fans react to the absence of some of their favourites? Do they stay away from games in even greater numbers? Is hockey hurt further? With their near-monopoly of best players, CSKA is hit hardest. How do CSKA fans react to losing more often, even to losing a championship? And what about the proud patriotic Soviet people – will they accept another country's flag raised at the world championship while many of their stars are playing somewhere else?

And what about the profound psychological implications this NHL connection brings? After more than forty years, it will mean for the Soviets turning their league into a farm system for the NHL, as the Swedes and Finns have done. It means accepting being second best, *always*. In time, young Soviet players will grow up with different dreams, with dreams of other places. CSKA and the Soviet national team will become mere stops along the way to the New Jersey Devils or St. Louis Blues. All this requires contortion of the mind, a "restructuring" or *perestroika*, that is boggling. Does it not twist the psyche even to the point of breaking?

For the Soviets, is there a better way, perhaps the long-discussed but never-created European professional league? That way the Soviet Federation could keep closer control. The league would be structured, as European leagues of all sports already are, with world championships and the Olympics in mind. But would European players turn their sights away from North America and stay at home? Could European teams afford the salary wars with the NHL that would follow? And in any event, does anyone have the stomach for the complications and fights such a new league guarantees?

While keeping that as an option and selling its players to NHL teams, the Soviet Federation has approved negotiations with the NHL that would put a Soviet team into the league. The scenario goes something like this: a corporate owner, likely North American, perhaps with European business interests, makes application for and is awarded an NHL expansion franchise. The owner pays the regular franchise price and any territorial indemnities. The team is sited in a North American city and in Moscow, with half of its home games played in each city. For five years, perhaps, the team is treated as a special case, with restrictions placed on the drafting or trading of Soviet players. At that point, the team becomes like any other NHL team.

The Soviet Federation and its agents in North America have already had discussions with prospective corporate owners. Their biggest roadblock will be the NHL. The NHL would prefer to avoid the messiness of special arrangements. It is already in a period of expansion and would like to spread around the Soviet players to all of its teams, so it could argue more effectively the public relations fight that the dilution of expansion this time is being counterbalanced by the influx of a new source of players. But mostly, the NHL does not want to deal in nationalities. In a corporate world, in a global world, nationalities are dangerous. They encourage, almost ensure, irrational, unpredictable behaviour. They run counter to the ideal business state of mind and business climate. In the past, the NHL has even balked at having Canadian and American divisions. A Soviet team creates immensely greater risks. For what happens if the Cold War heats up again? Would the Soviet players be withdrawn? Would the host country withdraw their visas? And what about the corporate owner's investment?

The most likely scenario is the one already begun – Soviet

players being sold to NHL teams. What is remarkable about the others is that they are even being thought about, discussed, sometimes agreed on, and taken seriously. This has to do, in part, with a general "globalization" in the world, and more particularly with Gorbachev's *glasnost* and *perestroika*. It also has to do with money. The Soviet Union is a poor country. In hockey, that shows itself in championship teams wearing nine different generations of hockey socks. It means hand-me-down and hand-me-down-again equipment even for the best young players. Fetisov remembers travelling to Canada for the first time in 1974, when he was sixteen years old. Someone gave him a pair of "Canadian" skates. "It changed how I played," he said. "The blade was so much stronger. I could skate differently. It was the difference between riding in a Cadillac or in some old car." In the years before the Canada-Russia series of 1972, Canadians had remarked on the excessive passing and poor shooting (with few slapshots) of the Soviets. But their sticks, like clubs, were heavy and awkward, broke easily, and were too costly to replace very often for most teams and players. How else could they play?

In all of the Soviet Union, with a population of about 286 million, there are 116 indoor arenas, not all of which are used for hockey. In all of Saskatchewan, population 1 million, there are 459. In Moscow, there are four teams in the top Soviet league. Those teams are part of sports clubs that sponsor boys' teams beginning at age eight. CSKA has approximately 400 boys in its minor hockey teams between the ages of eight and eighteen. Dynamo, Spartak, and Soviet Wings have about the same. Together, these 1,600 boys, plus another 800 at two other sports clubs in the city, are the only boys in Moscow, population 10 million, who have regular access to an indoor rink. And in Moscow, as in most of the populated hockey-playing areas of the country, outdoor ice is certain only two months a year. The Federation's priority is to build more rinks as efficiently and bare-bones as possible. Moscow's 1980 Olympics set back arena construction, and sports facility construction of all sorts, for almost a decade. Peter had to be robbed to pay Paul.

Soviet players are now sold to NHL teams to buy hockey sticks, skates, gloves, and socks to outfit and send on their way the next generation of Soviet players. Put another way, for one Soviet star, Fetisov perhaps, one new rink can be built, a rink with a life expectancy far longer than that of a thirty-one-year-old hockey player. It is the Soviets' rock-and-a-hard-place bargain. But this time it is butter instead of guns, automobiles instead of space stations, inside instead of outside.

Soviet hockey is not what it was supposed to be in 1972, in part because of the heavy thumb of Tikhonov and his generation. But someday even Tikhonov will pass. Poorness, their heaviest thumb, and the system that produced it define the Soviets' future.

In 1972, the Soviets held up a mirror to us and, for the first time, we saw ourselves. We looked a little rough around the edges, like street fighters, commanding in close quarters, in the corners, in front of their net and ours, flailing in the open ring, passionate, always on the emotional edge. They looked dazzling and quick, creative individually and as a team, disciplined and well-conditioned, unemotional, almost like robots. And the message in the mirror was undeniable: they were heading in the right direction and we were not.

What is in that mirror now? In 1987, fifteen years and many ups and downs later, the Canada Cup was won by Canada, two games to one, in a remarkably played and passionate series. The score in each game was 6–5, the same magic score that decided the first series in 1972. So what had really changed? This was no smashing victory. It gave us no claim on the future. The Soviets were good and would likely be better the next time – except that, maybe for the first time, we realized that we might be better, too.

We had had fifteen years to blow it, but it didn't happen. It had always happened to Canadians before. It had seemed our destiny. But not this time. In 1972, we saw us as we were, and them as they would be. And staring us in the eye was the future we could see. But we changed and so did they. We added system and science to instinct and natural resources and became more multidimensional. The Soviets improved, too, but have never quite realized the promise their model held out.

Now in 1989, we see us, and them, both as we are. And the future looks different. Our team play is still not all it should be. Our speed can pick up. But both are improved. Our passion, which once looked so primitive, set in this better direction, now seems remarkable, a mystery to the rest of the hockey world and its fans. In admiration, they shake their heads at the "never say die," "never quit" Canadians, at their most dangerous just when you think a game is won.

Once Canadians played too much like individuals. But now, set in the context of an improved team game, even that looks different to us. For in every team game, there is a moment when teammates can no longer help, when, out of space and time, facing a goalie or defender, it's up to you. You must do it yourself. Europeans once imported Canadian players to add skill and power to their teams, then decided to take Soviets and Czechoslovaks. Now it is Canadians again. Others, they found, nurtured on intricate team play, depend on their teammates tactically and psychologically. Canadians are more independent and resourceful. They can work with anyone, they've found; they can go it alone if they need to. With better team play our individuality has become a virtue.

The 1972 series is a national memory. The 1987 series was fun. Less was at stake; the burden of metaphor was not so overwhelming. We are now better able to lose and more likely to win. We've each gone through good times and bad times since 1972, and though we would never have believed it then, we've reached a kind of competitive equilibrium – they can't bury us; we can't bury them. Hockey and world affairs are played in a competitive pack. One you can leave behind, but never for long. Maybe size and power aren't destiny after all.

We entered the world in 1972 and were forever changed by it. Yet despite the messiness and uncertainty it caused, we managed to cope. Now it's the Soviets' turn. And if nothing here is now unimaginable, what's possible is another story. Their struggle, and ours, continues.

There are no final victories.

CHAPTER SIX

THE MAGIC OF PLAY

ROY MacGREGOR'S STORY

IT HITS ME THE MOMENT I AWAKE. I STARE OUT THE BEDROOM WINDOW through the gathered frost and the first light is made brighter by the knowledge that today there will be hockey. This knowledge, this heightened awareness, will be with me over breakfast. It will haunt me when I should be paying attention to other matters during the morning and again in the afternoon. I will think of plays over the lunch hour. I will imagine a breakaway and think about the relative advantages of deking over shooting. I will remind myself to knock down high passes with a glove rather than my stick whenever possible. I will daydream about tucking a puck in between a defenceman's skates and coming up with it again on the other side, home and free for the last-minute goal that breaks the tie. I will linger with this fantasy long enough to feel the rap of a winger's stick against my shinpads, the congratulatory cuff of a teammate's glove on my head, the ringing, surprising sound my own name makes when it bursts in a hollow arena. I will not fight it, even if it sometimes distracts me, for this is simply the way it is. On game day, from the moment I wake to the moment I fall asleep, I think about hockey.

I am forty-one years old.

Forty-one years old, yet I still carry hockey around in my head for the entire day that I am scheduled to play, rubbing up against it like a cat the way others might nurse a small flirtation. I go over my equipment and wonder if I have enough tape, if my skates need sharpening, if there are any goals left in the pock-marked Sherwood PMP 5030, left shot, No. 6 lie, illegal curve. I put new tape on, though none is needed. I eat at the correct time. No matter what the circumstances, I would refuse a drink, even a light beer. It might affect my game.

And yet, what is this *game*? It is played late at night in arenas that are absolutely empty unless a girlfriend happens to be so keen on a certain player she will undergo freezing cold and tortuous boredom and coffee that tastes like melted pucks to keep the relationship going. Once the relationship changes – either through marriage or breakup – she is never seen again. Ever. There are no standings kept, no scoring statistics, and most assuredly no scouts . . . and yet, if the game goes badly, the week goes badly; if the game goes well, all is well and right with the world. The dog gets a special pet when I burst in the door long after other responsible parents on the block have turned out the lights and gone to bed. I stay up an extra half-hour, savouring the moment that no one else noticed and no one else could possibly care about.

Like almost every other Canadian child, I had hockey handed to me the same way I eventually moved onto solid foods and chamberpots. Even as I write, there is a faded sepia photograph staring down at me of the 1927-28 Eganville Senior Hockey Team, D. MacGregor standing third from the right with his hair slicked and split down the middle straight as a plumb line, his gloved hand hanging onto a stick that is also dead straight, his hockey sweater, pants, socks, gloves, and skates seemingly out of another century, which they very nearly are. I cannot see my father when I stare at this picture, though I know it is him and have heard the stories of the cutters and buffalo blankets and the whole village of Eganville heading off down the line to see them play at Renfrew. He talks still – sixty-two years later – of the referee who blew his whistle on the Bonnechere River and brought the game to a halt while he skated slowly over to the bank, took a leisurely leak, and then returned to centre ice for a face-off. Still, it doesn't look like my father. It looks like a young man getting his picture taken with his teammates, his eyes as proud and filled with promise as little Jimmy Reeves, the team mascot who sits in front, little Jimmy Reeves who is himself now an old man.

My father is eighty-two now. The plumb line down the centre of his head has widened to a six-lane highway. But inside the head the game still dances as it did back in the season of 1927-28. He talks about Wayne Gretzky to my youngest child, a boy who is six, and it is as if they are the same age when they talk. We all share in common a game that makes everything else easier. My father came from the bush, a lumberman who worked outdoors all of his life and did not have a radio or television until he was almost seventy-five. I was born in a village where there was no electricity or running water and raised in a small town where, on a Saturday night, I would walk down the street to the widow Newton's, a lovely old woman in her eighties who would be sure to have chocolate chip cookies on a plate and Foster Hewitt on the radio. My son was born in a city and has always lived in one. He can watch a game a night on television if he wishes. Perhaps one day he will have the Montreal Canadiens and Moscow Red Army appearing as holographs in his finished basement. Three lives separated by time, society, and money – yet three lives that have in common a love of the game of hockey as much as they share an imperfect gene pool.

My father did not see me play my first games, and I remain indebted to God that he did not see me play some of my later games. I began the game on a pair of my older brother's skates, the rust removed with steel wool, the toes stuffed with three pairs of grey woollen socks. They were tied by my mother and I walked with my sister Ann, falling almost constantly, across the empty lot and past Munroe's barn to a spot where my friend Brent's father had shovelled all week long in a valiant attempt to level a sloping yard. Late each night Maurice Munroe had stood out there with a flashlight in one hand and a hose at full throttle in the other. The ice was brittle and pimpled, yet so shockingly slippery that my first hockey play brought tears to my own eyes, not those of any amused parent, when I fell straight back and struck my head with a sound not unlike two rocks colliding underwater.

Yet no one but me remembers those times. They are too true. The better memories – polished up and improved – sit in a red Empire Scrap Book that my mother had the good sense to store away when, for a short while, I believed that all I would ever require of life could be fitted into a backpack and stamped on a passport. She kept it and I am now glad she did, for it now brings back memories every bit as sweet and strong as the cancelled passport that took me through Europe and North Africa in the late sixties and early seventies.

The scrapbook is a cheap, manila folder, the price – 15 cents – still pencilled on the cover. The first page opens on me, eight years old, smiling out from a picture that was taken on a day when our little northern Ontario town put on a special display for the three Toronto daily newspapers to show that life goes on in cottage country in the winter as well. Below is a clipping from the *Huntsville Forester*: "Goals by MacGregor Gives Auxiliary Tie With Hay & Co. 2–2" The story begins:

> The Legion Auxiliary's Roy MacGregor turned two spectacular solo rushes into a 2–2 tie with Hay & Co. Saturday morning.
>
> A highlight of a Huntsville Hockey League Squirt playoff game, MacGregor's goals marked the second time Auxiliary had battled from behind a one-goal deficit.
>
> Young defenseman Michael Allemano was especially good for the Hookmen, breaking up many Auxiliary rushes. Both of the Hay & Company goals by Brent Munroe and John Newell, were scored on power plays.

It is important to remember here that this is squirt hockey, age seven and eight, that the full name of the team is the Legion Ladies' Auxiliary, and that the game was played on only one half the ice, a line of boards being temporarily erected so two games could go on at once. But no matter. This is what small-town hockey is all about. So what if there were no "spectacular solo rushes." I remember both goals vividly, one on a scramble, one on a slow shot the length of the ice that the goaltender fanned on. But the local paper knew what it was doing. Creating local heroes. And the day the paper came out there were grown-ups on Main Street who had noticed. An old relative even stopped me, opened her purse, pulled out the clipping, and said I'd soon be in the NHL. Damn right I would.

Today the glue has dried and some of the clippings fall out when the book is opened. "Pee Wee's Cut Down Orillia," "Pee Wee's Batter Burks Falls." The day we won the prestigious Wardell & Company trophy, the story began: "Anglo Canadian's one-two punch of Harry Snowden and Roy MacGregor continued to spark the Hidemen at the Arena on Tuesday night . . . " It was glorious. The teams had nicknames – the Hidemen meant you were sponsored by the local tannery, the Hookmen meant the local lumberyard – and the goalscorers were transformed magically in the local paper from goofy kids who had barely stopped wetting the bed into *somebodies*.

I see on one page of the scrapbook where I have practised writing my autograph. I see with the grace of time how totally absurd the notion was that anyone would ever want it. But I smile at the small-town myth for the harmless, happy days it gave me and God knows how many tens of thousands of others. Hockey, for most of us, was the first time – and so often the only time – we ever felt we truly mattered.

In a small town such as the one where I grew up in the north of Muskoka, hockey even mattered more than school. No one ever puzzled over the fact that, in all the town's history, there had been but one Ontario scholar, a grade 13 graduate with an average of more than 80 per cent. My sister came close, but no one noticed. When the town twisted in self-doubt, it was over why no one ever seemed to go on to a successful pro hockey career that seemed, in squirt and peewee and bantam and midget, such a sure thing. If you came close in hockey, though, it gave you status for life.

No one could understand this. The teams I played on, by

virtue of age and location, competed for several years against the Parry Sound all-star teams that included a blond brushcut named Bobby Orr. Year after year we would debate over who was the superior player, our Tim Kelly or their Bobby Orr. I can still vividly recall our coach, Mye Sedore – the full-time, *paid* all-star coach for our town of 3,000 – coming into the dressing room one day and holding up the game card so we could see where Orr had signed. "Lookit that signature!" Mye bellowed. "And you guys are worried about a kid who can't even write his goddamn name?" Well, it worked for a moment. But once we got on the ice and found out Bobby Orr was playing with a stick, not a ballpoint, it was quickly over, as usual.

One day Bobby Orr went over to the Oshawa Generals and Tim Kelly went off to the London Knights, and Orr went on to Boston and Kelly came back home and settled down and raised a lovely family. It happens everywhere, in every small town across the country, and today, when I hear a major-league scout or manager say that for every player who makes the NHL there is always one just as good who does not, I think about our Tim Kelly. Today he is a perfectly happy and contented human being who was, in a few memories, good enough to go just as far as he wanted. Which is exactly what he did.

When I think of hockey in the small town, I don't automatically think of the Huntsville Memorial Arena, though I cannot see the word "arena" without conjuring up the smell of Dustbane and the smooth hiss a wide broom makes on polished cement floors, the way the low lights glitter on the ice when you come in out of daylight for an afternoon practice, the sound of a freshly sharpened blade on the first untouched corner, the delicious sound of a puck off the crossbar. But I do not automatically see and hear and smell this arena when I think of hockey in a small town. No, there is more hockey played in a town like this on the roads and on the frozen bay and in the schoolyard than on the rink. One game a week and one practice. The rest of the time we would play on the streets or wait for the old cop, Sy Payne, to haul the hose out from the school basement, over the green boards, and onto the ice we had cleared with the shovels we carried from home. And when winter had settled in, we would shovel off the bay or the beaver pond, always with a drinking hole chopped to the side, a small but gaping hole down which, no matter where we placed it, the only puck we had would vanish at least once a winter.

But the greatest games were played on Dufferin Street, up by the reservoir. Hardly any traffic, and anyone who did come by had the courtesy to bridge the goalposts. Hockey from school's out to past dark; hockey on Saturday, on Sunday; hockey under the only streetlight on the rare nights when you and the tennis ball and a stick as thin as a toothpick could sneak out after supper. Brent Munroe and Eric Ruby and I were the "little guys," my brother Jim's gang the "big guys." One big guy equalled two little guys. Brent eventually hit 6'4" and Eric 6'2", and in the end they eventually scrapped that measure, but we were still a team unto our own, kids who would play "best out of ten" if there was no game to be had or shoot ice chunks if there was no ball to be found. In spring, when the town's interest gradually turned to lacrosse, there would be a month when the road was bare and the snowbanks crystal, and the rules would be bent so goaltenders could use lacrosse sticks and pass by throwing, but that was the only stated rule there ever was. Everything else was understood. Half ice after a goal. No golf shots. No slashing. No crosschecks. No quitting just because it's your ball. Fights would often carry on while everyone else took shots. When the sap was running Mrs. Wieler would offer up a pailful fresh from the tapped sugar maple near the road. The original Gatorade. And in return we would promise not to chase the ball into her raspberry bushes.

It is difficult now to convey how deeply hockey could penetrate a life back then. We had no television. My brother had a table-top hockey game, the kind where the metal players fit on and are controlled by steel rods running beneath. There were no slots, however, so the players could not go up and down the ice. All you could do was turn the rod between the thumb and finger so they could pass and shoot. All four defence rods eventually broke and we realized a shot was faster if we flicked the players from above rather than turned from below. And marbles were better than pucks. My brother found he could raise the marbles if he slightly bent his man. I suffered my first serious hockey injury wearing my pajamas in his bedroom.

Our father took us to Maple Leaf Gardens to see the Leafs play Detroit. Neither of us had ever seen lights so bright or felt air so alive. In an instant we more than doubled the number of other humans we had seen in our lives. The urinals spooked me. Our father pointed to Gordie Howe and said he was the greatest hockey player of all time. At least once a year in the thirty-odd years since he asks if we remember. We will always remember, even when he can no longer remind.

Out of hockey came all status. Brent and Eric and I played on the town lacrosse team that won the provincial championship, but we were lesser in some way than the great hockey stars who might only have made it to the district final. How could we argue? In summer the hot, stinking arena would be filled with parents who watched out of duty and tourists who came – once – out of curiosity. In winter on a Saturday night, the entire town would be at the hockey game, Mrs. Wieler with her cowbell, old Albert with his grenade-like cheers, Mr. Reynolds with his clipboard to handle the timekeeper's announcing. To say it was an event would be to do it a disservice. It was the only event.

We played right through until juvenile, sometimes making the all-star team, sometimes not. It cost two dollars to register. Those who could not afford equipment would get it somehow. Those who did not play were not only a minority, they were a curiosity. I had a strength, skating, but I had one enormous weakness, checking, and it seemed they would never come to any understanding. I also began wearing thick, ugly, horn-rimmed glasses and to this day I do not know if I gave up going into corners because I was afraid of opponents or more afraid of my mother if I walked in with yet another broken lug or snapped frame or shattered lens. Whatever, I cost as many goals as I ever scored. Coach Sedore gave up in frustration, and though I then blamed him wholly, I am now willing at least to share the blame for my own shortcomings. Perhaps when I am as old as my father I will be able to place the blame entirely where it needs to go. When I began to ride the all-star bench too much, I quit and played only house league. And eventually quit that as well.

My friends dropped out even earlier, Brent because he lacked speed and was proving to be a finer lacrosse player and Eric, the goaltender, because his parents grew weary of receiving letters from the town league executives concerning his behaviour. He could not explain to them that he had knocked another player unconscious only after a puck had taken out his own front teeth. Perhaps if he had hit the player who'd shot the puck and not some innocent teammate, it would have helped, but by then it was too late. A boy who not only looked like but acted like his cousin Eddie Shack, Eric could count on little understanding given his behaviour as a goalie. At fourteen, he'd already been suspended several times, and one season he didn't show up for the first practice or the second, and that was it.

Brent and Eric and I are remembered – entirely by ourselves – for one spectacular moment in Huntsville sports, but unfortunately it had nothing to do with anything that happened on the ice. We were at an awards ceremony at the Legion hall. Mayor Hubbell was speaking. I was praying I would win the bantam-level most valuable player trophy that my older brother and an older cousin already had their names on. The mayor was speaking and one of us – we have conveniently forgotten who – passed wind. It was such a wicked slapshot of a fart that it stopped His Worship in mid-sentence. Eric started giggling. Brent started giggling. I started giggling. In a moment we were all three of us underneath the table, hiding behind the white tablecloths and sputtering like tight balloons. Not a sound from the 300 players and coaches and managers and executives and honoured guests. Finally Mrs. Kelly – Tim's mother – from the ladies' auxiliary came out from the kitchen, stuck her head down under the tablecloths, and informed us, in a very loud voice, that "If you boys can't behave yourselves, you can leave."

I didn't win the trophy. *Brent* did. And Eric won for goaltenders. The five of us walked home up Lansdowne Street that night, Brent holding his Robin Hood Oats trophy, Eric holding his, and me holding back my tears, grateful for the poor street lighting our parents complained about.

After midget, the three of us came back together in hockey only once. We were all seventeen or eighteen and a few of the small towns and villages around were forming an "outlaw" league they didn't seem able to decide should be called "Juvenile" or "Junior D" hockey. Junior "Z" would have been rather more to the point. Baysville came after Brent and he talked Eric and me into going out. It was, as they say in that part of the country, a real "woodchoppers' league."

By the time the first – and only – season was through, we had won the district championship against Gravenhurst, but that is not what I remember. I don't recall the goals scored or the ones Eric stopped, but I do remember one of the players on our team was twenty-three years old and played on a younger brother's birth certificate. I remember he kept a lighted cigarette on the boards during warmup. I remember two brothers on the team and their father, all three of whom were usually drunk. I remember on the road trips we would have a case of twenty-four and open it from the bottom, one of the players convinced that, if a cop found a sealed beer case, he would search no further. I remember our sweaters – Boston, we were the "Baysville Bruins." And I remember the team rage was chewing tobacco and how I figured I'd rather try backchecking than dip my finger into one of those black tins and then into my mouth. And, of course, I remember the violence.

The most spectacular game we played was against Bracebridge. In the first period I was caught with my head down, as usual, and hit so hard at centre ice that I turned a complete circle in the air before landing again on my skates. That seemed to set the tone. I remember Brent getting into a fistfight with one of the Fuller brothers and suddenly the ice was flooded with Fullers from the stands. And I remember the one move I will regret to my grave, when I was racing a Bracebridge defenceman named Dave Cumberland for the puck in his end and decided I'd better hit him before he killed me. There was no glass around the boards then, nothing in fact until the icing lines where thick screen was strung from beams. Somewhere around the corner face-off circle I hit Cumberland from below and drove him up into the boards. But instead of flying into the seats, he hit right where the trussing began for the screen. It was a sickening sound. He snapped into the wood and went limp, falling back down onto the ice. Much later we would find out he had a broken elbow, a twisted knee, and cracked ribs, but as I say, that was much later. First there would be a riot.

Perhaps you have seen film footage of the Canadian junior team's disgraceful performance against the Soviets a few years ago, when the ice was covered with brawling players. Well, take away the television coverage and throw in a few parents, several cousins, a few drunks, the Fuller clan, and the Ontario Provincial Police and you'll have a rough idea of what it was like in the minutes that followed. Brent was still dealing with the Fuller family when a father of one of the Bracebridge players climbed over the boards and began charging across the ice. He grabbed a Bracebridge player's stick and began swinging it like a broadsword as he approached the area where Brent and I stood. Eric, who had been ignored in his goal crease all this time, raced up the ice and came on the man from behind. With one blow of the goalie stick the older man was left crumpled and moaning on the ice.

The focus instantly shifted to Eric, who had the good sense to keep on skating. Out through the doors he ran, his goalie skates screeching and sparking across the lobby, out in full equipment into the parking lot where he dove into a Huntsville car and locked all the doors. Back inside the arena, the police restored order, the game was called because we had no back-up goaltender, and we quickly changed and left without showering, walking out into a parking lot filled with the flashing lights of police cars, the flashing lights of the ambulance arriving from Orillia, and a snarling crowd that kept yelling for our goalie. Eric, still in full equipment, turned a window down far enough to shout *"He's already gone home!"* But no one was fooled. Had the police not been there, he might have been buried in full equipment as well.

I did not play after that remarkable season for a dozen years. My equipment vanished and I did not even skate. The Philadelphia Flyers came along and, for the longest time, I was convinced that the standards set by the Muskoka outlaw league had gone on to set the standards for professional hockey. It was no longer the game I had learned to love so much down on the bay and up on

Dufferin Street. The sole contact I had with the game was in writing about it for various magazines, and I was generally critical of what I saw.

But in 1975, I was sent on assignment by *Maclean's* to spend two weeks in Sweden with a Canadian team of bantam hockey players and I came back convinced that the Flyers were on the wrong track. The more I saw of European hockey, the more entranced I once again became with the inherent beauty of the game. If you looked past the Broad Street Bullies and their imitators, the *game* was still being played, if largely unnoticed. When the Montreal Canadiens won the Stanley Cup in 1975 through speed and passing, some of what had been lost was won back again. Lesser teams wanted to become like the champions, and for the first time in years the championship went to those who believed in skill over force. The Canadiens began a long domination and gradually, by the 1980s, the impact of Soviet and European hockey was also changing North American hockey into the game it had once been. I wrote articles on people like Guy Lafleur and Marcel Dionne and, strangely enough, I began to fantasize again about doing the impossible on a pair of skates.

I began playing shinny. I bought new equipment and, for the first time in my life, I was able to buy *good* equipment, not hand-me-downs or the cheapest skates Canadian Tire had in stock, but the kind of equipment the best players used to have. I got contact lenses and, for once, could see the wingers I'd spent my younger years ignoring. Not that it made much difference. By the time I'd decided to pass to teammates I could see so clearly for the first time, I no longer had the puck.

Soon shinny wasn't enough. I joined a Toronto group playing on Thursday nights with full equipment and different team sweaters, and soon Thursday became, for me, the most important day of the week. I moved to Ottawa and joined a full league, the Canterbury Rusty Blades, four different teams with bright sweaters, team captains, annual drafts. We played twice a week and soon two days out of the week were more special than the others. We formed a tournament team and now, four or five times a year, we play our hearts out for little plastic trophies and baseball caps while our children cheer from the stands, the exact reversal of the minor hockey experience. When we pick up a new player who had a stint in junior hockey or played professional in Europe, or we discover that the team we're up against has a player who made the American Hockey League or had a cup of coffee with the Detroit Red Wings, it suddenly, magically, makes all our past glories richer. We know this to be a fraud, but we bask willingly in its false warmth, treasuring the idea that we are somehow much better than we are.

Old-timers' hockey was different from anything I had experienced before. The dressing room was filled with the same crude jokes and vicious sarcasm, the characters had become even more exaggerated with time, but the act of "playing" the game bore little resemblance to what was last remembered. With no body contact it gave the better skaters the distinct advantage. When teammates got on me about never coming back, I could tell them that when you go bowling you don't have to set up your own pins. The pressure was gone, vanished. The emphasis was on laughs in the dressing room and fun on the ice, and the experience had an astonishing dividend to it that I had not expected. I had developed friendships in childhood that have lasted forever, friendships at school that seem like they will last forever, but the friendships formed after marriage and children seemed always more fleeting, as if somehow acquaintances were going to be the rule for the rest of life. Old-timers' hockey seemed to form fast friendships, team bonds that may well be childish and inexplicable, but if they are, so what? They have been new friendships to treasure.

In the spring of 1981, I joined a Toronto old-timers' team that was going to Finland. We called ourselves "The Toronto Maple Leaves" – a subtle joke in English; an impossible one in Finnish. In translation, we came out the "The ex-Toronto Maple Leafs" and Finnair, which was arranging this pioneer trip in the hopes of attracting more old-timers' teams to Europe, lined us up against the finest old-timer teams in the country. One team, in Lahti, had five former national team players on it. They beat us 12–5. I scored three times on three flukey shots, all to the Lahti goalie's glove side. It was not until later, when we lined up to shake hands, that we discovered that the Finnish goalie was weak to the glove side for the very reason that he had no hand on that side. I pretended not to notice, but my teammates did and continue to remind me to this day. Yet this small asterisk in no way diminishes the little white banner I was awarded for being the best of the worst on the ice. It is something I treasure as much as I would the Robin Hood Oats trophy that Brent Munroe stole from under my nose.

A few months ago Brent was in the hospital, recuperating from a minor heart scare. Because we come from a small town where so very little – as well as so very much – has changed, and since we were all children together in a town where our parents live still, we heard the news immediately, even though we are all now in our forties, live in different places, and do different things. Eric immediately drove down from Huntsville – where he still lives, now in his father's retail business – down to the Toronto hospital where they had transferred our friend. I telephoned later. Eric had cheered Brent up by telling him that he had come up with the perfect present for my upcoming birthday party: a little plastic hockey player standing on a plastic puck over a small plaque that says: "Robin Hood Oats MVP – Over 40 Class." I will treasure it forever.

With me on the line from Ottawa and Eric and Brent handing the phone back and forth in the hospital room, we remembered the mayor's speech and the heavy wind that had stopped it, and Brent got to giggling so hard that Eric thought they might have to dive under the bed and pull the sheets over the two of them until it went away.

Pretty childish, I know. Intensive care is no place to play and act like idiots. But then again, why not? Playing together was the most important thing we ever did together. It is what held us together then, what bonds us now, and what will keep a childhood friendship burning through three entire lives. And we don't plan to let it go now – not ever.

KEN DRYDEN'S STORY

With only a few seconds to go, the whistle blew. I turned around and looked up several rows of Forum seats to where I knew

Lynda was sitting, lifted my left arm, and waved. No smile, she waved back.

We had talked about it for years and months and days, careful never to come to a decision. But now time had run out on another year. Nothing had changed since we had last talked a few hours before, except suddenly for me it was clear, and when I raised my arm *she knew*. It was one last chance to do *something*, to mark a passing and create a separate memory that would someday extend recollected time and let me gather up the moment again.

The puck was shot around the boards, I skated after it, picked it up, the siren went, and I retired. I was thirty-one.

I thought some more about retiring in the days that followed, pretending to myself that so long as I had made no announcement and had nothing yet to undo, it would be easy to change my mind and keep on playing. But I was fooling myself. Emotionally, psychologically, the decision had been made. It wasn't until a few weeks later that I let everyone else know. I explained to a press conference that the reason for leaving had nothing to do with my contract, or with the team. It wasn't that I wanted to practise law. The duelling columns of "pros" and "cons" hadn't come down inexorably that way. It was a *feeling*. It was simply time to go.

I hung around our dressing room that Stanley Cup night longer than I ever had before. A videotape shows a long-side-burned, unspectacled, much younger me in the midst of an interview. Suddenly, champagne is streaming down my head, my face, my back. I looked startled, then, like a TV actress in a shower commercial, I yield to it, closing my eyes, tipping back my head, luxuriating in its bubbly coolness, in its championship glow. I jut out my jaw and catch its downflow with my lips, dabbing at it, licking it with my tongue.

I want to do other things, I explained. I wasn't sure what those other things were exactly, but it didn't matter. If the rest of my work life was not to be in hockey as an administrator or coach, I wanted to give myself time to be good at something else. Thirty-five years of work life is a long time to play out the string, I said.

I savoured long and hard those days of Stanley Cup celebration that followed. Our fourth annual parade to City Hall down hot and sweaty St. Catherine Street, people in Canadiens sweaters, Canadiens T-shirts, Canadiens baseball caps, waving from their office windows, hanging entwined around stoplights, hundreds of thousands of them on sidewalks and streets crushing up against our open-roof bus. For nearly three hours, we stopped and started, smiled, waved, shook hands, and signed autographs. I wanted to shake every hand, hear every generous season-over-championship-won word. I wanted to be adored one last time.

When the parade ended, it was on to a post-parade pub, then a shower, change of clothes, and to an evening-long party for players, coaches, management, and staff, their spouses, girl-friends or boyfriends, still later to a post-party restaurant. Before noon the next day, to Toe Blake's Tavern, Henri Richard's Brasserie . . .

I felt as if on a dangerous/exciting adventure, knowing what I knew and keeping it to myself – about to move on, but not just yet. The summer ahead was like the summer had always been: free of hockey, a time to catch up. Then on the first Monday in September, Labour Day, I walked into a crowded, makeshift lecture room in Ottawa, noisy with anxious soon-to-be lawyers, and began Ontario's bar admission course. That is when I felt it. It is then I retired.

The pattern to my life was suddenly changed. From September to spring to September again, I had lived to the seasonal rhythm of the school year and hockey year. For me, one year always ends and another begins on Labour Day. And for twenty-five years, Labour Day meant that last year's school and hockey laurels were about to become part of an irrelevant past and would need to be earned again. I would think no more of that in a few days time, but every Labour Day I felt a deep disquiet, not certain that last year's skills hadn't been mysteriously lost over the summer and not wanting to have to prove again that they were still there. Even now, Labour Day is the day of the year I hate most.

But on Labour Day, 1979, training camp was a few days away and my life was yet unchanged. Still, I felt lousy. As I sat down to listen to the lecturer's words I would fast need to learn, I heard nothing. If this "feeling" I have is so right, I wondered, if this really is the time to go, then why do I feel this way? A few hours later I delivered the first day's news back to Lynda in Montreal and cried into the telephone. The equipment that had always come down from the shelf would not come down again. It was really over.

Coiled, pacing this way and that, I wait. The puck squirts behind the net, players give chase, and quickly more get lured toward its scrum. It is a fatal attraction. *Now.* My body explodes forward, driven by no thought, no shouted instruction from the bench. It is instinct. Two or three strides and the forty feet from blueline to slot melts under my skates. The puck bounces free. Defenders, hopelessly trapped, look back in anguish. They tear at the ice; it is too late. I am clear. But no pass comes. Undiscouraged, I wheel back to the blueline. I will be back again.

There is another version to these events. An ungenerous opponent, even an ungenerous teammate, might doubt whether "explodes" quite captures what they saw, even whether "instinct" fully explains how and why I got to the net, though "driven by no thought" they might not quibble with. The camera's eye, too literal, is also blind in such cases. The different versions result from a common *trompe l'oeil.* Just as it was with Frank Mahovlich, just as it is now with Mario Lemieux, it often seems a big guy isn't moving as fast as he is. In any event, their versions don't count. For this is Monday night hockey!

The equipment that stayed up on the shelf has come down again. The boy becomes a man, the player a fan, a coach, a father, now a player again, and the game goes on.

We are a ragtag group. Helmets, pants, socks, skates, bodies of all ages and conditions; hairlines and waistlines toing and froing in all the wrong directions; hair colours and abilities across the entire visible spectrum, fading fast. There is no doubt about it: hockey, all physical life, is passing us by. But strangely, that seems not to matter. Just close your eyes and listen to the chirpy, irreverent, disrespectful sounds of the dressing room; to the banter on the bench and on the ice; to the laughter. Monday

MICHAEL BOLAND

PLAYERS

Kingston imagined,
1886:
Kingston, Ontario.

Sledge hockey for physically handicapped,
Ottawa, Ontario.

Top: left to right:
Ken Dryden, Gary Lautens, Roy MacGregor, Bill White.
Bottom: left to right:
Frank Mahovlich, Ron Ellis, Dave Dryden.

Floor hockey for mentally handicapped,
Montreal, Quebec.

Family game,
Bracebridge, Ontario.

MICHAEL BOLAND

When will the boys be home:
Toronto, Ontario.

MICHAEL BOLAND

night hockey is only a little bit about hockey. It is mostly about *play*. Fantasies, illusions, working up a sweat – it is about people, and getting together. Too old, too fat, too bald – no way. We *play* as well as we ever did. Maybe better.

In our lives, most of us are married, a few are divorced, most have kids. Two sell plumbing supplies, three sell sporting goods, one sells furniture, a few own or operate small businesses. We have three lawyers, a cop, a heavy machinery broker, an electrician, a gas station owner, two sheet metal men, a bank manager, fireman, beer store manager, and mechanic. We have an uncle and nephew, a son-in-law and father-in-law, and two brothers-in-law. We have lifelong friends and Monday night acquaintances. We have co-workers, employers and employees, and some who do business together.

We call each other by first names or nicknames. They are "Corky" and "Red"; from alliterative first and last names, "JJ" and "Double R"; identifiable last names bring obvious nicknames, and so Mullen is "Moon" and Rizzuto is "Scooter." One player was born in England, has lived for decades in Toronto, but for a few years as a child he lived in Newfoundland. Naturally, he is a "Newf." For most of the rest, we use jock-talk/dressing-room diminutives: "Bobby," "Billy," "Johnny," "Lenny," "Frankie." I am "Kenny." Only now as I think of it, I realize that most last names I have never heard or learned.

One guy is twenty-four, another is sixty, but most are older than I am, I think. (I hope; they sure look old.) Two once played in the NHL, one played minor pro, another in college, and a few played junior hockey. Many became better players as adults in industrial and old-timers' leagues than they ever were as kids. One preferred other sports as a child and only last year, at forty-three, really took up hockey. Now he plays with the born-again zest of someone who is actually improving. The rest of us aren't. We have our stars – Billy, Double R, Corky – and our strugglers. We have guys who weave down the ice with the puck – their teammates in a race to catch up and, catching up, darting this way and that to find open ice for a pass – and who weave over centre, over the blueline, into the corner, behind the net, who would weave through the end boards and out onto the street before they would pass. We have guys with no sense of time, who pace themselves and save their strength, their teammates going off, coming on, going off, coming on, who need a hook and a rope to get them off the ice. Worse, we have others who wheeze off after thirty seconds, before anyone else has had time to stop wheezing himself. We have guys who, with a chance, never miss, and guys who, year after year, *always* miss; some who rarely say anything, and one guy, of course, who laughs louder, talks louder, and never shuts up. He is "the Shithawk." Turmoil is his game. He creates it and stirs it up, is always at its centre. I once asked Bob, the nominal head of our group, his highlight of the week? "When the Shithawk falls on his ass." Yet when he isn't around, Monday night isn't the same.

What is it that makes grown men rearrange schedules and ink into their appointment books every Monday night from October to March from 9:15 to 10:30? "It's the guys," says Bob. "Sure, it's exercise," Double R explains, "and it can get competitive sometimes, especially when new young guys come out. But it's more a social thing." "It's such a change from the rest of the day," John adds. "All the problems and worries that fill your mind, at night, you just want something to let you forget them." "It's nice to find an hour or two, no pressures, and just get away from the realities of life," continues the Shithawk. "To have a few laughs, then to get back to it." "You know, once I would've said I did it for the exercise," John says with a pensive nod. "But at some point the exercise-friendship lines on the graph crossed. It's the guys."

It is the largely fantasy world of the lifestyle beer commercial – grinning, laughing, youth-loving, life-loving, arm-around-the-shoulder – just "Bob and the boys." In this world everyone is a buddy, everything is fair, there are winners and losers but, all together at the end, no one cares. Not so much an escape from real life, it is an escape *to* life as we wish it to be. When the fantasy of skating end-to-end and scoring fades, this fantasy glows brighter. Monday night hockey has a lot more to do with psychological health than physical health.

Years ago, before I joined the group, they divided up into the "Blacks" and "Whites," and the teams have stayed mostly the same ever since. The Whites, a team of independent thinkers, wear a variety of white sweaters. The Blacks, like sheep, bought L.A. Kings sweaters when Gretzky made them fashionable. Newf wears #99. The Blacks, here as elsewhere, are the bad guys. And if the truth must be told (why must it?), they are annoyingly, frustratingly, slightly better than we are. Each year it's the same. They have more snipers, and their goaltending is a little more consistent. For if "Moon," our goalie, is never short of fabulous – splitting, sprawling, spinning around his crease like a break dancer – and is better at his position than most of us are at ours, he is not always good. Moon lets in the occasional long one. "Jee-zus Christ, Moon!!" we wail from the bench. "What the hell's he doin'?!" No one has an answer. Moon may cover up for me, as a defenceman, several times a game, but in the last few years I've changed my mind. It *is* the goalie's fault.

The first team to score five goals wins the game. When one game ends, another begins. Usually we don't quite finish two games in a night. It is never quite clear whether a lead in a partially completed game "counts" as a win. On Monday nights, things are left purposely unclear. So depending on the score, one week we argue one way, the next another, and everyone is ill-mannered enough to remember. We keep no standings, only a vague running tab of the results in our heads. Our estimates are more reliable than theirs. And when the Whites do win, no matter our past futility, we say something like, "Jee-zus, that was easy. I mean, I can't even remember when you guys won the last time . . ." In the wonderful world of Monday nights, saying it makes it so.

We have no referees for our games, no coaches or captains, no authority figures of any kind like those that crowd the rest of our day. This is *our* game. We play by our own rules and apply them ourselves. We have face-offs only to start each game. We dispense with icings and centre-ice offsides entirely. They make a game more of a challenge to play and at our age, with our skills, playing is challenge enough. As for a blueline offside, if the offensive team chooses not to notice it, the defensive team surely will. "Offside!" they chorus, from the bench and ice, and the game accepts it. With a close game, a good scoring chance, there is a huge temptation to "cry wolf," to see high-flying would-be goal scorers hilariously slam on the brakes. I don't remember it ever happening. The game could survive the joke, but only to get it out of its system. For play survives on trust.

It is like a kids' game, in a backyard or on a pond or playing field. There, kids learn to sort things out themselves, to decide their own rules; they learn to be fair. Introduce a referee, a judge, a higher authority, and everything changes. Broken rules unseen become rules unbroken. Unfairness is penalized sometimes, fairness is rewarded sometimes, but so is "getting away with it." It becomes its own game, often as important as the game itself. But with no referee you become your own referee, and "getting away with it" ceases to be a game. And a game becomes play.

It seems the most natural thing in the world, yet rarely do we play. Everyone on that ice is used to, and accepts, the invisible hooking and holding, the gamesmanship that is part of hockey and everything else they do, so much so that on Monday nights when old instincts take over, as they sometimes do, we are almost afraid to complain. Our words sound so naive to worldly ears. Yet even if we are used to gamesmanship, even if the victims don't often complain, we rarely violate the "player's" unspoken code. We know somehow that he who abuses the power risks destroying the game and himself in it. That every game survives only on a thousand and one little understandings that we all must abide by – no slapshots, no intentional icings, no staying on the ice too long, no saying a puck isn't in if it is – and mostly we do. We may be high-spirited, free-spirited, get-the-edge-on-the-other-guy types as much as anyone else, but here we are people at play. Serious play.

It is play we seek. I schedule other things around Monday nights and every Monday night I'm not here, I resent whatever keeps me from it. I love the physicality, the feeling of moving. I may skate with a curious wide-gaited stride, clunking around as if I'm still in my goalie pads, but that isn't the way it feels to me. I feel powerful, even graceful, when I skate. I am amazed at how recklessly, excitingly fast I can go, able to feel my own crisp breeze, to bite loud, crunching ridges into the ice as I move. And when I turn over my wrists, or wrong-footed and stylelessly swing at a puck, I can't quite believe how it flies off my stick with actual force.

I love the feeling of being put through something: a goal down, a chase for the puck, a scramble, a two-on-one, working, trying, feeling my lungs ignite and keep on going; and when it's over sitting on the bench and sensing the temperature of my scalp rise. Sometimes I succeed, sometimes not, yet blocking a shot and feeling its pain brings exhilaration, as does the morning after, waking up tired and brittle, knowing I earned it.

I love the self-discovery. Life off ice is so complicated, its outcomes smudged, its motivations rationalized and finessed, the picture you get of yourself so unclear. On the ice, you see your elemental self, whether you like it or not – do you try hard? do you quit? are you fair? are you selfish? do you forgive? are you willing to take risks? do you care too much or too little? do you fit in with a team on the ice, and off? When I was young and an NHL player, I took little notice. My elemental self seemed shapeless and unfrozen. I *was* and I *would be*; only now it is also what I am *not*. In Monday night hockey, most often, you discover something you like that makes you feel better about yourself, that you can take home with you and make part of your life. According to child psychologists, kids experience the world for the first time through play. For adults, play may be the most vivid way for us to experience that world again, and ourselves in it.

I love the feeling of "team": the Blacks against the Whites – our bench yapping at their bench, their bench yapping at ours; cheering the good pass, the good save, and, when things go wrong, listening as each bench turns on itself and yaps even more. To watch sweaty, tired, middle-age faces coming alive, snapping with energy, as the score mounts, in tandem, toward five – 3–3; 4–3; 4–4 – is to see something natural, true, right.

As a player, I am at best what a friend, thinking himself generous, described me to be – "competent." It was not a word I was looking to hear. Competence is probably a good thing in brain surgery, but it sure kills fantasies and that's what Monday nights are for. Do you know anyone who actually dreams of being competent?! – *a hundred thousand people fill the stadium, billions at home watch on TV. The whole country is behind me. I step into the starting blocks. The track races beneath me. I throw my chest at the tape . . . then race to celebrate in front of my proud, flag-waving fans. A solid fourth.* Fourth happens. On Mondays, I want to be a star.

I always imagined I would be. For twenty-five years I tried to decide, if fate had been different, whether I would have been a forceful, elegant Beliveau-type centre, a power-skating, slap-shooting, Hull-like winger, perhaps a dashing, all-over-the-ice Orr-clone on defence. When I left the Canadiens for one season in mid-career, I even imagined starting again as a forward. This was post-1972, sports scientists were brimming with confidence, and perhaps player creation was possible. I wondered, if I put myself into their hands, maybe I could work my way up and make it to the NHL another way.

Never adept outside my crease as a goalie, I should have had a hint, but I didn't. My task as a goalie had seemed easy enough – get quickly back to the boards to stop the puck; look up; set up the puck for our mobile defence or, occasionally reading trouble in the play, make a pass myself to an unguarded winger along the boards. But I could never master the complexity. I could do any two of the three things asked of me, but the third overloaded my circuits. If I looked up and took time to read the play, I was too slow and got in the way of it. If I didn't, I'd panic and pass the puck around the boards, often taking it right off the stick of an unpressured defenceman. I was able to talk and chew gum at the same time, it was the breathing that did me in. My problem was fear, I think – of running out of time, making the wrong play, getting hit.

I was too much a goalie. Still, I thought that once I took off my pads and worked at it, I would overcome my fear and things would change. I didn't, and they didn't. As an old-timer, I made the mistake of trying to play forward in my goalie skates. Goalie skates have long, flat, unrockered blades which give to a goalie the stability and balance he needs. Unfortunately, with so much blade touching the ice at one time, it is hard to turn, which is not what a forward needs. I would race up the ice; suddenly the play would go the other way. It was like swinging on the end of a long, slow rope. As I turned, the game flashed back and forth in front of me. I seemed always in the middle of a turn. Changing to forward's skates, my fantasies returned. My feet were now able to pivot more sharply (I could turn on a dime and give a nickel's change, it seemed to me), but this time inner-ear problems held me back. For twenty-five years, my whole equilibrium had been geared to wide, graceful turns. Now when my feet turned like a forward's feet and my body tried to follow, alarms went off. Feeling as if I was falling on my head, instinctively my body shook itself upright and, in my brand-new forward's skates, I went back to my never-ending turns.

Also at forward, I never had enough time. There was always someone around, tapping at my arms, at my legs or stick. Unused to the distractions, I would hurry my play and make the wrong play, which may be inherent in being a forward but is unforgivable for a goalie. I found I couldn't accept all the mistakes I was making and instead did my best to avoid them altogether by avoiding the puck as much as I could. So I gave up dreams of Beliveau and Hull, to become Orr. Defence gives me more of the time I need, yet if anyone comes near me I still lose my poise with frightening ease. I have also come to realize that a lifetime without body contact has left me unprepared for even the most casual bumping that comes in old-timers' hockey. Now when there is a fight for the puck, I react with overwrought fury, as if I'm being mugged, and forget to breathe. If the battle goes on more than a few seconds, I'm left panting and weak and useless for the rest of my shift. And when I get ambitious and look to stun the Blacks with a rifleshot breakout pass, I have the remarkable ability to spot quickly my best target and be stone-blind to the Blacks' Lennie or Double R standing in direct line between me and the puck's target.

It is altogether not very encouraging. Still, I can never see a reason why next week will not be different. It is the opportunity for fantasy that made me decide that Stanley Cup-winning night never to play goal again. I wanted finally to skate and be untethered from the net. I wanted to score goals. But more than that, I wanted to do something at which I could actually get better. As a goalie, I could only chase the phantom of what I had been and come quickly to choke on its dust. I had no fantasies left as a goalie. But as a forward or defenceman, I can get outside myself, out of the shadow of "me," and be what every player wants and needs – to be someone else. As a defenceman, I have new fantasies.

It helps, of course, that the other guys aren't so perfect either. It is much easier to imagine I am Bobby Orr, or will be, if no one makes me feel too inept too often. And while we represent a rat's nest of ages, shapes, and abilities, remarkably no one is so good or so bad as not to belong. When someone does come out who is too good or too bad, the effect is stunning. Our regulars may be here every Monday night because of the "guys," but the friendly, fun-to-be-around guy is no guy to have around if he takes the puck from end to end or messes up every play that comes near him. He ruins the game, and the game and its fantasy still matter.

We keep score in our games because winning and losing are important to us. Just as it is with all kids at play, it is part of our fun. Every Monday night I want to win just as much as I wanted to win every Saturday night at the Montreal Forum and every other night and game I ever played. It bothers me when a shot hits a skate or banks in off a knee and the Blacks win again. But if at one time I would have gone home and shut out the rest of the world until the next game had been played, and won, now by the time I'm back in the dressing room, the feeling of losing is largely forgotten. Double R and the Shithawk do their best to resurrect it, of course, but that is another game. Monday night hockey, winning and losing, ends the moment I leave the dressing room to go out to my car. I don't take hockey home anymore.

That is mostly true. I can lose 5–3 every game, every week, and still have fun. I can mindlessly give away the puck three or four times a night and do nothing more than direct forgettable anger at myself. Lose by a bigger score, give the puck away more often, and that's embarrassing; that's not fun. I don't need to win or be a star but I do need to play *well enough* so that my mind doesn't shift from thoughts of the game to matters of self-image, self-respect, age. For me, a game is first and last a contest with myself and it always has been. The other team helps determine the contest, wins and losses offer hints of how I'm doing, but they are not the final scoreboard. That is a feeling, and that comes from standards and expectations within me which I can do little about. It is the same, I think, for everyone. Only when the personal battles are won can the buddyness and fantasies, the full spirit of Monday night hockey, come through. And so we make those battles as easy to win as we can.

I don't play goal now because as a goalie that personal battle is too hard to win and I don't want to fight that hard anymore. I want just to skate, try hard, sneak in occasionally from the point for a shot on net, hope, pretend I'm Bobby Orr, or will be, and beat the Blacks at least sometimes. I want to play. And as a klutzy defenceman, full of fantasies but not expecting much, I can.

I retired from the Canadiens because of a feeling. The right thing to do at the right time, it's only now that I realize where that feeling came from. At age thirty-one, in a lifelong contest with myself, I was beginning to lose. And in losing, the fantasies, the buddyness – the play – that had driven me into frigid back-yards and Saturday-morning arenas, that kept me at it year after year and wouldn't let me go, were fading. I retired because I had lost my reason to continue. In Monday night hockey, I have found it again.

THE GAME AND REAL LIFE

Why do we love this game? What makes millions of Canadians sit and watch tiny flickering images scores of nights a year? What makes grown men and women buy T-shirts and sweat-shirts, coffee mugs, posters and key chains of favourite teams and favourite players and talk with passion about those teams and players as if they were family? Why do certain phrases buckle our knees – "the river," "fathers and sons," "Foster Hewitt," "my first sweater," "1972," "the year we won the championship"? What hold does hockey have on us? It doesn't put food on our tables or roofs over our heads. It doesn't cure the sick, raise the downtrodden, spark our minds to do great deeds and think great things. It is just a game. We are serious, ambitious people. We have kids and jobs and bombs to worry about. There are drugs on the streets. Isn't this attention, this preoccupation, misplaced; this money, time, and energy misspent? Don't we have our priorities wrong?

Aren't we just being manipulated? "Our" Montreal Canadiens, "our" Edmonton Oilers – do you think Peter Pocklington really cares about us? Do you think Carling O'Keefe, Molson's, Gretzky, and all the knickknack makers care? *Hockey Night in Canada*, radio and newspaper sports, public appearances, ads, endorsements, "nice guy," "good guy" images – aren't they just a web of creations to support a fiction, ways to make a buck?

Why should this game matter? Why *does* it matter? It matters because communities matter. Kids matter. Kids and parents and grandparents matter. Friends matter. Dreams, hopes, passions; common stories, common experiences, common memories; myths and legends; common imaginations; things that tell us about how we were, how we are, how we might be – they matter. Links, bonds, connections – young-old, past-present, East-West, French-English, men-women, able-disabled; things in common, things to share – they matter. And that is why hockey matters.

There is nothing innately superior about hockey as a game, nor about any game. The act of skating, its speed, may be extraordinary, but there is nothing uniquely compelling about slapshots, forward passes, three-on-twos, and the rest. Hockey's appeal to Canadians still mystifies most Englishmen. The English love cricket, the world loves soccer, and Canadians and Americans scratch their heads and wonder why. A game's aesthetics have little to do with its appeal. All the requisite elements of entertainment – excitement, drama, confrontation – can be present, and still few might play or watch. Hockey's speed and rawness seem perfect for an American audience, but hockey in the U.S. has never quite caught on. Its cultural roots are too thin.

The average American fan sees only the hockey game in front of him – the speed, the collisions – the full power of which never reaches him in his living room. He doesn't hear names with rich,

THE MAGIC OF PLAY

complicated histories. He doesn't see ghosts of players past, games and teams past, a whole lifetime of them, cavorting across his TV screen with every second of the present. He has no childhood stories, no childhood heroes to remember. He can see baseball's ghosts – for baseball is America's game. Football might make more sense, may come into fashion and be better suited to television, but baseball has the history and the mythology. The mistress may be beautiful, but someone else is under the American fan's skin. That is where the depth of passion lies.

Hockey is Canada's game. Nothing else is; nothing else will be.

Hockey is no "never-never" land. It disappoints us often: fighting and excessive violence that will not go away; alcohol, drugs, players who take the money and run; Harold Ballard, Peter Pocklington; minor hockey's prodigy life for kids and parents; endless playoffs; discomfiting commercialization and spectacle; gamesmanship. It seems a long way from sport's sylvan age, when sport existed, in memory at least, as an idealized world apart, with its own special higher code of behaviour – sportsmanship, fair play, sport for sport's sake. But if sport was ever like that, it was because it truly inhabited a world apart: a late nineteenth-century, early twentieth-century world of the rich – no one else had the time and energy to play games – embodied best in the Victorian image of the English public schools and *Tom Brown's School Days*. Sport was viewed as a test. Sport teaches morals and discipline; it engenders community spirit. It was Matthew Arnold's "muscular Christianity" with the Christianity removed. Sport builds character; character builds empires.

Hockey in Canada today doesn't much resemble Tom Brown's world. Many of those same ideals remain, but their realization continues to elude us. And each time it does, we feel the distress. It is as if we see sport as a societal barometer; if an idealized world can't exist in sport, what hope is there for the rest? But sport is no longer a world apart. Today, hockey is dead-square in the mainstream of Canadian life. It has taken on life's purposes and ambitions; it suffers life's conflicts and temptations, its weaknesses and abuses. It has become indistinguishable from life itself.

267

The same is true of sport in general. In September, 1988, Ben Johnson won the Olympic 100-metre dash in Seoul, Korea, then three days later, found to have taken banned drugs, he was stripped of his gold medal. No event in recent years so dominated the Canadian mood and conversation. Is this what sport has come to? It was the national question. If Johnson had run his Olympic race at almost any other time this century, few would have noticed: stadium spectators, some newspaper readers, friends at home, in total, perhaps a few hundred thousand people. Technology could not yet connect the world and give to certain events importance. Winning and losing in the Olympic Games meant less to fewer people.

In 1988, billions of people were watching. Millions of dollars, national pride, and professional futures were at stake. The Canadian Olympic team needed Johnson to win. Four years before in Los Angeles, many easier-to-earn, boycott-tarnished medals had been won. Expectations for Seoul were unreachably high. If we couldn't win many medals, we had to win the big one. Charlie Francis, Johnson's coach, needed him to win, and so did Johnson's personal doctor, his personal masseur, his agents. So did Nike, Diadora, Toshiba, and his other corporate sponsors. So did the Canadian government. So did the Canadian people.

So did his parents, his brothers and sisters, not rich, not even comfortably well off. Everyone was counting on him. Above all, Johnson needed to win for himself.

Ben Johnson could have said "no." Cheating, hurting his body, he should have said "no." It was his own fault. He was wrong.

It was easier to say "no" in 1896, not much harder in 1936 and 1972. There was much less temptation for athletes, coaches, and officials to try and alter fate. And without temptation, we are all unbreakably strong. In an idealized world apart, there are few temptations. In 1988, in sport today, temptations were and are everywhere. The more sport becomes like real life, the more we behave in sport like it is real life. Expectations change, codes get winked at, athletes react like real people. Some will be honest, others afraid; some will seek only to win.

Real life caught up to Ben Johnson.

Less than a month after Johnson's disqualification, wobbly-legged Kirk Gibson came off the Los Angeles Dodgers' bench and, in the World Series, hit a ninth-inning, game-winning Hollywood home run. And millions at home, who just weeks before had decided finally and forever to turn their backs on sport, stood and cheered. Kirk Gibson is real life, too. So are Joe Tutt and Radisson, Saskatchewan, so are Bill Hunter, Wayne Gretzky, Phil Esposito, and Rocket Richard. Cynicism is a powerful voice and an infectious style, but cynicism can never quite transcend. Hockey, all sport, is inherently optimistic. There is always a new season. There's always hope. It's never over until it's over. It may stretch credibility to say that any boy or girl can grow up to be Prime Minister of President, but say the Toronto Maple Leafs can win the Stanley Cup – why not!

Hockey is people, lots of them, everywhere: Greg Koehler and his parents; Kevin Kaminski; Mark Messier and Guy Carbonneau, the scorer and the checker, head to head for pride and team. It is women and old-timers, the two fastest-growing segments of hockey in Canada; it is the physically and mentally handicapped, the blind, after years on the outside, saying – hey, what about us? We want to play, too. They will never win a Stanley Cup or earn a million dollars. But watch them at play, on the ice, in dressing rooms – different sizes, different shapes, different skills from those of the Montreal Canadiens or Edmonton Oilers, but their eyes, their sounds, are the same. And in their heads, in their imaginations, they are playing the same game.

ROY: REGRETS, LIES, AND RIPPLING

I have been hearing about regret all my life: regret that I didn't try harder, regret that expansion came too late for me, regret that I didn't have my head screwed on right then, regret that I didn't have such bad knees or weak eyes or such unbelievable jerks for coaches – regret, in a thousand different forms, *that I didn't make it*.

But if it were as simple as that, the NHL would have long since had to expand into places like Peggy's Cove and Hornpayne and Peebles just to absorb the vast supply of qualified players. The regret is based on a lie everyone sees through, even the teller, but it is oddly comforting in a country where one game seems to matter more than anything else.

I personally knew I would never make it by the time I was twelve. Limited ability. Poor attitude. Not enough desire. My own great regret now is that I stopped playing for the best fifteen years of my life, something that would never have happened if the game of choice had been, say, tennis. But, like so many thousands of others who drop into hockey's black hole around midget, I was gone when I should have been playing hardest. Still, I'm glad I came back to it. I loved it then; I love it now; we just fell out of touch with each other. I came back because old-timer hockey came along and there were enough baby boomers clinging to childhood fantasies to make it economically viable. My father had no such luck. He could stay on only as a fan, and though his enjoyment is rich, he is still poorer than the balding son who gets to play twice each week.

I also came back through my children. Kerry, now thirteen, began when she was still in a walker. I used her supposed interest in the game as an excuse to buy something I had never had, a hockey net, and set it up in my basement where I could take shots and fantasize in complete privacy. Christine, now eleven, wanted to play organized hockey and when I signed her up they signed me up as well, to coach. I had to take a ridiculous course and became a level II coach complete with crest and frameable certificate. They taught us break-out patterns. The children we were coaching were five years old.

For two years, in two different cities, I coached. The kids were terrific. Most parents were wonderful. In the last game of the last season I found a father bribing another man's son by offering him a mittful of dollar bills, one for every goal he would score. I didn't volunteer when the next season rolled around.

While I coached I tried out the pylons, but I never knew what to do with them. Most of the kids couldn't skate, let alone skate around them. I began to believe more in what my brother Jim said one day after his son's practice: "I'd like to be the coach. I'd bar the parents from the arena, drop a pail of pucks over the boards, and just walk away." In my opinion, he's as much a visionary as Tarasov.

In winter I help flood the schoolyard down from our house. I do it with a man named Dave who shares my love of the game and still plays old-timer hockey. We *talk* hockey while we work. We talk better than we play. We're never so close to the game as on a bitter January night when the hoses freeze and we have to breathe through our mouths because our nostrils keep locking up on us and we can stand there and bitch happily about how kids don't play shinny anymore the way we did when we were kids.

Dave's son Danny and my son Gordie are both six and have started playing on this rink. Sometimes his daughter Rebecca and my eight-year-old daughter Jocelyn join in. And over the last two winters an older group of neighbourhood boys, the ones we'd given up on, have started coming out to play as well. We were pleasantly surprised. First time out they asked me if I'd referee and I foolishly agreed. Then they spent ten minutes arguing about rules. Where would they have the face-offs? How many "steamboats" would they have to count off for a penalty? I threw the puck down and walked home where, from a bedroom window, I was able to see that eventually they worked everything out. No face-offs, no penalties, and they played magnificently for three hours and went back the next afternoon for more.

So don't tell me there's no hope for this game. The National Hockey League may have come to the conclusion that clutching and grabbing is as much a part of the game as scoring goals, they may have convinced themselves that violence is a necessary evil when it is necessary in no other sport, but hockey has not been destroyed by such persistent stupidity. Organized hockey may be out of control, greed may be too much in control – but when a game can still draw children to a raw outdoor rink in February there is reason to cheer.

And even though I'm far too wise to waste time on false and

vain regret, don't tell me, either, that there is no hope for me. In the final game of the tournament we played in last year, there were eleven fans in the stands and at the end, though we had lost, one of them came into the dressing room and said that at one point the action had gotten so furious he could actually see our sweaters "rippling" out there.

Rippling – just like the pros. The way they have been moving through our imaginations all our lives. With many years to go.

KEN: I THINK I WILL PLAY FOREVER

I am asked all the time if I miss playing. It's hard to tell people "no," even though that is what I feel. I am sure if I do, having lived out so many of their fantasies, they will think I must never really have loved to play. Or that I never really loved it the way play deserves to be loved, that I took for granted the privilege I had, that, hard-bitten and money-driven, I had exploited play. Or, I will see in their eyes a sympathetic sadness, a look that says, *You are lying to yourself but I understand. Who could not regret the passing of play and time? "No" is the dance of denial we all must do, rationalizing away yesterday to make today seem brighter.* I miss not being so mindlessly at ease with my body. Going into the hole after a ground ball, my left arm stretched to its limits, I miss wrapping my hand around that ball, pivoting and firing it to first as surely I still could if only I was able to find those extra few inches to reach it. I miss the dressing room, the sounds, the energy, a team's nostril-flaring solidarity. But miss playing? I play all the time.

I have a wife and kids to play with. Michael, now eleven, is my alter ego, my childhood self. He plays everything – hockey, baseball, tennis, basketball, lacrosse, golf – and finds the latest game the most irresistible. He attacks play, sweaty and dirty, his eyes fired with delight, the world tuned out. Put him near a baseball park and, like me at forty-two, he will slide.

Until a year ago, Sarah, age fourteen, never played hockey or very much of anything. There was a reserve and control about her that girls seem to have or learn, that seems expected of them, that resists the kind of physical disorder – awkwardness, dishevelment, dirtyness, and (ugh!) sweat – which comes with active play. But last fall she played field hockey and when winter came, to our surprise, she decided to join a hockey team. In her first game, reaching for the puck with an opponent, she bumped accidentally against her and knocked her down. She was horrified. She became to us "Sarah, the goon." There was something wonderful about watching her on that ice, losing herself in the game, unafraid of looking awkward and, after a rare win, joining her teammates in a pile of celebration. And it was just as wonderful seeing her little girl's face when she emerged from the dressing room, her freckled cheeks crimson with effort, sweating.

Once, I asked three middle-aged Monday night hockey players what would make them stop playing. They were stunned. "I've never thought about that," said Double R. "I don't know. Health problems, maybe. Maybe if I couldn't skate anymore." Double R, fluid and smooth, loves to skate. "Short of a heart attack," the Shithawk rasps, "I don't think I would. The quality of hockey isn't the same as ten years ago, but the fun's still there. Hell, you're never too old to enjoy life." John went quiet. "Maybe if I reached a level of incompetence that embarrassed me," he mused. Then realizing what a Monday night dressing room would do to his words, he began to laugh. "Obviously, I don't embarrass easily." He went on. "I don't know if you really stop. Maybe you just slow down, play less and less, until you haven't played in a year or two, though you always keep intending to."

When I was a kid, I just played. In September the equipment came out, and in arenas and backyards the games began: one practice, two games a week; at lunch time, from school-end until dinner, Saturdays, Sundays, and holidays, from morning to floodlit night. In March the equipment was packed away again. It was the pattern and shape of my years, and the seasons passed. From September to March to September again, until some day some coach, burying his chin in his chest, would mutter, "Sorry son, maybe next year." And it would be over. I kept expecting this would happen, but it never did, and I saw no reason to stop.

Now, on Monday nights, we have no coaches. I pay my $10 each night and no one can tell me to go home. The pattern to my years continues. It is the Canadian cycle of life – the boy becomes a man, the player a fan, a coach, a father, a player again – and the game goes on.

I think I will play forever.

EPILOGUE

IT WAS A MYTHICAL CANADIAN SPRING – SUDDEN, INTENSE, AND SHORT-lived. Day after day, Saskatoon had squinted into white-bright sunshine that filled its immense sky, turning it a pale, pale blue. Daytime temperatures never dipped much below the high twenties. Doors, shut tight by the winter, suddenly opened, and life emerged. Cyclists and joggers busied the streets; lunch-time strollers, brown bags and paperbacks in hand, meandered down to the park near the river to lie on the grass and feel the sun melt winter from their faces. And the prevailing winds that affect so much of life in this province this time arrived as a gentle breeze, just strong enough to blow the bugs away.

A few miles from downtown, farmers ploughed their fields, fine rooster-tails of dust kicking up behind their tractors. Tiny wraith-like dust twisters came out of nowhere, danced over the land, and were gone. After last year's disastrous drought, this year looked good, the farmers said. So far. There was moisture in the ground. Then one day in the midst of this mythical spring, the wind picked up and the pale blue sky that had covered most of south-central Saskatchewan turned to an amber fog. Highways going south were closed, visibility at times near zero. It was a prairie dust storm, a reminder of times past, a reminder of the vulnerability of life here, a reminder of who was boss.

If the storm had come a few days earlier, before the seed had taken root, farmers would have harvested in the fall what their

275

neighbours had planted in the spring. If the dust had come a few days later, the stubble of new growth would have been several inches out of the ground. And like sandpaper, the tiny particles of dust would have eaten and gouged and sawn it away tiny bit by tiny bit until, by morning, there would be nothing left. The crop would have vanished. But this time the fates were smiling and by the following morning puffy white clouds were again tumbling across the bright spring sky.

The storm proved a great show for Canada's best junior hockey players assembled in Saskatoon for the Memorial Cup. The stuff of high school history books had come suddenly to real life. Television's cameras could bring back to family and friends in suburban Laval, Quebec, and small-city provincial Peterborough, Ontario, the story of the faraway games. But the young players would return home with a more fascinating tale to tell, of the day when the winds blew, the dust filled their nostrils and caught in their teeth, and the sun disappeared. An image of another Canada.

The Memorial Cup exceeded even Saskatoon's high hopes for it: accounts of Stanley Cup games from nearby Calgary were pushed back into the nether pages of the *Star-Phoenix* sports section; SaskPlace filled to its expanded 9,100 seat capacity; the tournament's games proved almost uniformly close. And left standing at the end, after Peterborough and Laval, champions from the East, had departed for home, were two Saskatchewan teams, the home-town, big-city Blades and the Broncos from tiny 15,000-person "Speedy Crick" – Swift Current. Once again, it was town against town. And by convoy up highways 4 and 7 came Bronco fans by the hundreds, in their blue-green-and-white jerseys and badges, supporting their boys on the road when they needed it most.

Two years earlier, four Bronco players had been killed when the team's bus slid off an icy highway only six kilometres outside of Swift Current. The Broncos were on their way to a game in Regina. The team, and the town, struggled to piece themselves together and this season the Broncos finished first in the Western Hockey League, Eastern Division, twenty-five points ahead of the second-place Blades. Now they were on the verge of a Memorial

Cup. Some of the accident's survivors were still on the team, as were Trevor and Darren Kruger, brothers of one of the victims. This would be their last chance to create a legacy to their fallen teammates. Yet Broncos' management had refused to use the accident as a team rallying point. Only discreet four-leaf clovers had been added to the sleeves of the players' jerseys. They decided that anything more would put dangerous pressure on the backs of young people who had already gone through too much.

The Blades took a 3–2 lead into the third period, but the Broncos tied the game with fourteen minutes remaining. The game went into overtime. At 3:35, Tim Tisdale scored and the Broncos were Memorial Cup champions. Few among the 9,100 who left the arena were unhappy. The right team had won. Kevin Kaminski spent several uncontrollable minutes at game's end sitting by himself on the Blades' bench, his head down, in tears. He had just come through the worst year of his junior hockey life: twenty-five goals and forty-three assists. He had rebounded in the Memorial Cup and was one of the Blades' leading scorers. Still, as he said later, "I could've handled the loss better if it had been 7–1." Disconsolate, he was met by his father, Julian, as he emerged from the Blades' dressing room. Julian took him aside. "Forget about this game," he said. "Think about Minnesota."

Early in June, Kevin got a telephone call from the Minnesota North Stars. He was told to report to the North Stars' offices in Bloomington, Minnesota, on July 2. He'd then spend a few days in the Mayo Clinic where, once and for all, they'd find out what was wrong with his back. Then he'd stay on for some special power-skating sessions and a strict fitness program to get him in shape for the opening of training camp. He could feel next year suddenly, excitingly upon him and in Saskatoon he began to work out in earnest. Then he got another call. Minnesota had traded him to the Quebec Nordiques for veteran defensive forward Gaetan Duchesne.

Kevin was stunned. He had always been a team player. It was in his character, a point of his pride. Others would get a little too excited by their own goals and assists; he became the jersey he was wearing. And so the moment he was drafted by the

North Stars, Bryan Trottier's New York Islanders became a childhood flirtation. The North Stars were his team. Now, the North Stars had decided they weren't.

Now he would be going to a French-speaking city where he had never been before and he spoke not a word of French. Still, Duchesne was a pretty good player *and* Québécois, Kevin thought; the Nordiques must want him a lot. It took a few days, but then the Nordiques became Kevin's team. And when training camp opened in September, he would show them that neither size, nor speed, nor temper would keep him from his dream. No one at that camp would want it more. He was going to make it.

* * *

Greg Koehler's road to Quebec had been bumpy early in the season, but for the most part the year had turned out well. The solution to Greg's early slump turned out to be an old trick practised by parents on children for as long as games have been played: a little recognition, some talk, some praise – and a small reward at the end that paid off twice.

Ed and Cathy Koehler, in a rare quiet moment in their Scarborough home, sat down with Greg and had a long talk. Greg was told to quit taking the game and himself so seriously. Enjoy yourself, they said. Play. And to help him do this, they created a game of their own. Every time, from now on, that Greg picked up a point in a game, Ed would take out his jackknife and put a notch in Greg's hockey stick – "just like a gunfighter." And once the stick was filled with notches, well, they'd have to buy a new one, wouldn't they? Next game, Greg scored four points, and he never looked back.

His Toronto Marlboros team did not win at Quebec, but they fell just one game short of playing for the tournament's Grand Championship, a much better result than they would have imagined earlier in the season. Marlboros defeated teams from Chicago and Detroit, then in double overtime beat Montreal before losing to the "New York Rangers," a team from Rye, New York. Then small-town Drummondville, Quebec, defeated Rye to win Quebec's top prize.

Ed and Cathy Koehler followed the games via Greg's telephone calls home; with seven kids, the cost and complications of travelling to Quebec were too great. They spent their week, as usual, in Toronto's arenas watching their other sons play. Bob and Gerry Taylor took time off work and with other parents accompanied their children on the train to Quebec. Bob's plan had been to have Chris keep fit while still in his cast, hoping the cast might come off in time for the tournament. The plan worked, and Chris dressed for each game, skated on Colisée ice during warm-ups, and watched anxiously from the bench during his team's games. But getting that close and no closer proved difficult for Chris and Bob. At that distance they couldn't quite taste the dream.

Yet in every other way, Quebec had been for Greg and Chris like spending a week in the NHL. There had been autographs and TV cameras. They had walked the long corridor from their dressing room to the ice and, just as Scott Parker had described, they were transfixed by the wall of people – thousands and thousands of people, and among them some French-speaking Quebec City girls who thought that fourteen-year-old hockey-playing Toronto boys were pretty special. Down from their bedroom walls, new fantasies were just beginning to become part of real life.

When their season ended, both Greg and Chris were asked to play again with the Marlies next year, this time at the minor bantam level, and they accepted. The dream that began for them in early childhood, reinforced at every turn by gleaming trophies, NHL-like jerseys, parents, newspapers, and TV screens, would be with them one more year at least. And early in June at the NHL Television Awards Special, where she was making a presentation, Alyssa Milano heard about Greg and her picture five times on his bedroom wall, and wrote, "To Greg Koehler, With Love, Alyssa Milano."

* * *

About the time of their 7–5 victory over the Edmonton Oilers on November 26, Canadiens' coach Pat Burns decided once and for all to do things his own way. He and his veteran players grew gradually to trust each other, and the team lost only nine of their remaining fifty-four games, becoming Stanley Cup contenders again. At season's end, Burns would be named the NHL's coach of the year; November's scoring star, Guy Carbonneau, again won the Selke Trophy as the NHL's best defensive forward; Chris Chelios was the league's best defenceman and Patrick Roy the best goaltender. But Jyrki Lumme did not score again and twenty games later, after the twenty-first game of his NHL career, he missed a team curfew and was sent to the Sherbrooke Canadiens of the American Hockey League and did not return the rest of the year. Bob Gainey continued his strong play until a slapshot broke his foot; then, after his return, he reinjured the same knee that had caused him so much difficulty the year before. Healthy, Gainey had proved that he still could play as he once had, but the 1988-89 season had proved to him that he could not stay healthy for long. His style invited injury, age made it more likely, and there was no other way for him to play. After the Canadiens had lost the all-Canadian Stanley Cup final to the Calgary Flames, Gainey took time to consider his future. He decided to leave the NHL and move with his family to France, where he would play for and coach a team in the French league. He would gain coaching experience, become more fluent in French, and, after living all his adult life to the same pattern, learn to live a different way. In two years' time, when his contract is up, he would be better able to decide what the future should hold.

His teammate, Larry Robinson, became the last link to the great Canadiens' teams of the 1970s, but not for long. The California fantasy that Wayne Gretzky and Bruce McNall had brought even to hockey proved irresistible. Robinson decided to leave Montreal and finish his career as a King. His likely replacement on the Montreal blueline – Jyrki Lumme.

* * *

For Gretzky and McNall, it had been an unforgettable year. The Kings improved from eighteenth in the NHL to fourth, and Los

RICHARD MARJAN

The Kaminskis,
Saskatoon.

Greg Koehler,
Quebec.

MICHAEL BOLAND

MICHAEL BOLAND

PLACE

RICHARD MARJAN

Getting together,
Radisson, Saskatchewan.

The ball game,
Radisson, Saskatchewan.

When the railroad comes...
Bill Hunter.

MICHAEL BOLAND

MICHAEL BOLAND

Spring: Alfons Hajt's farm
near Radisson, Saskatchewan.

Another season.

Angeles fans supported them in record numbers. Gretzky showed once more that he was the league's most valuable player, and was so judged, winning his ninth Hart Trophy. No one else, perhaps ever, had meant so much to his teammates, to his franchise, to the status of his sport in the city where he plays. And appropriately, in the first round of the Stanley Cup playoffs, the Gretzky-led Kings met the Gretzky-less Oilers.

Edmonton took a commanding series lead, three games to one, before Los Angeles began to come back. When Gretzky scored into an empty net to clinch victory in the seventh game and in the series, the look on his face told the story – triumph, relief, a little surprise, a little wonder, a little sweet revenge. Four months later, Gretzky was back in Edmonton where a statue of him was unveiled at Northlands Coliseum. It showed him in characteristic pose, the captain of the Stanley Cup champions, carrying above his head his treasured prize.

The break-up of the Oilers continued in the off-season. Goaltender Grant Fuhr announced his retirement, citing a lack of respect from Oiler teammates and management. Late in the summer, he decided to reconsider. On August 9, the first anniversary of *the trade*, Peter Pocklington reaffirmed his belief that it would turn out to be in the best interests of the team. But the real sign that the Oiler era had ended came weeks earlier when Glen Sather stepped down as coach in favour of his long-time assistant, John Muckler. The message was clear. Sather's time would be best spent in his general manager's role – scouting, drafting, trading, putting together the next generation of Oilers for another run at the Stanley Cup a few years from now.

As for the Kings, no one was quite certain whether Larry Robinson at age thirty-eight could help them much, but his signing offered its own clear message. Once again, Bruce McNall had been willing to part with his money to buy the best player available. He was reaffirming his commitment to Gretzky and telling Kings' players, coaches, management, fans, and media: I am out to win the Stanley Cup. McNall, the good partner, was doing his part. Now, he was telling them, you do yours.

* * *

Perhaps the biggest news of the summer (indeed any summer in which Gretzky isn't traded) was the arrival of the Soviets. Sergei Priakhin, internationally a rather obscure forward, had been the first, joining Calgary late in the season. But post-season, the Soviet Union's endlessly surprising floodgates opened without General Marushak or Colonel Viktor Tikhonov intervening to stop them. This time, genuine stars arrived, the four top players from the Soviet Union. Vyacheslav Fetisov signed with New Jersey, Sergei Makarov with Calgary, Igor Larionov and Vladimir Krutov with the Vancouver Canucks. Others came as well. Goaltender Sergei Mylnikov joined the Quebec Nordiques, Helmut Balderis the Minnesota North Stars. Also signing with New Jersey was Irina Starikova's husband, Sergei.

In the Soviet Union, Tikhonov remained at his post as coach of CSKA and the national team. But as Tikhonov once told Larionov, the system can outwait anyone. And this time it waits – for Tikhonov. And the system always wins.

*　　*　　*

Back in Saskatoon, the wait is over for the old arena. A symbol of small-town Saskatoon, it was levelled and carted away, its usefulness gone. For Bill Hunter the wait continues. The NHL has announced its plans to expand; Hunter is ready to make his application on behalf of Saskatoon and the province. But ahead he faces a tougher fight than that his Prairie predecessors waged a century ago. Then, Saskatchewan seemed the land of opportunity. Now, in NHL minds at least, that opportunity resides in Dallas and Milwaukee, San Francisco or Seattle or San Jose.

But forty miles up the Yellowhead Highway, there has been a major new development. As the rink fund crept closer to its ground-breaking goal, Radisson town council and the Saskatchewan Trappers Association held a joint press conference to announce that Radisson had been chosen as the site of the new provincial fur depot. Northern trappers would now reach their southern markets through Radisson. The volume of furs expected to be received by the new depot is estimated at between $3 million and $10 million a year. There will be need for a proper hotel. There is talk of new restaurants. The depot will need to hire staff. There will be spinoff jobs. The decision was, declared school principal Walter Kyliuk, "the most significant news here since the railway came through."

For the past two years, through bottle drives and box socials, banquets and billboards, Joe Tutt's ride, and the World Mud Volleyball Championships, Radisson has been delivering its ringing message to banks, car dealers, farm equipment dealers, people in town and out of town, and finally, it turns out, to the Saskatchewan Trappers Association – *we will make it*. In Radisson, Saskatchewan, where its highway sign reads "Town With A Future!" and where the hockey-community connection always seemed literal and absolute, it has turned out just that way.

And back in Toronto and Ottawa, two old-timers work and play through a hot, busy summer, their skates and pads packed away onto summer shelves and forgotten. But soon, as if imbued with a spirit of their own, they will come down again for another season.